1997 Read

to accompany

Mishkin
THE ECONOMICS OF MONEY, BANKING, AND FINANCIAL MARKETS
Fourth Edition

Edited by

James W. Eaton
Bridgewater College

Frederic S. Mishkin
Federal Reserve Bank of New York and Columbia University

An imprint of Addison Wesley Longman, Inc.

Reading, Massachusetts • Menlo Park, California • New York
Harlow, England • Don Mills, Ontario • Sydney
Mexico City • Madrid • Amsterdam

1997 Readings to accompany Mishkin, *Economics of Money, Banking & Financial Markets,* Fourth Edition

Copyright © 1997 Addison Wesley Longman, Inc.

All rights reserved. Printed in the United States of America. No part of this book may be used or reproduced in any manner whatsoever without written permission from the publisher, except testing materials and transparency masters may be copied for classroom use. For information, address Addison Wesley Educational Publishers Inc., One Jacob Way, Reading, Massachusetts 01867-3999.

ISBN: 0-673-52499-X

96 97 98 99 00 9 8 7 6 5 4 3 2 1

CONTENTS

PREFACE vii

PART ONE   *INTRODUCTION* 1

    Reading 1   ***The Money Market*** 3
                            Timothy Q. Cook and Robert K. LaRoche

    Reading 2   ***Logging On To Electronic Means of Payment*** 9
                            Michelle L. Kezar

    Reading 3   ***The Changing Meaning of Money*** 19
                            John V. Duca

PART TWO   *FINANCIAL MARKETS* 27

    Reading 4   ***Investment Improvement: Adding Duration to the Toolbox*** 29
                            Michelle Clark Neely

    Reading 5   ***Inflation-Indexed Bonds*** 34
                            Chan Huh

    Reading 6   ***The Yield Curve as a Predictor of U.S. Recessions*** 39
                            Arturo Estrella and Frederic S. Mishkin

    Reading 7   ***McCurrencies: Where's The Beef?*** 48

    Reading 8   ***Budget Deficit Cuts and the Dollar*** 52
                            Ramon Moreno

    Reading 9   ***The Dollar and the Federal Funds Rate*** 57
                            Charles L. Evans

PART THREE   *FINANCIAL INSTITUTIONS* 65

    Reading 10   ***A Look At America's Corporate Finance Markets*** 69
                            Stephen D. Prowse

Reading 11	*Solving the Mystery of High Credit Card Rates* 79 Randall J. Pozdena	
Reading 12	*Financial Fragility and the Lender of Last Resort* 85 Desiree Schaan & Timothy Cogley	
Reading 13	*Derivative Mechanics: The CMO* 90 Joseph G. Haubrich	
Reading 14	*Small Business Lending and Bank Consolidation: Is There Cause for Concern?* 97 Philip E. Strahan and James Weston	
Reading 15	*The Rhyme and Reason of Bank Mergers* 108 Elizabeth Laderman	
Reading 16	*Russian Banking* 114 Dwight Jaffee and Mark Levonian	
Reading 17	*The Decline of Traditional Banking: Implications for Financial Stability and Regulatory Policy* 120 Franklin R. Edwards and Frederic S. Mishkin	
Reading 18	*Reduced Deposit Insurance Risk* 144 Mark E. Levonian and Fred Furlong	
Reading 19	*Making Sense of Mark to Market* 150 Michelle A. Clark	
Reading 20	*Glass-Steagall and the Regulatory Dialectic* 155 João Cabral dos Santos	

PART FOUR THE MONEY SUPPLY PROCESS 163

Reading 21	*Where Is All the U.S. Currency Hiding?* 165 John B. Carlson and Benjamin D. Keen	

PART FIVE — THE FEDERAL RESERVE SYSTEM AND THE CONDUCT OF MONETARY POLICY 173

Reading 22 *Why Central Bank Independence Helps to Mitigate Inflationary Bias* 175
Timothy Cogley

Reading 23 *The Natural Rate and Inflationary Pressures* 180
Stuart E. Weiner

Reading 24 *A Primer on Monetary Policy Part I: Goals and Instruments* 186
Carl E. Walsh

Reading 25 *A Primer on Monetary Policy Part II: Targets and Indicators* 191
Carl E. Walsh

Reading 26 *U.S. Foreign Exchange Operations* 197
Kristina Jacobson

PART SIX — MONETARY THEORY 213

Reading 27 *M2 Growth in 1995: A Return to Normalcy?* 215
John B. Carlson and Benjamin D. Keen

Reading 28 *Is There an Output-Inflation Trade-Off?* 222
Evan F. Koenig and Mark A. Wynne

Reading 29 *Bank Lending and the Transmission of Monetary Policy* 228
Bharat Trehan

Reading 30 *What Causes Inflation?* 233
Laurence Ball

Reading 31 *Challenges to Stock Market Efficiency: Evidence from Mean Reversion Studies* 246
Charles Engel and Charles S. Morris

Reading 32 *Activist Monetary Policy for Good or Evil? The New Keynesians vs. the New Classicals* 263
Tom Stark and Herb Taylor

PREFACE

This *Reader* helps make *The Economics of Money, Banking, and Financial Markets* a unique teaching package to meet the needs of both professors and students. A basic problem of textbooks in the Money and Banking or Financial Markets and Institutions fields is that current events and financial innovation make many of the facts in the textbooks obsolete soon after they are published. To minimize this problem, *The Economics of Money, Banking, and Financial Markets* stresses a few basic economic principles that never go out of date, rather than a set of facts that quickly do so, to understand the role of money in the economy and the structure of financial markets and institutions. To make this economic approach to teaching Money and Banking or Financial Markets and Institutions even more effective, it is important to keep the textbook analysis up to date by supplementing it with current articles on money, financial markets and institutions. This is what this *Reader* does.

UNIQUE FEATURES OF THIS READER

Up-to-date

In contrast to other readers in the Money and Banking or Financial Markets and Institutions field, this *Reader* is updated annually, with half or more of the articles new each year. For example, sixteen of the thirty-two articles in this *Reader* are new to this edition; nine articles were published in 1996 and eight during the second half of 1995. These include articles on electronic means of payment, inflation-indexed bonds, the yield curve as a predictor of recessions, the effect of budget deficit cuts on the dollar, corporate finance markets, small business lending, bank mergers, Russian banking, foreign holdings of U.S. currency, central bank independence, and recent M2 growth. No other reader in the field is as current, and this will continue to be the case with the appearance of a new edition of the *Reader* every year.

A New Way to Teach Financial Markets and Institutions

The fourth edition of *The Economics of Money, Banking, and Financial Markets* develops a unifying economic framework to organize students' thinking about financial markets and institutions so that they can make sense of, rather than be confused by, all the facts about our financial system. The strength of this approach, in contrast to the approach used in other textbooks which focus on a set of facts about financial institutions, is that it will not go out of date. Because this approach stresses lasting economic concepts, it allows instructors to discuss the latest developments in financial markets and institutions. As part of this approach to teaching financial markets and institutions, instructors will want to use current articles in class to illustrate the economic forces that are driving changes in financial markets. This *Reader* is designed to make it easier for instructors to do this and keep their teaching current. Over half of the readings are devoted to financial markets and institutions. Because the need for current discussion of financial markets and institutions is so important to teaching Money and Banking or Financial Markets and Institutions, future annual editions of the *Reader* will make a special effort to have a similarly high proportion of current articles focus on financial markets and institutions.

The numerous, current readings on financial markets and institutions that will appear annually in this and future editions of the *Reader* and the stress on economic analysis in the textbook provide a whole new way of teaching financial markets and institutions. This new approach will make it less likely that students will memorize a mass of facts that will be forgotten after the final exam and that soon become obsolete because of the rapid pace of financial innovation. Instead, they will have an understanding of the dynamism of our financial markets and institutions and will see that what they have learned applies to current developments in financial markets, illustrating the relevance of their course work.

Pedagogical Aids

Each of the *Reader*'s six parts begins with an introduction (written by James Eaton) which provides the student with a brief summary of each article. In addition, the introduction suggests the chapter(s) with which the reading might be assigned, thus helping instructors decide how to organize their courses. We suggest that instructors read through all the part introductions as they plan their courses to become aware of the various options for matching readings with the text chapters they assign.

James Eaton has also written several discussion questions which follow each reading in order to encourage students to think about how the reading relates to material in the text. Instructors may find these questions useful for class discussions of the reading or as written assignments in problem sets.

Low Price

Because we believe that this *Reader* is such an important supplement to courses in Money and Banking or Financial Markets and Institutions, it will be sold with the text at a particularly low price. This should give students the benefit of the *Reader* without making its cost prohibitive.

SUGGESTIONS AND ACKNOWLEDGMENTS

It is hoped that both students and instructors who use this *Reader* will indeed find it an effective pedagogical tool. The editors look forward to receiving any comments or suggestions concerning the articles in this edition of the *Reader* or ones which would be appropriate for future editions. Please send your comments and suggestions to:

>   James W. Eaton
>   Department of Economics and Business
>   Bridgewater College
>   Bridgewater, Virginia 22812
>   *jeaton@bridgewater.edu*

We owe sincere thanks to several people who have given expert assistance in the preparation of this *Reader*. Special thanks go to Elizabeth Middleton, who once again skillfully retyped each article to give the *Reader* its uniform, polished appearance; to Bruce Kaplan, development editor; and to Julie Zasloff, associate editor for finance at Addison Wesley Longman, for her advice and encouragement. Above all, we would like to thank our wives Mary and Sally, and our children Amanda, Elizabeth and Matthew (for Eaton) and Matthew and Laura (for Mishkin), who put up with us while projects like this claim a large share of our time. We hope they know that they are infinitely more important to us than a book.

1997 READINGS

to accompany

Mishkin
THE ECONOMICS OF MONEY, BANKING, AND FINANCIAL MARKETS
Fourth Edition

PART ONE

INTRODUCTION

The three readings for Part One introduce some of the institutions and issues critical to the successful operation of the financial system—the money market, money itself and the forms in which it is evolving, and the difficulties of defining a monetary aggregate that will be an accurate guide for monetary policy.

In Reading 1, **"The Money Market,"** Timothy Q. Cook and Robert K. LaRoche provide an overview of money market participants and financial instruments. This reading supplements Chapter 2's introduction to the financial system.

Reading 2, **"Logging on to Electronic Means of Payment"** by Michelle L. Kezar, surveys electronic alternatives to cash and checks and obstacles impeding their rapid adoption by businesses and consumers. This reading can be used early in the course with Chapter 3's introduction of money or reserved for use with the discussion of financial innovation in Chapter 10.

John V. Duca in Reading 3, **"The Changing Meaning of Money,"** explains how changes in technology, demographics, and preferences haves weakened monetary aggregates' usefulness as economic indicators. The reading shows the difficulty of formulating an empirical definition of money and can supplement Chapter 3's distinction between theoretical and empirical definitions of money or Chapter 21's discussion of the conduct of monetary policy.

READING 1

The Money Market

Timothy Q. Cook and Robert K. LaRoche

The major purpose of financial markets is to transfer funds from lenders to borrowers. Financial market participants commonly distinguish between the "capital market" and the "money market," with the latter term generally referring to borrowing and lending for periods of a year or less. The United States money market is very efficient in that it enables large sums of money to be transferred quickly and at a low cost from one economic unit (business, government, bank, etc.) to another for relatively short periods of time.

The need for a money market arises because receipts of economic units do not coincide with their expenditures. These units can hold money balances—that is, transactions balances in the form of currency, demand deposits, or NOW accounts—to insure that planned expenditures can be maintained independently of cash receipts. Holding these balances, however, involves a cost in the form of foregone interest. To minimize this cost, economic units usually seek to hold the minimum money balances required for day-to-day transactions. They supplement these balances with holdings of money market instruments that can be converted to cash quickly and at a relatively low cost and that have low price risk due to their short maturities. Economic units can also meet their short-term cash demands by maintaining access to the money market and raising funds there when required.

Money market instruments are generally characterized by a high degree of safety of principal and are most commonly issued in units of $1 million or more. Maturities range from one day to one year; the most common are three months or less. Active secondary markets for most of the instruments allow them to be sold prior to maturity. Unlike organized securities or commodities exchanges, the money market has no specific location. It is centered in New York, but since it is primarily a telephone market it is easily accessible from all parts of the nation as well as from foreign financial centers.

The money market encompasses a group of short-term credit market instruments, futures market instruments, and the Federal Reserve's discount window. The table summarizes the instruments of the money market. The major participants in the money market are commercial banks, governments, corporations, government-sponsored enterprises, money market mutual funds,

Reprinted from *Instruments of the Money Market* edited by Timothy Q. Cook and Robert K. LaRoche, Federal Reserve Bank of Richmond, 1993, 1-5.

PART I Introduction

The Money Market

Instrument	Principal Borrowers
Federal Funds	Banks
Discount Window	Banks
Negotiable Certificates of Deposit (CDs)	Banks
Eurodollar Time Deposits and CDs	Banks
Repurchase Agreements	Securities dealers, banks, nonfinancial corporations, governments (principal participants)
Treasury Bills	U.S. government
Municipal Notes	State and local governments
Commercial Paper	Nonfinancial and financial businesses
Bankers Acceptances	Nonfinancial and financial businesses
Government-Sponsored Enterprise Securities	Farm Credit System, Federal Home Loan Bank System, Federal National Mortgage Association
Shares in Money Market Instruments	Money market funds, local government investment pools, short-term investment funds
Futures Contracts	Dealers, banks (principal users)
Futures Options	Dealers, banks (principal users)
Swaps	Banks (principal dealers)

futures market exchanges, brokers and dealers, and the Federal Reserve.

COMMERCIAL BANKS

Banks play three important roles in the money market. First, they borrow in the

READING 1 The Money Market

money market to fund their loan portfolios and to acquire funds to satisfy noninterest-bearing reserve requirements at Federal Reserve Banks. Banks are the major participants in the market for federal funds, which are very short-term—chiefly overnight—loans of immediately available money; that is, funds that can be transferred between banks within a single business day. The funds market efficiently distributes reserves throughout the banking system. The borrowing and lending of reserves takes place at a competitively determined interest rate known as the federal funds rate.

Banks and other depository institutions can also borrow on a short-term basis at the Federal Reserve discount window and pay a rate of interest set by the Federal Reserve called the discount rate. A bank's decision to borrow at the discount window depends on the relation of the discount rate to the federal funds rate, as well as on the administrative arrangements surrounding the use of the window.

Banks also borrow funds in the money market for longer periods by issuing large negotiable certificates of deposit (CDs) and by acquiring funds in the Eurodollar market. A large denomination CD is a certificate issued by a bank as evidence that a certain amount of money has been deposited for a period of time—usually ranging from one to six months—and will be redeemed with interest at maturity. Eurodollars are dollar-denominated deposit liabilities of banks located outside the United States (or of International Banking Facilities in the United States). They can be either large CDs or nonnegotiable time deposits. U.S. banks raise funds in the Eurodollar market through their overseas branches and subsidiaries.

A final way banks raise funds in the money market is through repurchase agreements (RPs). An RP is a sale of securities with a simultaneous agreement by the seller to repurchase them at a later date. (For the lender—that is, the buyer of the securities in such a transaction—the agreement is often called a reverse RP.) In effect this agreement (when properly executed) is a short-term collateralized loan. Most RPs involve U.S. government securities or securities issued by government-sponsored enterprises. Banks are active participants on the borrowing side of the RP market.

A second important role of banks in the money market is as dealers in the market for over-the-counter interest rate derivatives, which has grown rapidly in recent years. Over-the-counter interest rate derivatives set terms for the exchange of cash payments based on subsequent changes in market interest rates. For example, in an interest rate swap, the parties to the agreement exchange cash payments to one another based on movements in specified market interest rates. Banks frequently act as middleman in swap transactions by serving as a counterparty to both sides of the transaction.

A third role of banks in the money market is to provide, in exchange for fees, commitments that help insure that investors in money market securities will be paid on a timely basis. One type of commitment is a backup line of credit to issuers of money market securities, which is typically dependent on the financial condition of the issuer and can be withdrawn if that condition deteriorates.

PART I Introduction

Another type of commitment is a credit enhancement—generally in the form of a letter of credit—that guarantees that the bank will redeem a security upon maturity if the issuer does not. Backup lines of credit and letters of credit are widely used by commercial paper issuers and by issuers of municipal securities.

GOVERNMENTS

The U.S. Treasury and state and local governments raise large sums in the money market. The Treasury raises funds in the money market by selling short-term obligations of the U.S. government called Treasury bills. Bills have the largest volume outstanding and the most active secondary market of any money market instrument. Because bills are generally considered to be free of default risk, while other money market instruments have some default risk, bills typically have the lowest interest rate at a given maturity. State and local governments raise funds in the money market through the sale of both fixed-and variable-rate securities. A key feature of state and local securities is that their interest income is generally exempt from federal income taxes, which makes them particularly attractive to investors in high income tax brackets.

CORPORATIONS

Nonfinancial and nonbank financial businesses raise funds in the money market primarily by issuing commercial paper, which is a short-term unsecured promissory note. In recent years an increasing number of firms have gained access to this market, and commercial paper has grown at a rapid pace. Business enterprises—generally those involved in international trade—also raise funds in the money market through bankers acceptances. A bankers acceptance is a time draft drawn on and accepted by a bank (after which the draft becomes an unconditional liability of the bank). In a typical bankers acceptance a bank accepts a time draft from an importer and then discounts it (gives the importer slightly less than the face value of the draft). The importer then uses the proceeds to pay the exporter. The bank may hold the acceptance itself or rediscount (sell) it in the secondary market.

GOVERNMENT-SPONSORED ENTERPRISES

Government-sponsored enterprises are a group of privately owned financial intermediaries with certain unique ties to the federal government. These agencies borrow funds in the financial markets and channel these funds primarily to the farming and housing sectors of the economy. They raise a substantial part of their funds in the money market.

MONEY MARKET MUTUAL FUNDS AND OTHER SHORT-TERM INVESTMENT POOLS

Short-term investment pools are a highly specialized group of money market intermediaries that includes money market mutual funds, local government investment pools, and short-term investment funds of bank trust departments. These intermediaries purchase large pools of money market instruments and sell shares in these instruments to investors. In doing so they enable individuals and other small investors to earn the yields available on money market instruments. These pools, which were virtually nonexistent before the mid-1970s, have grown to be one of the largest financial intermediaries in the United States.

FUTURES EXCHANGES

Money market futures contracts and futures options are traded on organized exchanges which set and enforce trading rules. A money market futures contract is a standardized agreement to buy or sell a money market security at a particular price on a specified future date. There are actively traded contracts for 13-week Treasury bills, three-month Eurodollar time deposits, and one-month Eurodollar time deposits. There is also a futures contract based on a 30-day average of the daily federal funds rate.

A money market futures option gives the holder the right, but not the obligation, to buy or sell a money market futures contract at a set price on or before a specified date. Options are currently traded on three-month Treasury bill futures, three-month Eurodollar futures, and one-month Eurodollar futures.

DEALERS AND BROKERS

The smooth functioning of the money market depends critically on brokers and dealers, who play a key role in marketing new issues of money market instruments and in providing secondary markets where outstanding issues can be sole prior to maturity. Dealers use RPs to finance their inventories of securities. Dealers also act as intermediaries between other participants in the RP market by making loans to those wishing to borrow in the market and borrowing from those wishing to lend in the market.

Brokers match buyers and sellers of money market instruments on a commission basis. Brokers play a major role in linking borrowers and lenders in the federal funds market and are also active in a number of other markets as intermediaries in trade between dealers.

FEDERAL RESERVE

The Federal Reserve is a key participant in the money market. The Federal Reserve controls the supply of reserves available to banks and other depository institutions primarily through the purchase and sale of Treasury bills, either outright in the bill

PART I Introduction

market or on a temporary basis in the market for repurchase agreements. By controlling the supply of reserves, the Federal Reserve is able to influence the federal funds rate. Movements in this rate, in turn, can have pervasive effects on other money market rates. The Federal Reserve's purchases and sales of Treasury bills—called "open market operations"—are carried out by the Open Market Trading Desk at the Federal Reserve Bank of New York. The Trading Desk frequently engages in billions of dollars of open market operations in a single day.

The Federal Reserve can also influence reserves and money market rates through its administration of the discount window and the discount rate. Under certain Federal Reserve operating procedures, changes in the discount rate have a strong direct effect on the funds rate and other money market rates. Because of their roles in the implementation of monetary policy, the discount window and the discount rate are of widespread interest in the financial markets.

QUESTIONS

1. What is the money market? Why does it exist? What are the basic characteristics of money market instruments?

2. Who are the principal borrowers in the money market? Through what instruments do they borrow?

3. Describe banks' various roles in the money market.

READING 2

Logging On To Electronic Means of Payment

Michelle L. Kezar

Stretched out on the couch, you flip on the TV. You skip past the nature channel to the banking channel and select your checking account. As you scan the register, you realize that you forgot to buy a birthday present for your mother.

Not to worry. You go upstairs and flick on your personal computer. You log onto the Internet and look for a present at the virtual mall. Within an hour, you find the perfect gift: a recipe book. You run your debit card through the card reader built into your computer. You know that the bank will automatically deduct the cost of the purchase from your checking account, and that the present will be mailed to your mother in time.

As you leave the mall, though, you hear a digitized voice coming from your computer: "Your rental payment is overdue." Quickly, you tell your PC to pay the rent. As you log off, the phone on your other line rings. It is your landlord asking for your late rent payment. "It's in the e-mail," you say smugly.

Some day soon this scenario could be a reality. Debit cards, smart cards, electronic cash, electronic checks—all of these electronic means of payment (EMOP) are now coming into use. Slowly, they are beginning to replace paper checks and paper cash.

Electronic means of payment are a big step beyond credit cards, the first and now widespread alternative to payment by cash or check. A credit card issuer acts as an intermediary between the merchant and the consumer. For the merchant, it takes on, for a fee, the burden of verification and debt collection. For the consumer, it consolidates transactions, puts off the due date, and acts as a buffer in disputes.

EMOP often eliminate the intermediary. When a customer makes a purchase, his bank account is debited. For the merchant, payment is guaranteed and almost immediate. For the consumer, EMOP offer convenience, instant proof that the "money" is good, and automated bookkeeping.

Not surprisingly, EMOP are widely touted as the wave of the future. But the hype was there 20 years ago, too. *Business Week* in 1975 predicted that EMOP soon "will revolutionize the very concept of money itself." Less than two years later, though, the same magazine noted, "Suddenly it appears

---

Reprinted from Federal Reserve Bank of Richmond *Cross Sections*, 12, 4 (Winter 1995/96), 10-18. The views expressed in *Cross Sections* are those of the contributors and not necessarily those of the Federal Reserve Bank of Richmond or the Federal Reserve System.

PART I Introduction

that the great electronic ... revolution that has been 'just around the corner' for a decade may never arrive at all."

What happened was that revolutions take time. People were unlikely to give up writing checks overnight. They were going to require other reasons to invest in the home PCs needed for some EMOP transactions. Merchants also were hesitant to embrace EMOP because they faced start-up costs. Another problem was that the communication networks and supporting tools were not established. Software programmers had hardly begun the work needed to address the prickly issue of privacy or the major threats of theft and fraud. And the standardization of equipment and networks that would be needed to minimize cost and complexity for both consumers and merchants was far from complete.

In the last few years there has been enormous progress in making electronic means of payment a reality. Many consumers, for example, can use their ATM cards as debit cards to pay retailers. And today some 44 percent of American households surveyed now contain at least one PC, according to an *American Banker*/Gallup report. A consumer now can navigate the Internet, likely to be the major communications link for electronic payments, with user-friendly software. Entrepreneurs, banks, and other financial institutions are working vigorously on the details of various EMOP transactions. And a growing number of these transactions are now being tested in marketplace trials.

Still, the obstacles to EMOP remain immense. So the transition to a cashless society is certain to be a bumpy one—unlikely to be concluded within the next decade or two. Changes in the payment system, notes Thomas Hoenig, president of the Federal Reserve Bank of Kansas City, "tend to be evolutionary, not revolutionary."

EMOP TRANSACTIONS

Whatever the timetable for the arrival of a cashless society, experts agree that someday everyone will be EMOP users. Use of debit cards and smart cards will grow most rapidly. The use of electronic cash and checks, which require computer access, will increase more slowly.

Debit Cards. Like a credit card, a debit card has a magnetic strip from which a card reader can extract data. When consumers use a debit card issued by a bank to make purchases, they authorize deductions from their checking accounts at that bank. If the merchant processes the card on-line, which is usually the case, the deduction is immediate. For the consumer's protection, the user must furnish a separate personal identification number (PIN) when the card is used.

The Bank of Delaware launched the first debit card program in 1966. Several other banks ran pilot programs through the mid-1970s, but major efforts to launch debit cards did not develop until the early 1980s. Currently, most banks and many nonbank companies such as Visa and Mastercard issue debit cards or ATM cards that also can function as debit cards. A consumer can use debit cards in many of the places that accept credit cards, such as gas stations, supermarkets, and other retail stores.

READING 2 Logging on to Electronic Means of Payment

Smart Cards. Unlike a debit card, which deducts money from a bank account after a purchase, a smart card requires an outlay from the user's account prior to a purchase. A smart card, as the name implies, can do much more than a simple debit card can do. That's because it has an embedded microprocessor chip, which makes it possible to store, retrieve, and in some cases to manipulate data.

There are two basic types of smart cards. The simpler type, known as "stored value," is one a consumer buys with a preset dollar amount and then spends down. It is, in effect, disposable. The more versatile type, commonly termed "intelligent," is loaded with value from a user's bank account whenever needed. The user can do this at an ATM. Instead of "spitting out money," the ATM adds value to the card representing a specific amount, such as $100, according to Bob Gilson, executive director of the Smart Card Forum, a multi-industry group that is promoting the smart card. Some banks offer cards that can have value added to them using a PC or a specially equipped telephone.

Potentially, the intelligent smart card would be able to store not only cash balances, but also data on shopping patterns, store coupons, citizenship status, and medical history. Card users eventually may be able to pay for a night on the town, including money for the babysitter with nothing more than a smart card. Consumers already are seeing the benefit of the cards—more than 30 million cards are being used worldwide.

Smart card technology was first developed by a French journalist, Roland Moreno, in 1974. France has been driving the technology ever since, running the first trial of smart cards in 1982. Several U.S. banks and other financial organizations recently have announced smart-card trials. The list includes Citibank, Chemical Bank, and Electronic Payment Services.

A major test in connection with the 1996 Olympics in Atlanta is planned by three banks—First Union Bank, Wachovia, and NationsBank—that are teaming up with Visa. As part of the team project, First Union, headquartered in Charlotte, N.C., expects to issue about a million cards in the Atlanta area. About 70 percent of the cards will be disposable, stored-value cards. The remaining 30 percent will be rechargeable cards.

One company that has added a twist to the smart card is the London-based Mondex. It developed a smart card that enables individuals to transfer value electronically—not just between buyers and sellers, but between any individuals. To transfer value from one card to another, a cardholder uses a handheld wireless device that has been dubbed an electronic wallet. The wallet stores five currencies simultaneously and displays the stored value on a screen.

The electronic wallet moniker is not an idle overstatement, according to Benjamin Miller, publisher and editor of *Personal Identification Newsletter*. In the future, he says, such a device will store everything that is currently kept in a conventional wallet—money, identification, allergy warnings, licenses, credit cards, phone numbers, and, yes, other smart cards. Predicts Miller: "Someday everyone will carry an electronic wallet."

PART I Introduction

Mondex started testing the card in Swindon, England, in July 1995. In August, Wells Fargo Bank in San Francisco announced that it will distribute 90 cards to employees—the first U.S. test for Mondex.

Electronic Cash. The Internet offers plenty of opportunities to shop on-line. Already, the estimated 30 million Internet users loom as an enticing new market waiting to be reached by marketers worldwide. According to *Internet World*, the Internet "represents the cheapest new business opportunity in history .... Many businesses will use the Internet as an alternative form of distribution because of its large reach and relatively low cost."

Technology companies have attempted to stimulate the growth of the on-line marketplace by developing electronic cash, also known as e-cash. E-cash is nothing more than a digital representation of money. To get e-cash, a consumer funds an account with a bank connected to the Internet. The bank converts funds from the user's account to e-cash. The bank then transfers the e-cash to the consumer's PC.

A consumer who wants to buy something using e-cash, for example, "travels" to an Internet store. After selecting an item, the consumer selects the "buy" option, which automatically transfers e-cash from the consumer's computer to the merchant's computer. The merchant's computer automatically contacts the Internet bank to verify that the e-cash is valid; if so, the bank approves the transaction and credits the merchant's account. The Internet store then ships the items to the user.

DigiCash, based in Amsterdam, appears to be taking the lead in developing e-cash systems for the Internet. In a year-old trial still underway, it is giving 10,000 volunteers $100 of Cyberbucks, DigiCash's version of e-cash. The recipients cannot exchange Cyberbucks for any existing currency, but they can use them to purchase goods at any of the 75 participating Internet shops, which include such disparate businesses as Encyclopedia Britannica and the Road Runner Shop. The $100 may not seem like much for a shopping expedition these days, but it's a useful amount for Internet shopping. Many shops in DigiCash's trial program are selling wares for less than a dollar.

Merchants worldwide who want to tap more deeply into the market for small cash transactions, ones for less than $10, are helping to fuel the work on EMOP. An estimate by *The Economist* puts this global market at $2 trillion. According to Smart Card Forum, 88 percent of U.S. commercial transactions are made with cash or checks and 83 percent of those transactions are for less than $10.

Glenn Edelman, assistant to the vice president of e-cash business development for DigiCash, believes that a majority of payments on the Internet will be small. One reason for this, notes Edelman, is that there is a need to be able to sell parts of products, such as an article from a magazine instead of the entire issue. Although credit card transactions for small amounts are costly for merchants, with e-cash, Edelman believes, many merchants are more likely to offer low-priced products and services.

READING 2 Logging on to Electronic Means of Payment

KEY TERMS

Debit card. A debit card is a plastic card issued by a bank or other financial institution by which purchases are deducted directly from the cardholder's checking account.

E-cash. E-cash is a digital representation of money that consists of binary code. Consumers will be able to use e-cash to buy goods and services from stores on the Internet. To get e-cash, consumers fund an account with a bank connected to the Internet. The bank converts funds from the user's account to e-cash. The bank then transfers the e-cash to the consumer's PC.

E-check. An e-check is the electronic equivalent of a paper check that can be used when the parties and banks involved are connected to an electronic network, such as the Internet. A consumer writes an e-check using a PC and sends the "check" over the network to the other party. The recipient forwards the e-check to his bank for deposit. The bank then forwards the e-check to the consumer's bank for collection.

Internet. This is a collection of international computer networks that links schools and universities, businesses, government agencies, libraries, nonprofit organizations and individuals. It is an outgrowth of a government research project called Arpanet, created to link government agencies and universities. When it was developed in 1969, electronic commerce was nowhere in the plan. Now businesses run over 60 percent of the networks that comprise the Internet. CommerceNet estimates that more than 20 million people in 140 countries have access.

Smart card. A smart card is a plastic card, issued by a bank or other financial institution, that has cash value. The card has an embedded microprocessor chip that can store, retrieve, and in some cases manipulate data to transfer value and track a person's cash balance. An intelligent type can be reloaded with cash value and can store much more data, such as a person's medical history, shopping patterns, or citizenship status.

The current DigiCash project is intended in part to "gauge popularity and to deal with any glitches" in its e-cash system, says Edelman. The system moved another step toward reality this past October when Mark Twain Bancshares, a regional bank holding company based in St. Louis, agreed to set up e-cash accounts on the Internet. Using technology developed by DigiCash, Mark Twain Bancshares will be the first issuer of e-cash for payments by personal computer. The bank initially is limiting the trial to 10,000 accounts and keeping transactions among its account holders.

PART I   Introduction

Electronic Checks. As more people sign onto the Internet, interest in electronic checks also is growing. With such a system, a purchaser uses a PC to write the equivalent of a check and then sends the "check" to the seller who, in turn, forwards it to his bank. The seller's bank verifies that the e-check is valid, then transfers money from the purchaser's bank account to the seller's bank account. E-checks also can be used for transactions with other individuals, provided all users are connected to the same network.

For purchasers, there is a downside to using e-checks instead of paper checks: Purchasers lose much of their float—the time between when a transaction is charged to an account and when money is taken out of an account. That's because the receiving bank need not wait for the couriers required to transport paper checks.

For sellers, though, there is an enormous upside in greatly reduced costs of check processing. Some compelling numbers come from the Financial Services Technology Consortium (FSTC), a group of banks, technology companies, and government research and development projects. FSTC says that the cost of an average paper-check transaction, including paper, printing, postage, and processing, is 84 cents. In comparison, the cost of an e-check is only 29 cents.

One organization already using e-checks is the Commonwealth of Virginia. In May 1994, its Department of Accounts started paying some of the state's bills with e-checks. Richard Davis, the department's assistant fiscal manager, estimates that in general the cost of making electronic payments is 30 percent below the cost of printing and mailing paper checks.

REVOLUTIONS TAKE TIME

Considering the development of EMOP and their supporting technology, it's hard to see why electronic payments have not made more rapid inroads in the financial system. but developers had to overcome major obstacles before EMOP could become commonplace. And while present real-world tests seem to promise rapid advances for EMOP, some major issues remain.

Technical Standardization. One big reason that EMOP progress has been slow to date is that businesses lacked a common set of technical standards for collecting and processing payments data. When businesses use a multitude of systems and there are a large number of people involved, "it may be extremely difficult to achieve the coordination necessary to obtain a common set of standards," noted the Federal Reserve's Hoenig in a speech.

Success in standardization to date differs widely among EMOP transactions. For example, both the information on the magnetic strip of a debit card and the characteristics of the machine that reads it must be standardized to gain wide acceptance by merchants. That task has been largely achieved. One reason is that debit-card standards have advanced with ATM standards. By 1993, as a result of bank mergers, a handful of ATM networks controlled more than half the market, making technical coordination much easier than before.

READING 2 Logging on to Electronic Means of Payment

Compared with debit cards, much standardization is still needed with smart cards. A major player in the standardization effort is the Smart Card Forum whose mission, says Executive Director Gilson, is finding "a way for all the networks to learn to talk to one another."

As for the Internet, until recently it was a network used to connect universities and government agencies. Now that transactions over the Internet are developing, says Cathy Medich, executive director of CommerceNet, "procedures that are consistent are important for [electronic means of payment] to go forward."

CommerceNet, a consortium of companies that includes Bank of America, Intel, Netscape, and Hewlett Packard, was founded in 1993 to "look at the issues of [creating] an electronic [marketplace] on the Internet," Medich says. The companies involved hope that they will be able to develop standards that will make e-cash almost as common as real cash.

Start-up Costs. For merchants, all EMOP transactions involve significant up-front costs for infrastructure. A merchant who accepts debit cards, for example, would have to lay out between $100 and $600 for each on-line card reader. For smart cards, that figure might be as much as $1,000. "The issue of infrastructure," says Edgar Brown, senior vice president at First Union, "is the biggest stumbling block to the growth of any kind of transaction product."

For consumers, debit cards and smart cards have no up-front costs beyond the cash needed to fund them. But for those without a PC at home—an estimated 56 percent today—getting onto the Internet to use e-cash or e-checks will require an outlay of about $1,500 to $2,000, which for some could be significant. And even for those who already own PCs, Internet access adds another monthly bill to pay.

Consumer Resistance. Start-up costs aside, many consumers have balked at the idea of abandoning paper checks for their transactions. One reason is that consumers are largely comfortable with the recordkeeping that canceled paper checks provide. Another is the time and effort required to learn to use the new technologies.

Perhaps just as important is the loss of float with EMOP. The use of a paper check typically gives purchasers several days of float. As noted earlier, an e-check eliminates most of that float. When a person uses a debit card online, he gets zero float. And with a smart card or e-cash, he gets what might be called negative float: The stored value may sit for days or weeks before being used and earns no interest the entire time.

Even so, consumer acceptance of debit-card transactions has been growing at a healthy clip. According to *Bank Network News*, the number of debit-card transactions grew 30 percent between 1990 and 1993, to more than 700 million transactions. And in 1994 the number of on-line installed terminals doubled to 344,000 units.

At the same time, consumers are showing undeniable signs of interest in e-cash and e-checks. A 1995 *American Banker*/Gallup Consumer Survey found that 12 percent of respondents who own PCs have used them for electronic means of payment transactions. People still are "exploring," says

PART I   Introduction

CommerceNet's Medich, "but they are much more used to the on-line world now."

Privacy and Security. As consumers become more knowledgeable about smart cards and the Internet, they are likely to become more concerned about potential loss of privacy. A smart card, for example, can store a vast amount of personal data. Privacy advocates worry that employers, insurers, and government officials, not to mention marketers, may obtain that data. Some worry that a smart card may be the precursor to a national ID card—complete with such personal details as prior criminal record or a person's medical history.

For many, the Internet is even more scary. Its inherently open structure gives users access to any transaction that occurs on the Internet. Such accessibility does not merely threaten privacy. It makes all too easy the theft and wrongful use of account numbers, which may lead to financial loss for Internet users. The current inability to provide confidentiality is why credit card information for Internet transactions is sent separately by phone or fax.

Finding a solution to this problem is critical to the future of e-cash and e-checks. "A lot of digital cash approaches are basically begging people to try to break them," says Kawika Daguio, federal representative for regulatory and trust affairs at the American Bankers Association (ABA).

The solution for on-line credit card purchases, e-cash, and e-checks may lie in encryption. Encryption uses complex mathematical formulas to garble messages. Companies such as CyberCash Inc., based in Reston, Va., are working on codes intended to prevent snoopers from reading, and criminals from stealing, confidential information on the Internet.

CyberCash signed an agreement with First National Bank of Omaha under which merchants honoring the bank's credit card will use CyberCash software to process credit card payments on the Internet while maintaining confidentiality. According to *American Banker*, more than 44,000 merchants will have access to the system.

Some e-cash developers maintain that the key to privacy is anonymity—a feature that DigiCash and Mondex are building into their systems. Dan Eldridge, vice president of e-cash business development for DigiCash, believes that the ability to make anonymous transactions with e-cash will prove to be an important plus for e-cash compared to other EMOP transactions.

Other EMOP experts, however, believe that it will be necessary to compromise on privacy to achieve the best protection against fraud. ABA's Daguio notes that the data that a credit card issuer now has on a user's spending habits allows it to identify atypical transactions and alert the user to the possibility of illegal card use. "The real battle," says Daguio, "is between anonymity and accountability."

DigiCash is certain that, given a choice, consumers will opt for anonymity. One reason for this is the perils of loss from Internet transactions are invisible and somewhat abstract. With smart cards, though, the possibilities for physical loss or theft are easier to visualize. Carrying a smart card is just like carrying cash: If the card is lost, the

READING 2 Logging on to Electronic Means of Payment

money stored on it, as well as any stored information, is gone.

If that happens, a person's maximum loss may or may not be limited under current law. Under the Electronic Fund Transfer Act (EFTA), a loss resulting from illegal use of an ATM or debit card is limited to $50. Under debate is whether smart cards fall under EFTA. A reload of a rechargeable type of smart card resembles an ATM withdrawal, but a disposable stored-value card has little in common with either an ATM or a debit card.

If, in fact, losses resulting from a misplaced or stolen smart card are covered to any degree, there remains the problem of proving how much value was stored on the card. With anonymous transactions, there is little chance of making a case.

EMOP raise two other security issues as well—not so much for individual users as for the public as a whole. Some EMOP transactions may make it easier to launder money. Transactions with a smart card such as Mondex's leave no audit trail. So criminals who need to move large amounts of money could easily do so with on plastic card instead of suitcases. The same problem applies to unrecorded transfers via e-cash.

The other concern is counterfeiting. By reproducing the binary code of e-cash, for example, a forger could reproduce e-cash. "All you have to do is break into the system once ... and you can do whatever you want," says ABA's Daguio. He believes that the counterfeiting threat has received too little attention. He noted that precautions are taken with paper currency and the same should hold true for e-cash. "We don't put five billion dollars in cash in trucks and send them out on the highway because we look at the risks," he says. Some of the developers of e-cash who are out there, he claims, don't look at the possible risks.

Reproducing binary code might not be any easier than counterfeiting paper money, however, especially with the advent of high-quality photocopying and laser printing. Smart card developers expect to rely in part on encryption techniques and in part on operating procedures. And DigiCash and its competitors hope to protect e-cash by building an electronic signature or "watermark" into it.

All of the privacy and security issues of EMOP represent not just technical and marketing challenges, but also, at least potentially, public policy concerns. Outside of EFTA, these concerns have yet to be reflected in legislation or regulation. If EMOP make inroads into the nation's payments system, which now seems likely to happen over the next decade or so, there will almost certainly be a perceived need for regulation that addresses the potential hazards of the new environment.

For now, many technical and marketing issues still await resolution. But resolution appears a lot closer than it was when EMOP were first hyped 20 years ago.

PART I Introduction

> **QUESTIONS**
>
> 1. Is the electronic means of payment revolution more likely to occur now than when it was first anticipated 20 years ago? Why?
>
> 2. What electronic alternatives exist for cash and checks—the most common means of payment today? How do these EMOP work?
>
> 3. What are the main obstacles to widespread use of EMOP? Can they be easily overcome? Explain.
>
> 4. What costs do consumers incur in using EMOP?

READING 3

The Changing Meaning of Money

John V. Duca

Because inflation can quickly disrupt an economy, central banks have tried to develop policies to keep inflation in check. One approach assumes that there is a stable relationship between economic activity and the measured money supply. Recently, this relationship has been changing because people have been changing how they handle their finances and how they pay for goods and services. As a result, what the measured money supply means, in terms of what it reveals about economic activity, has also changed.

DOES M2 STILL MEASURE UP?

Money and economic activity are linked by the famous equation of exchange:

money × money's velocity = the price level × real GDP,

or

$$M \times V = P \times Y.$$

In other words, changing hands V times during a year, the money stock, M, facilitates the transaction of Y goods, which each cost P dollars. Converting this equation into growth rates yields two important relationships:

$$\text{inflation} = \text{money supply growth} + \text{velocity growth} - \text{real output growth}$$

and

$$\text{nominal GDP growth} = \text{money supply growth} + \text{velocity growth}$$

where *nominal GDP growth* equals growth in the dollar volume of gross domestic production (output growth plus inflation). U.S. output typically grows at about 2.5 percent annually. Thus, the equation of exchange strongly suggests that over the long run, inflation can be kept at zero by limiting money supply growth to equal 2.5 percent minus growth in velocity.

Money holdings typically fall and velocity rises as the spread between a riskless short-term market interest rate and the average yield on monetary assets rises. The stability of the relationship between interest rates and velocity

Reprinted from Federal Reserve Bank of Dallas *The Southwest Economy*, Issue 6, 1995, 6–9.

PART I Introduction

is what makes it possible for money to be a useful indicator of not only inflation, but also of nominal GDP *(P x Y)*, since GDP data are available after a long lag, unlike data on money and interest rates. If velocity is predictable, then by controlling money supply growth, the Federal Reserve can control long-run inflation. While this sounds easy, shifts in how people conduct their finances and how they pay for goods can undermine the stability of the money—GDP relationship, thus making the Fed's inflation-fighting job more difficult in practice.

History bears this out. The M1 monetary aggregate that measures the money supply as checking deposits plus currency was once touted as the "holy grail" by monetarists. But M1 began to fall from grace in the mid-1970s when its velocity was unusually high, and M1 growth underpredicted real GDP, based on prior velocity behavior. Then in the early 1980s, the interest-rate sensitivity of M1 jumped as financial innovations and deregulation created new deposits that combined savings and transactions features and helped firms avoid holding non-interest-bearing demand deposits. As a result, attention turned to M2, a broader and less interest-rate-sensitive aggregate that was created in 1980.

M2 was redefined to include not only conventional M1, passbook savings accounts and small time deposits, but also new types of money market mutual funds, overnight instruments and, in 1982, money market deposit accounts. M2 had a stable relationship with nominal GDP during the 1980s (Small and Porter 1989). However, this relationship broke down in the 1990s as M2 became more sensitive to bond yields and as households shifted toward bond and stock mutual funds and toward Treasury securities (see Duca 1995b for references).

Such breakdowns in the link between money and nominal output have spurred efforts to either redefine money to include new types of "money" or revise money models to account for changing relationships between money and nominal output.[1] Understanding why the money—income relationship can shift is critical to finding new ways of deriving information from money.

WHY THE MONEY—NOMINAL GDP RELATIONSHIP CAN SHIFT

A stable link between M2 and nominal GDP will hold as long as people handle their finances in the same way.[2] However, a market economy will continuously create new financial products and markets will react to fundamental changes in the tastes of households (*Table 1*).

Since the early 1980s, the attractiveness to households of owning non-M2 assets has increased because of two types of technological change: lower costs of transferring funds from nonmonetary assets to transactions deposits (from bond mutual funds to money market funds, for instance) and greater use of financial services from nonasset products (such as credit cards). Nonmonetary assets are any assets not included in the definition of the monetary aggregates, while nonasset products are instruments or ways of conducting transactions that do not directly

Table 1
How Market Forces Can Cause Unusual Weakness in Money

Fundamental type of factor	Examples
Technological innovations	
Lower transfer costs	Lower mutual fund commission (load) fees Easier purchase of Treasury securities Electronic banking Easier banking and investing by phone
Financial services from nonassets	More widespread credit cards and lines Automatic teller machines Electronic wires and transfers
Demographics, preferences and learning	
Demographic shifts	Rising population share of middle-aged people preparing for retirement
Preferences and financial sophistication	Rising share of households sophistication with portable pensions due to IRA/Keogh laws and increased job uncertainty Greater tolerance of investment risk

and immediately involve holding an asset (for example, using a credit card to pay for something) until final settlement is made. As the cost of shifting between non-M2 assets and checkable deposits falls, the incentive to hold checking deposits to avoid transfer costs declines. Since households balance the transfer cost savings from holding money against the higher yields on alternative assets, lower transfer costs have induced lower money holdings. For example, over the past 10 years, the costs of shifting from a bond mutual fund to a checkable money market fund have fallen as transfer fees have fallen and as transfers have become easier. As a result, when longer term interest rates (on bond funds) are high relative to short-term rates (on money market funds), people are more likely to hold bond funds today than 10 years ago when transfers involved higher fees and greater headaches.

Thanks to improvements in financial products, households and firms can now better coordinate cash inflow with cash outflow. As a result, they can reduce check usage by consolidating many purchases into fewer check

PART I Introduction

payments. They also have less need to hold checking balances for unexpected expenses.

Aside from technological changes, a rise in households' awareness of assets outside of M2 and their tolerance for risk can lead to unusual weakness in M2. For example, if households needed less extra return on stocks to compensate them for the extra investment risk, then at a given gap between the yields on M2 and stocks, they will hold less M2 and more stocks.

TECHNOLOGY AND NEW PRODUCTS

Lower Asset Transfer Costs

The costs of shifting between non-M2 and checkable M2 assets have fallen in several ways. First, load (commission) fees on mutual funds have fallen sharply over the past two decades.[3] Furthermore, many mutual funds now also allow a greater number of free transfers among funds in asset management accounts. These accounts offer a host of investments, including bonds and equities, and allow no-cost shifts among investments within mutual fund families that typically include a checkable money market fund. So, a person who unexpectedly gets hit with a big car repair bill can use the phone to shift funds from an equity fund to a money market fund (without incurring a fee) and then write a money market fund check. Furthermore, many banks now offer mutual funds and allow customers to jointly manage their mutual fund and deposit balances. Additionally, the Federal Reserve has made it easier for people to buy Treasury securities, a change that, coupled with interest rates, encouraged people to take money out of M2 deposits and buy Treasury securities.[4]

More generally, the spread of better information technology is lowering transfer costs. In particular, the rise of electronic banking (especially via personal computer) poses potentially large reductions in the pecuniary and convenience costs of making such transfers.[5] Unfortunately, continuous data on asset transfer costs over long periods are lacking. Nevertheless, the limited evidence implies that lower transfer costs have led people to reduce M2 balances. In particular, lower transfer costs of using bond and equity funds likely explains why most of the unusual weakness in M2 during the 1990s has been in small time deposits (which compete with stocks and bonds) and money market mutual funds (which were unusually weak when relative yields on stocks and bonds yields were high).

Financial Services from Nonassets

In the 1970s and 1980s, technological advances and high interest rates induced firms to avoid using non-interest-bearing demand deposits to conduct transactions. Cash management techniques, coupled with the increased use of electronic transfers, allowed firms to more easily and cheaply tap nonmonetary assets to meet cash shortfalls. Breaking with the tradition of holding a lot of non-interest-bearing demand deposits, firms adopted cash management techniques that enabled them to better predict their cash needs. Also, firms increasingly used wire transfers when they needed to shift funds. The result was a decline in demand deposits held by firms.

Financial innovations later spread to households after improvements in computer software made such innovations cost-effective for people. By providing liquidity and by enabling households to weather temporary changes in asset prices (such as stock prices), credit cards and credit lines likely induced many households to hold less money and more nonmoney assets.

For example, using 1983 data, Duca and Whitesell (1995) find that each 10-percentage-point rise in the probability of owning a credit card lowers checking accounts by 9 percent and checkable money market mutual funds and money market deposit accounts by 11 percent. The impact of credit cards on checkable balances is likely larger today because credit cards are more widely accepted, credit card purchases are more quickly processed, and consumers are now offered greater incentives to use credit cards. Another important innovation is the spread of automatic teller machines (ATMs). ATMs have reduced the need for people to carry extra cash by allowing them to easily withdraw cash from their checking or savings accounts.[6]

Evidence shows that because people gained a greater choice in how to pay for goods, the composition of M2 had shifted away from transactions and toward nontransactions accounts. Coupled with lower transfer costs, greater use of nonmoney ways of making payments could now be lowering M2, in addition to altering its composition.

ARE DEMOGRAPHICS, PREFERENCES AND LEARNING PLAYING A ROLE?

Greater tolerance of investment risk can stem from changes in employment patterns, demographics and in other factors that boost financial awareness.

Demographics

According to the life-cycle theory of consumption, people borrow when they are young because their income is below that of later years, save in middle age when their income is highest and then draw down their savings in retirement. An implication of this theory is that savings rates and the share of wealth invested in higher earning non-M2 assets should rise in the peak earning years before retirement. By increasing the average need to fund retirement, demographic trends may be inducing an overall shift toward risky assets with higher expected long-term yields and away from lowering earning M2 deposits. Alternatively, as people reach their peak earning years, their ratio of income to spending falls. As this ratio falls, so too will the public's demand for low-transactions cost M2 deposits.

Consistent with these implications, Duca and Whitesell (1995) find that small time and savings deposits are higher for older age groups, after controlling for income and wealth. Furthermore, Morgan (1994) finds that the average share of household assets held in stocks and bonds rises with the population share of 35- to 54-year-old people.

PART I Introduction

Changing Preferences and Learning

Two factors that could be depressing M2 holdings are households' increased awareness of investments outside of M2 and an associated rise in households' willingness to tolerate risk in the assets they control. Aside from new technology and financial products, increased job uncertainty and the liberalization of IRA/401K accounts have induced a shift toward portable (defined contribution) retirement plans that have given households a greater role in managing their retirement assets. This shift, in turn, has induced households to incur large, one-time costs to learn more about bond and equity investments for retirement. In addition, with many mutual funds, people can count their IRA/Keogh mutual fund balances along with other mutual fund holdings toward meeting the minimum balances requirements for opening asset management accounts. As a result, IRA and Keogh assets effectively reduce the minimum balance requirement on non-IRA/Keogh mutual fund assets. Consistent with this, both IRA/Keogh and non-IRA/Keogh bond and equity fund assets rose in the mid-1980s after tax laws were eased and in the early 1990s.[7] Cross-section data confirm a big shift in household portfolios toward bond and equity funds and away from bank CDs since the late 1980s.[8]

CONCLUSION

The recent breakdown in the link between nominal GDP and conventionally defined M2 reflects how technological changes have enabled households to hold less money and more nonmonetary assets. Such innovations have reduced the costs of transferring funds from other assets to checking accounts, or, as in the case of credit cards and lines, have reduced the need to hold money that arises from mismatches of cash inflow and outflow. Changes in tastes and the age composition of the U.S. population may also be heightening the extent to which people can substitute other financial assets for money.

The information revolution will likely further reduce the benefits from holding traditional forms of money by fostering the spread of new electronic types of money, banking through personal computer, credit lines and financial management software. Together with these advances, a likely continuing shift toward portable (defined contribution) retirement plans and tax incentives will likely increase peoples' role in managing their retirement assets. These factors will likely lead people to further reduce their holdings of conventionally defined "money" and increase their investments in higher earning alternative assets. As a result, what growth in conventionally measured money means for inflation will continue to change.

ENDNOTES

I thank the late Stephen Goldfeld and my many colleagues throughout the Federal Reserve System for sharing their insights on money with me over the years.

1. For example, see Collins and Edwards (1994), Duca (1995a and 1994) and Koenig (1995).
2. For a more technical discussion, see Duca's (1995b) modified version of Milbourne's (1986) model of money.
3. For evidence, see Orphanides, Reid and Small (1994).
4. See Feinman and Porter (1992).
5. For more details, see Holland and Cortese (1995) and Lewis (1995).
6. Daniels and Murphy (1994a) find that a 100-percentage-point rise in the probability of ATM use increased the velocity of currency (transactions/currency) by 40 to 45 percent for transactions account holders, while Daniels and Murphy (1994b) estimate that a 5-percent rise in the proportion of ATM users would boost average transactions account balances by 4.5 percent. Together, these studies imply that ATMs induced households to shift from holding cash to holding transactions balances in the mid-1980s.
7. See Duca (1995a) for evidence.
8. See Kennickell and Starr-McCluer (1994) for cross-section evidence. These factors are consistent with a study by Blanchard (1993), who found that the extra return that investors demand from equities over bonds has trended downward since the 1940s and abruptly fell in the early 1980s.

REFERENCES

Blanchard, Olivier J. (1993), "Movements in the Equity Premium," *Brookings Papers on Economic Activity*, no. 2: 75-138.

Collins, Sean, and Cheryl L. Edwards (1994), "Redefining M2 to Include Bond and Equity Mutual Funds," Federal Reserve Bank of St. Louis *Review*, November/December, 7-30.

Daniels, Kenneth N. and Neil B. Murphy (1994a), "The Impact of Technological Change on the Currency Behavior of Households: An Empirical Cross-Section Study," *Journal of Money, Credit, and Banking* 26 (November): 867-74.

_____, and _____ (1994b), "The Impact of Technological Change on Transactions Account Balances: An Empirical Cross-Section Study," *Journal of Financial Services Research* 17 (January): 113-19.

Duca, John V. (1995a), "Should Bond Funds Be Included in M2?" *Journal of Banking and Finance* 19 (April): 131-52.

_____ (1995b), "Sources of Money Instability," Federal Reserve Bank of Dallas *Economic Review*, Fourth Quarter.

_____ (1994), "Would the Addition of Bond or Equity Funds Make M2 a Better Indicator of Nominal GDP?" Federal Reserve Bank of Dallas *Economic Review*, Fourth Quarter, 1-14.

_____, and William C. Whitesell (1995), "Credit Cards and Money Demand: A Cross-Sectional Study," *Journal of Money, Credit, and Banking* 27 (May): 604-23.

Feinman, Joshua, and Richard D. Porter (1992), "The Continued Weakness in M2," FEDS Working Paper no. 209, Board of Governors of the Federal Reserve System (Washington, September).

Holland, Kelley, and Amy Cortese (1995), "The Future of Money," *Business Week*, June 12, 66-78.

Kennickell, Arthur B., and Martha Starr-McCluer (1994), "Changes in Family Finances from 1989 to 1992: Evidence from the Survey of Consumer Finances," *Federal Reserve Bulletin*, October, 861-82.

Koenig, Evan F. (1995), "Long-Term Interest Rates and the Recent Weakness in M2," manuscript, Federal Reserve Bank of Dallas, June.

Lewis, Peter H. (1995), "Chemical Aims to Expand Electronic Banking," *New York Times*, July 7, D5.

PART I Introduction

Milbourne, Ross (1986), "Financial Innovation and the Demand for Liquid Assets," *Journal of Money, Credit, and Banking* 18 (November): 506-11.

Morgan, Donald P. (1994), "Will the Shift to Stocks and Bonds by Households Be Destabilizing?" Federal Reserve Bank of Kansas City *Economic Review*, Second Quarter, 31-44.

Orphanides, Athanasios, Brian Reid, and David H. Small (1994), "Empirical Properties of a Monetary Aggregate that Adds Bond and Stock Funds to M2," Federal Reserve Bank of St. Louis *Review*, November/December, 31-52.

Small, David H., and Richard D. Porter (1989), "Understanding the Behavior of M2 and V2," *Federal Reserve Bulletin*, April 244-54.

QUESTIONS

1. What is the equation of exchange? What insights does it provide into the causes of inflation?

2. How has the use of ATMs and credit cards affected money's velocity? Why?

3. What is the life-cycle theory of consumption? According to this theory, what should happen to velocity as the population ages? Why?

4. What is an *empirical* definition of money? Do the factors Duca discusses make M2 a better or a poorer empirical definition of money? Explain.

PART TWO

FINANCIAL MARKETS

Interest rates and exchange rates are among the most important variables in the economy and explaining how they are determined is an essential part of courses on money, banking, and financial markets. The readings for Part Two provide examples for discussing interest rate determination, the risk and term structure of interest rates, and exchange rate determination.

Reading 4, **"Investment Improvement: Adding Duration to the Toolbox"** by Michelle Clark Neely, discusses several types of risks bond investors face and the use of duration for assessing risk and measuring a bond's price sensitivity to interest rate changes. This reading augments Chapter 4's coverage of the relation between bond prices and interest rates and the distinction between yield and rate of return on a bond.

In Reading 5, **"Inflation-Indexed Bonds,"** Chan Huh describes the workings and benefits of inflation-indexed bonds and suggests governments issue them to demonstrate their commitment to low-inflation policies. This reading can be used with the discussion of the relation between inflation and interest rates in Chapter 6, monetary policy indicators in Chapter 21, or policy credibility in Chapters 28 and 20.

"The Yield Curve as a Predictor of U.S. Recessions" by Arturo Estrella and Frederic S. Mishkin, Reading 6, advocates using the spread between interest rates on ten-year Treasury notes and three-month Treasury bills for forecasting economic activity and recessions. This reading gives students a practical application of the yield curve presented in Chapter 7.

Reading 7, **"McCurrencies: Where's the Beef?"** compares Big Mac prices in several countries to estimate the purchasing power parity value of the dollar. For use with Chapter 8, this reading gives students a palatable introduction to long-run exchange rate determination.

In Reading 8, **"Budget Deficit Cuts and the Dollar,"** Ramon Moreno attempts to reconcile opposing views regarding how cutting the government budget deficit will affect the U.S. dollar. He considers the short- and long-run impacts on the balance of payments, capital flows, expected inflation, productivity, and the composition of demand. This reading supplements Chapter 8's treatment of exchange rate determination.

Why did the dollar depreciate, rather than appreciate, against the yen and the mark as the federal funds rate rose from 3% to 4.25% over the first half of 1994? Charles L. Evans's **"The Dollar and the Federal Funds Rate,"** Reading 9, investigates the empirical relationship between the federal funds rate and the yen/dollar and mark/dollar exchange rates during the 1980s and 1990s to shed some light on this question. The reading goes with Chapter 8's discussion of short-run exchange rate determination.

READING 4

Investment Improvement: Adding Duration to the Toolbox

Michelle Clark Neely

An increasing number of Americans are taking control of personal investment decisions—whether to meet retirement, children's college education or other financial goals. To do this, they're seeking useful, understandable tools that will guide them in making profitable choices. One tool that investors in fixed-income securities—individual bonds or bond mutual funds—have for assessing risk versus reward is an economic formula known as *duration*. Although it is far from a perfect measure of risk, duration is a useful supplement to more common, traditionally used measures, like a bond's credit rating and maturity.

BOND RISK BASICS

Bond investors face several types of risk. One is credit or default risk; that is, the risk that the bond issuer will not repay the principal invested. Since very few debt issuers default on their obligations, however, it is less of a worry for most investors than another major risk, interest rate risk. This is the risk that the market value of an investment—the price an investor would receive if an asset were sold today—will change because of changing market interest rates.

The degree of interest rate risk associated with a given fixed-income security (or bond) depends on the size and timing of the cash flows—interest and principal—from that bond. To see this, consider a zero coupon bond, a bond that pays no interest until maturity.[1] Because no interest is received until maturity, an investor in a zero coupon bond loses out on any opportunity to reinvest potential earnings at higher market interest rates. In addition, if the investor were forced to sell prior to maturity, he could face a substantial loss if current interest rates on a comparable bond were higher than the interest rate on his zero coupon bond.

However, if the same investor were to purchase a coupon-paying bond—like a U.S. Treasury bond—instead, his interest rate risk in a rising interest rate environment would be reduced since interest or coupon payments received at six-month or year intervals could be reinvested at higher interest rates. This would offset some of the loss that might occur if the investor needed to sell the bond prior to maturity.

Reprinted from Federal Reserve Bank of St. Louis *The Regional Economist*, April 1996, 10-11.

PART II Financial Markets

Interest rate risk, then, comprises two distinct types of risks, which frequently counteract each other: price or *market risk* and *reinvestment risk*. Market risk is the risk that an already-issued bond's market price will fluctuate because of changes in market interest rates. It arises because of the inverse relationship between market interest rates and a bond's price. The longer the maturity of the bond, the greater the market risk since the purchaser of an existing bond with a below-market yield will be stuck with it for as long as he holds the bond. Of course, market risk is not an issue for investors who hold bonds to maturity because the face value, not the market value, of the bond is received at maturity.

Reinvestment risk encompasses the risk that cash flows received from an existing investment, like semiannual coupon payments, could be reinvested at different interest rates than those paid on the existing security. When the market interest rates rise, reinvestment risk works in the investor's favor because the cash flows received can be reinvested in higher-yielding securities. When rates fall, however, reinvestment risk works against the investor.

An investor faces market risk whenever his planned holding period for a fixed-income security is less than its maturity. These risks tend to work in opposite directions, however: Rising market interest rates increase market risk but decrease reinvestment risk, while declining interest rates decrease market risk but increase reinvestment risk. In other words, an initial capital loss (from rising market interest rates) may, in time, be more than offset by greater returns from reinvested earnings and vice versa.

DURATION: THE NET EFFECT

So how does an investor know how much interest rate risk—the net effect of market and reinvestment risk—he's assuming when purchasing a bond or shares in a bond mutual fund? That's where duration comes in. Basically, duration measures the average life of a fixed-income security or a portfolio of securities. It is a more precise measure of the life of a bond than maturity because it takes into consideration any cash flows that are received prior to maturity. In general, the sooner cash flows are received and the larger the amount, the lower the duration, or interest rate risk, of the bond.

More specifically, duration is calculated as the weighted average time to maturity of a bond, using the relative present values of the cash flows from the bond as weights. The calculation yields a single number called *Macaulay's duration* that is expressed in units of time, which correspond to the receipt of cash flows.[2] Macaulay's duration depends on the number of cash flow payment periods and the interval between them, the size of the cash flows and the current yield to maturity of the instrument.[3]

To see how duration can be used to judge the riskiness of a fixed-income security, consider two bonds, A and B, which on the surface, at least, appear to be very similar. Bond A is a coupon bond with a face value of $1,000 and a maturity of 20 years; its coupon rate is 8 percent, and it pays interest annually.

Bond B is a zero coupon U.S. Treasury bond that pays principal and interest of $2,600 at maturity. The current yield to maturity on 20-year bonds is 10 percent. Both bonds yield combined principal and interest of $2,600 over 20 years. Which bond, then, has the most interest rate risk?

Although the total cash flows from bonds A and B are equal at maturity, their risk profiles for the intervening years are very different. Bond A has a duration of 9.75 years while Bond B, the zero coupon bond, has a duration of 20 years, equal to its maturity. Bond A has the lower duration and is, therefore the least risky of the two because the investor will start receiving cash flows much sooner than the holder of Bond B. If an investor were in a position where he would need to sell a bond—all else equal—his capital loss would be lowest with Bond A. The duration of Bond B is twice as large as the duration of Bond A because all of the interest is deferred until maturity.

DURATION DYNAMICS

The example above illustrates how differences in the timing of cash flows change the duration of a bond. Listed below are several other properties of duration that an investor can use either to differentiate the risk characteristics of similar bonds or to anticipate how changes in bond characteristics alter its duration.

- *The duration of a bond is always less than its maturity, except for a zero coupon bond, whose duration is always equal to its maturity.*

- *Duration declines as the coupon rate rises, holding maturity and yield to maturity constant.*

- *Duration declines as the yield to maturity rises, holding the coupon rate and maturity constant.*

- *Duration increases as maturity increases, holding the coupon rate and yield to maturity constant.*[4]

Another useful feature of duration is that, by rearranging the duration equation, it can be used to predict the sensitivity of a bond's price to very small increases in interest rates. This rearranged calculation is called *modified duration*.[5] The percentage change in the price of a bond can be approximated by multiplying the percentage point change in the yield to maturity by negative one and the bond's modified duration. The modified duration for Bond A, the 20-year coupon bond with a duration of 9.75 years, is 8.86 years. If market interest rates rise one percentage point to 11 percent, the price of this bond will decline about 8.9 percent to $911.40. For Bond B, the zero coupon bond, a one percentage point increase in market interest rates would lead to a whopping 18.2 percent *decline* in price. Of course, if interest rates decline one percentage point, Bondholder A would enjoy about a 9 percent capital gain, and Bondholder B would reap an 18 percent gain.

This simple relationship between duration, interest rates and bond prices can help an investor determine an optimal investment strategy based on his expectations about future interest rates.[6] For example, if an investor expects interest rates to rise in the near future, he would likely want to keep the duration of his bonds or bond mutual fund short to minimize any potential losses, should a sale become necessary.[7] Conversely, in a falling interest rate environment, an investor may want to lengthen the duration of his fixed-income securities, for two reasons; first, he may be able to sell them for a nice gain and second, a longer duration positions an investor to take advantage of a rebound in interest rates, which could lead to profitable reinvestment opportunities. An investor may also wish to use duration to partially hedge or immunize interest rate risk: Market risk and reinvestment risk almost completely offset each other when the duration of a security is equal to the investor's planned holding period.

Duration has been used to measure and hedge interest rate risk to varying degrees by financial institutions and other institutional investors for decades. With an increasing number of brokers and bond mutual fund managers calculating and keeping an eye on duration, individual investors would be wise to add it to their investment toolbox, too.

ENDNOTES

1. Zero coupon bonds, like T-bills and certain other instruments, are frequently sold at a discount from their face value and do not pay periodic interest or a coupon. The return, or compounded interest, on these investments is the difference between the discounted purchase price and the face value of the instrument.

2. The mathematical formula for Macaulay's duration (D) is:

$$D = \frac{\sum_{t=1}^{N} \frac{t \cdot C_t}{(1+r)^t}}{\sum_{t=1}^{N} \frac{C_t}{(1+r)^t}}$$

where N = number of cash flows, t = time to receipt of the cash flow, C_t = cash flow amount in period t, and r = yield to maturity. The expression $C_t/(1+r)^t$ is the present discounted value of the cash flow received in each period t. The sum of all these cash flows is equal to the market value or price of the bond.

3. The yield to maturity is the expected rate of return, or interest rate, on a given debt security held until maturity. Because the yield to maturity can be difficult to calculate, the current market interest rate on comparable securities is usually used in the duration calculation.

4. This last property only holds true for par and premium bonds. For deep-discount bonds, duration increases with maturity to a distant point and then declines. That's because bonds with really long maturities behave like *perpetuities*, bonds that pay coupons forever. See Bierwag (1987) or Kritzman (1992) for details.

5. The modified duration calculation is: $D_m = D/(1+r)$ where D_m is modified duration, D is Macaulay's duration and r is the yield to maturity or current market interest rate.

6. Duration has its limitations, mostly because it is based on some unrealistic assumptions. For example, duration and modified duration calculations implicitly assume that short-term and long-term interest rates are equal, i.e., the yield curve is flat. See Bierwag (1987).

7. The duration of a bond mutual fund is the weighted average of the durations of the individual bonds in the fund.

FOR FURTHER READING

Bierwag, Gerald O. *Duration Analysis: Managing Interest Rate Risk* (Ballinger Publishing Co., 1987).

Kritzman, Mark. "What Practitioners Need to Know About Duration and Convexity," *Financial Analysts Journal* (November/December 1992), pp. 17-20.

Saunders, Anthony. *Financial Institutions Management: A Modern Perspective* (Irwin, 1994), Chapter 6.

Williams, Gordon. "Deciphering Duration," *Financial World* (October 12, 1993), pp. 80-82.

QUESTIONS

1. Define and compare default risk, interest rate risk, market risk, and reinvestment risk.

2. How do market risk and reinvestment risk affect an investor when interest rates fall?

3. During a period of falling interest rates, would you prefer to be holding a 15-year coupon bond or a 15-year zero-coupon bond? Explain why using the duration concept.

READING 5

Inflation-Indexed Bonds

Chan Huh

A number of industrial countries have recently started issuing inflation-indexed government securities: that is, bonds with yields that rise and fall with inflation. The U.K. was among the earliest, inaugurating such bonds in 1981, followed by Australia in 1986, and by Sweden and Canada in the early 1990s; New Zealand is expected to join the ranks in the near future. Whether or not the U.S. also will offer such bonds is a matter of ongoing public discussion. A congressional hearing on the topic in 1992 was the most recent example.

This *Weekly Letter* examines the basic mechanics of inflation-indexed bonds and their purported benefit in aiding monetary policymakers. With a stock of indexed bonds outstanding, the nominal cost of the government's debt financing automatically increases as inflation goes up. This feature of indexed bonds makes them a good mechanism for enhancing the credibility of a government's commitment to a low-inflation policy in the future. Indeed, this feature might be an important reason for the recent popularity of inflation-indexed bonds among industrial economies.

HOW INFLATION-INDEXED BONDS WORK

A typical long-term government security is redeemed at its face value at maturity, and periodic coupon payments are fixed in nominal terms. So at any date, its real yield at maturity is uncertain, as inflation and thus the purchasing power of money in the future is uncertain. In comparison, an inflation-indexed bond guarantees holders a real rate of return by compensating them for the eroded purchasing power of nominal payments due to inflation. For example, consider the U.K. version of indexed bonds, which are called "indexed gilt." Their semiannual coupon payments are based on the inflation-adjusted face value of the bond over time. The adjustment for inflation is made using the Retail Price Index (RPI) with an eight-month lag. At maturity, the redemption value also is adjusted for the actual inflation between the initial indexation date and eight months prior to the maturity date. Because of this indexation lag, an indexed gilt will be exposed to inflation risk in the final eight-month period. However, this does not appear to be crucial, since many indexed gilts have maturities over fifteen years.

Reprinted from Federal Reserve Bank of San Francisco *Weekly Letter* no. 95-32, September 29, 1995.

READING 5 Inflation-Indexed Bonds

At a theoretical level, the provision of an asset that is free from inflation risk should improve the general welfare, both on the buyers' side and on the sellers' side. On the buyers' side, such an asset offers a means of adjusting portfolios for individual investors with different risk and return preferences. For example, investors, such as pension funds, that want to secure a predictable flow of cash payments could include indexed bonds in their portfolios. Indeed, when they were first issued in 1981, indexed gilts were offered only to pension funds. This restriction was lifted in 1982, but data from 1994 show that pension funds and insurance companies still held close to 50 percent of the outstanding stock of indexed gilts.

On the sellers' side, the issuing government may end up with lower borrowing costs in certain situations. For example, long-term government bonds generally sell at a discount, which reflects the yield the market demands. The discount will be deeper after a high-inflation period, because markets assess a large premium in interest rates for expected inflation, as well as a premium for an inflation risk for holding a nominal asset whose real value is uncertain over time. Such a premium might be unacceptably high for a government that genuinely intends to impose monetary and fiscal discipline in order to bring about and maintain low and stable inflation. This situation is like that faced by the Thatcher administration in 1981, when it started issuing inflation-indexed bonds (Woodward 1990, de Kock 1991, Shen 1995).

INFLATION-INDEXED BONDS AND THE EFFECTIVENESS OF MONETARY POLICY

One of the key benefits of having inflation-indexed bonds in addition to conventional nominal bonds is that together they offer a means of measuring markets' expectations about future inflation. The problem with obtaining such a measure from the yield on conventional bonds alone is that the yield consists of expected inflation, an inflation risk premium, and the expected real rate—and it is very difficult, if not impossible, to measure one separately from the other. But since the yield on indexed bonds reflects only the expected real interest rate, the problem is solved, theoretically, at least (that is, assuming that inflation risk is small and well-behaved over time): One can simply take the difference between the yields on indexed and nominal bonds with the same maturities, and the result is a measure of inflation expectations. Such a measure of inflation expectations can aid a monetary authority by offering timely, market-based feed-back regarding the inflationary consequences of its actions. Presumably, changes in this difference would convey valuable information on changes in expected inflation that could be incorporated in determining short-term monetary policy.

In practice, however, the problem is not so easy to solve. Certain preconditions need to be met for policymakers to use information from indexed bonds in this way. First, the nominal bonds and indexed bonds have to have similar characteristics, such as maturity and coupon rate. Thus it would be preferable to have a variety of indexed bonds that match the characteristics of current U.S. Treasury securities. This would afford a more precise reading of markets' expectations at different horizons (Hetzel 1992).

Second, there has to be sufficient liquidity in the indexed bond market. The usefulness of indexed bonds as an indicator hinges on how correctly changes in their prices reflect changes in the underlying inflation expectations. Therefore, it is imperative that the market have sufficient depth and breadth so that non-fundamental factors will not cause large changes in their yields.

Third, the quality of the price indexes used for inflation indexation must be high; that is, the candidate price index has to reflect changes in the purchasing power of money accurately. It would be especially problematic if the bias in the price index varied over time. For example, there is currently some concern about potential bias in the U.S. Consumer Price Index. A bias arises due to imprecise measurement of improvements in the quality of goods, the introduction of new goods, or substitution on the part of consumers between different goods and retail outlets (Wynne and Sigalla 1993). This could become an issue concerning indexed bonds, if and when they come into being in the U.S.

INDEXED BONDS AS A COMMITMENT MECHANISM

When a government issues inflation-indexed bonds, it is signaling its intention to control inflation in the future, since the nominal cost of debt financing automatically increases as inflation goes up. For example, with ordinary nominal bonds a government faces a stream of known, fixed, nominal obligations whose real burden can be reduced by future inflation. With indexed bonds, the government faces unknown nominal obligations that will balloon with higher future inflation. This automatic escalation of indexed-debt costs offers a potentially binding mechanism committing the government to non-inflationary policies in the future.

This appears to be an important element of the move by the U.K., Australia, Sweden, and Canada to begin issuing inflation-indexed bonds. At least two out of the following three characteristics applied to those countries when they started issuing indexed bonds: (1) a recent history of a high inflation and large government deficits, (2) a relatively new and fiscally conservative government that supported lowering inflation, (3) a central bank with relatively less institutional independence.

Under such circumstances, issuances of inflation-indexed bonds was perhaps a practical way to signal the governments' commitment to low inflation in the future. For example, a much more difficult way to send the signal would have been to make the central bank more independent. According to studies such as Cukierman, Webb, and Neyapti (1992), in industrialized countries there is a negative correlation between the degree of a central bank's institutional independence and a country's inflation rate. But changing the institutional structure of a country's central bank would involve a major legislative effort. Clearly, providing indexed bonds as an incentive to keep inflation under control would be much easier to accomplish.

The experiences of the U.K. and Canada seem to support this view. In the U.K., the Conservative party won the election in 1979, following a decade marked by both high inflation and substantial government budget deficits. The Thatcher administration implemented policies aimed at cutting government spending and debt and controlling inflation, which were the subject of rancorous disagreement, even within the ruling party. Hence, negotiating a drastic change in the traditional relationship between the government and the Bank of England might have been out of the question. Indexed bonds may have offered a more practical solution.

Canada is another interesting case. Though its economy was stable throughout the 1980s, there was a strong effort to establish price stability as the official, single goal of monetary policy. A legislative initiative to do so was pushed forward by the Conservative administration, though it eventually failed in Parliament in the fall of 1991. The first issuance of indexed bonds immediately followed at the end of 1991.

CONCLUSION

The provision of inflation-indexed government bonds appears to be a useful innovation. First, it would provide an indicator of the markets' assessment of the monetary authority's commitment to low inflation when indexed and nominal bonds with matching characteristics coexist, and this could be valuable in aiding short-run monetary policy deliberations. Second, it could play an important role in signaling governments' commitment to policies of low inflation in the future. The existence of indexed bonds adds to the credibility of the commitment, since the government's cost of debt financing automatically escalates in tandem with inflation.

REFERENCES

Cukierman, A., S.B. Webb, and B. Neyapti. 1992. "Measuring the Independence of Central Banks and Its Effect on Policy Outcomes." *The World Bank Economic Review* (September) pp. 358-398.

de Kock, G. 1991. "Expected Inflation and Real Interest Rates Based on Index-Linked Bond Prices: The U.K. Experience." *Federal Reserve Bank of New York Quarterly Review* (Fall) pp. 47-60.

Hetzel, R. 1992. "Indexed Bonds as an Aid to Monetary Policy." *Federal Reserve Bank of Richmond Economic Review* (January/February) pp. 13-23.

Shen, P. 1995. "Benefits and Limitations of Inflation Indexed Treasury Bonds." *Federal Reserve Bank of Kansas City Economic Review* (Third Quarter) pp. 41-56.

Woodward, G.T. 1990. "The Real Thing: A Dynamic Profile of the Term Structure of Real Interest Rates in the United Kingdom, 1982-1989." *Journal of Business*, 63, pp. 373-398.

Wynne, M. and F. Sigalla. 1993. "A Survey of Measurement Biases in Price Indexes." Federal Reserve Bank of Dallas Research Paper No. 9340.

PART II Financial Markets

QUESTIONS

1. How does an inflation-indexed bond differ from an ordinary "nominal" bond? Will a change in expected inflation have similar effects on both types of bonds?

2. How would issuance of inflation-indexed bonds provide a measure of inflation expectations? Why can't conventional bonds provide this measure?

3. Will issuance of inflation-indexed bonds affect a government's incentives to pursue inflationary policies? Why?

4. Governments of several industrial countries have begun issuing inflation-indexed bonds. Do you expect this has raised or lowered their costs of borrowing? Why?

READING 6

The Yield Curve as a Predictor of U.S. Recessions

Arturo Estrella and Frederic S. Mishkin

Economists often use complex mathematical models to forecast the path of the U.S. economy and the likelihood of recession. But simpler indicators such as interest rates, stock price indexes, and monetary aggregates also contain information about future economic activity. In this edition of *Current Issues*, we examine the usefulness of one such indicator—the yield curve or, more specifically, the spread between the interest rates on the ten-year Treasury note and the three-month Treasury bill. To get a sense of the relative power of this variable, we compare it with other financial and macroeconomic variables used to predict economic events.

Our analysis differs in two important respects from earlier studies of the predictive power of financial variables[1] First, we focus simply on the ability of these variables to forecast recessions rather than on their success in producing quantitative measures of future economic activity. We believe this is a useful approach because evidence of an oncoming recession is of clear interest to policymakers and market participants. Second, we choose to examine out-of-sample, rather than in-sample, performance—that is, we look at accuracy in predictions for quarters beyond the period over which the model is estimated. This feature of our study is particularly important because out-of-sample performance provides a much truer test of an indicator's real-world forecasting ability.

WHY CONSIDER THE YIELD CURVE?

The steepness of the yield should be an excellent indicator of a possible future recession for several reasons. Current monetary policy has a significant influence on the yield curve spread and hence on real activity over the next several quarters. A rise in the short rate tends to flatten the yield curve as well as to slow real growth in the near term. This relationship, however, is only one part of the explanation for the yield curve's usefulness as a forecasting tool.[2] Expectations of future inflation and real interest rates contained in the yield curve spread also seem to play an important role in the prediction of economic activity. The yield curve spread variable examined here corresponds to a forward interest rate

Reprinted from Federal Reserve Bank of New York *Current Issues in Economics and Finance*, June 1996.

PART II Financial Markets

applicable from three months to ten years into the future. As explained in Mishkin (1990a, 1990b), this rate can be decomposed into expected real interest rate and expected inflation components, each of which may be helpful in forecasting. The expected real rate may be associated with expectations of future monetary policy and hence of future real growth. Moreover, because inflation tends to be positively related to activity, the expected inflation component may also be informative about future growth.

Although the yield curve has clear advantages as a predictor of future economic events, several other variables have been widely used to forecast the path of the economy. Among financial variables, stock prices have received much attention. Finance theory suggests that stock prices are determined by expectations about future dividend streams, which in turn are related to the future state of the economy. Among macroeconomic variables, the Commerce Department's (now the conference Board's) index of leading economic indicators appears to have an established performance record in predicting real economic activity. Nevertheless, its record has not always been subjected to careful comparison tests. In addition, because this index has often been revised after the fact to improve its performance, its success could be overstated. An alternative index of leading indicators, developed in Stock and Watson (1989), appears to perform better than the Commerce Department's index of leading economic indicators. In the discussion below, we compare the predictive power of all three of these variables with that of the yield curve.[3]

ESTIMATING THE PROBABILITY OF RECESSION

To assess how well each indicator variable predicts recessions, we use the so-called probit model, which, in our application, directly relates the probability of being in a recession to a specific explanatory variable such as the yield curve spread.[4] For example, one of the most successful models in our study estimates the probability of recession four quarters in the future as a function of the current value of the yield curve spread between the ten-year Treasury note and the three-month Treasury bill. The results of the model, based on data from the first quarter of 1960 to the first quarter of 1995, are presented in a table showing the values of the yield curve spread that correspond to estimated probabilities of a recession four quarters in the future. As the table indicates, the estimated probability of a recession four quarters ahead estimated from this model is 10 percent when the spread averages 0.76 percentage points over the quarter, 50 percent when the spread averages -0.82 percentage points, and 90 percent when the spread averages -2.40 percentage points.

The usefulness of the model can be illustrated through the following examples. Consider that in the third quarter of 1994, the spread averaged 2.74 percentage points. The corresponding predicted probability of recession in the third quarter of 1995 was only 0.2 percent, and indeed, a recession did not materialize. In contrast, the yield curve spread averaged -2.18 percentage points in the first quarter of 1981, implying a probability of recession of 86.5 percent four quarters later.

Estimated Recession Probabilities for Probit Model Using the Yield Curve Spread
Four Quarters Ahead

Recession Probability (Percent)	Value of Spread (Percentage Points)
5	1.21
10	0.76
15	0.46
20	0.22
25	0.02
30	-0.17
40	-0.50
50	-0.82
60	-1.13
70	-1.46
80	-1.85
90	-2.40

Note: The yield curve spread is defined as the spread between the interest rate on the ten-year Treasury note and the three-month Treasury bill.

As predicted, the first quarter of 1982 was in fact designated a recession quarter by the National Bureau of Economic Research.

TRACKING THE PERFORMANCE OF THE VARIABLES

Using the results of our model, we can compare the forecasting performance of the yield curve spread with that of the New York Stock Exchange (NYSE) stock price index, the Commerce Department's index of leading economic indicators, and the Stock-Watson index. For each of these four variables, the chart plots the forecasted probabilities of a recession in the United States for one, two, four, and six quarters in the future together with the actual periods of recession (the shaded areas).[5]

To understand how to read the chart, consider the forecast for the fourth quarter of 1990, which is the first quarter after the peak of the business cycle and is thus at the start of the last shaded recession region in each panel. In Panel 1, which shows the forecast one quarter ahead, the probability of recession from the probit model using the yield curve spread variable (Spread) forecasted in the third quarter of 1990 for the fourth quarter of 1990 is 13 percent. Similarly, in Panel 7, which shows forecasts six quarters ahead, the forecasted probability of recession for the fourth quarter of 1990—22 percent—is generated from a model using the yield curve spread as of the second quarter of 1989.

In assessing these panels, note that even a probability of recession that is considerably less than one can be a strong signal of recession. Because in any given quarter the probability of recession is quite low, a forecasted probability of, say, 50 percent is going to be quite unusual. Indeed, the successful forecasting model described in the table yields probabilities of recession that are typically below 10 percent in nonrecession (unshaded) periods (as shown in Panel 5). Thus, even a probability of recession of 25 percent—the figure forecast for the fourth quarter of 1990 from data on the yield curve spread one year earlier—was a relatively strong signal in the fourth quarter of 1989 that a recession might come one year in the future.

PART II Financial Markets

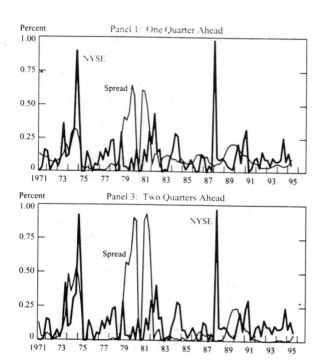
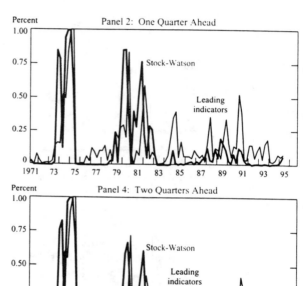

READING 6 The Yield Curve as a Predictor of U.S. Recessions

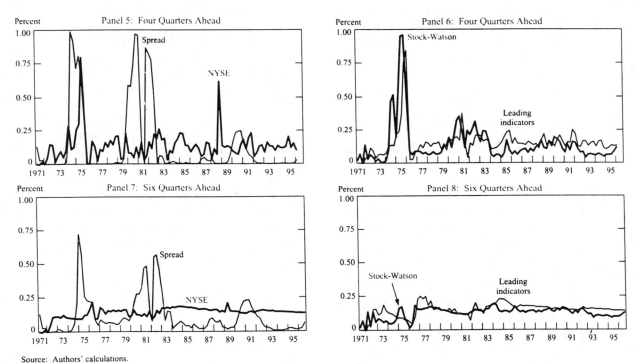

Source: Authors' calculations.

Notes: The probabilities in this chart are derived from out-of-sample forecasts one, two, four, and six quarters ahead. For example, the forecasted probabilities in Panels 1 and 2 are for one quarter ahead—that is, the probability shown is a forecast for the quarter indicated, using data from one quarter earlier—while for Panels 7 and 8, the forecasted probabilities are for six quarters ahead. *Spread* denotes the forecasts from the model using the yield curve spread (the difference between the interest rates on ten-year Treasury notes and three-month Treasury bills, both on a bond-equivalent basis) as the explanatory variable. *NYSE* denotes the results from the model using the quarterly percentage change in the New York Stock Exchange stock price index as the explanatory variable. *Leading indicators* denotes the forecasts from the model using the quarterly percentage change in the Commerce Department's (now the Conference Board's) index of leading indicators as the explanatory variable. *Stock-Watson* denotes the forecasts using the quarterly percentage change in the Stock-Watson (1989) leading economic indicator index as the explanatory variable. Shaded areas designate "recessions" starting with the first quarter after a business cycle peak and continuing through the trough quarter. The peak and trough dates are the standard ones issued by the National Bureau of Economic Research.

PART II Financial Markets

The chart invites two basic conclusions about the performance of the four variables.[6]

- Although all the variables examined have some forecasting ability one quarter ahead, the leading economic indicator indexes, particularly the Stock-Watson index, produce the best forecasts over this horizon.

- In predicting recessions two or more quarters in the future, the yield curve dominates the other variables, and this dominance increases as the forecast horizon grows.

Let's look in more detail at the probability forecasts in Panels 1-8. Panels 1 and 2 show that the indexes of leading economic indicators typically outperform the yield curve spread and the NYSE stock price index for forecasts one quarter ahead. For the 1973-75, 1980, and 1981-82 recessions, both indexes of leading economic indicators, and particularly the Stock-Watson index, are quite accurate, outperforming the yield curve spread and the NYSE stock price index with a high predicted probability during the recession periods. However, despite excellent performance in these earlier recessions, the Commerce Department indicator provides several incorrect signals in the 1982-90 boom period, and the Stock-Watson index completely misses the most recent recession in 1990-91.[7] Although the financial variables—the yield curve spread and the NYSE stock price index—are not quite as accurate as the leading economic indicators in predicting the 1973-75, 1980, and 1981-82 recessions one quarter ahead, they do provide a somewhat clearer signal of an imminent recession in 1990.

As the forecasting horizon lengthens to two quarters ahead and beyond, the performance of the NYSE stock price index and the leading economic indicator indexes deteriorates substantially (Panels 3-8). Indeed, at a six-quarter horizon, the probabilities estimated using the three indexes are essentially flat, indicating that these variables have no ability to forecast recessions. In contrast, the performance of the yield curve spread improves considerably as the forecast horizon lengthens to two and four quarters. The estimated probabilities of recession for 1973-75, 1980, and 1981-82 based on the yield curve spread are substantially higher than at the one-quarter horizon, and the signal for the 1981-82 recession no longer comes too early (compare Panel 5 with Panel 1).

Furthermore, in contrast to other variables, the yield curve spread gives a relatively strong signal in forecasting the 1990-91 recession four quarters ahead. Although the forecasted probability is lower than in previous recessions, it does reach 25 percent (Panel 5).

There are two reasons why the signal for this recession may have been weaker than for the earlier recessions. First, restrictive monetary policy probably induced the 1973-75, 1980, and 1981-82 recessions, but it played a much smaller role in the 1990-91 recession. Because the tightening of monetary policy also affects the yield curve, we would expect the signal to be more pronounced at such times. Second, the amount of variation in the yield curve spread has changed over time and was much less in the 1990s than in the early 1980s, making a strong signal for the 1990-91 recession difficult to obtain.[8]

When we look at how well the yield curve spread forecasts recessions six quarters in the future (Panel 7), we see that the performance deteriorates from the four-quarter-ahead predictions. Nonetheless, unlike the other variables considered, the yield curve spread continues to have some ability to forecast recessions six quarters ahead.

CONCLUSION

This article has examined the performance of the yield curve spread and several other financial and macroeconomic variables in predicting U.S. recessions. The results obtained from a model using the yield curve spread are encouraging and suggest that the yield curve spread can have a useful role in macroeconomic prediction, particularly with longer lead times. Policymakers value longer term forecasts because policy actions typically take effect on the economy with long time lags. Thus, the fact that the yield curve strongly outperforms other variables at longer horizons makes its use as a forecasting tool even more compelling.

With the existence of large-scale macroeconomic models and the judgmental assessments of knowledgeable market observers, why should we care about the predictive ability of the yield curve? There is no question that judgmental and macroeconometric forecasts are quite helpful. Nevertheless, the yield curve can usefully supplement large econometric models and other forecasts for three reasons. First, forecasting with the yield curve has the distinct advantage of being quick and simple. With a glance at the ten-year note and three-month bill rates on the computer screen, anyone can compute a probability forecast of recession almost instantaneously by using a table such as ours.

Second, a simple financial indicator such as the yield curve can be used to double-check both econometric and judgmental predictions by flagging a problem that might otherwise have gone unidentified. For example, if forecasts from an econometric model and the yield curve agree, confidence in the model's results can be enhanced. In contrast, if the yield curve indicator gives a different signal, it may be worthwhile to review the assumptions and relationships that led to the prediction. Third, using the yield curve to forecast within the framework outlined here produces a probability of future recession, a probability that is of interest in its own right.

ENDNOTES

1. A list of references on this literature can be found in Estrella and Mishkin (1996).
2. The analyses in Estrella and Hardouvelis (1990, 1991) and Estrella and Mishkin (1995) suggest why the yield curve contains information beyond that related to monetary policy.

PART II Financial Markets

3. In Estrella and Mishkin (1996), we have examined in detail the predictive ability of these and other variables, including interest rates by themselves, other stock market indexes, interest rate spreads, monetary aggregates (both nominal and real), the component series of the index of leading economic indicators, and an additional experimental index of leading indicators developed in Stock and Watson (1992). Of all the variables, the four singled out in this article have the best ability to predict recessions.

4. For a technical discussion of this model and how it is estimated, see Estrella and Mishkin (1996). The economy is designated as "in recession" starting with the first quarter after a business cycle peak and continuing through the trough quarter. The peak and trough dates are the standard ones issued by the National Bureau of Economic Research (NBER) and used in most business cycle analysis. These dates are not without controversy, however, because the NBER methodology makes implicit assumptions in arriving at these dates.

5. Note that the forecasts in these panels are true out-of-sample results, obtained in the following way: First, a given model is estimated using past data up to a particular date, say the first quarter of 1970. Then these estimates are used to form the forecasts, say four quarters ahead. In this case, the projection would apply to the first quarter of 1971. After adding one more quarter to the estimation period, the procedure is repeated. That is, data up to the second quarter of 1970 are used to make a forecast for the second quarter of 1971. In this way, the procedure mimics what a forecaster would have predicted with the information available at any point in the past.

6. Note that all conclusions drawn from looking at the charts are confirmed by more precise statistical measures of out-of-sample fit in Estrella and Mishkin (1996).

7. these results have already been noted in very useful postmortem analyses by Watson (1991) and Stock and Watson (1992).

8. Another potential explanation is that the 1990-91 recession was relatively mild and so a weaker signal might be expected. However, as shown in Estrella and Hardouvelis (1991), the yield curve spread also provides much weaker signals for recessions in the 1950s, even though they were not mild. Furthermore, the signal for the 1969-70 recession is strong, although the recession itself was mild. Thus, the severity of the recessions does not seem to be associated with the strength of the signal from the yield curve.

REFERENCES

Estrella, Arturo, and Gikas Hardouvelis. 1990. "Possible Roles of the Yield Curve in Monetary analysis." In *Intermediate Targets and Indicators for Monetary Policy*, Federal Reserve Bank of New York.

———. 1991. "The term Structure as a Predictor of Real Economic Activity." *Journal of Finance* 46, no. 2 (June).

Estrella, Arturo, and Frederic S. Mishkin. 1995. "The Term Structure of Interest Rates and Its Role in Monetary Policy for the European Central Bank." National Bureau of Economic Research Working Paper no. 5279, September.

———. 1996. "Predicting U.S. Recessions: Financial Variables as Leading Indicators." Federal Reserve Bank of New York Research Paper no. 9609, May.

Mishkin, Frederic S. 1990a. "What Does the Term Structure Tell Us About Future Inflation?" *Journal of Monetary Economics* 25 (January): 77-95.

———. 1990b. "The Information in the Longer-Maturity Term Structure About Future Inflation." *Quarterly Journal of Economics* 55 (August): 815-28.

Stock, James and Mark Watson, 1989. "New Indexes of Coincident and Leading Indicators." In Olivier Blanchard and Stanley Fischer, eds., *NBER Macroeconomic Annual* 4.

———. 1992. "A Procedure for Predicting Recessions with Leading Indicators: Econometric Issues and Recent Performance." Federal Reserve Bank of Chicago Working Paper WP-92-7, April.

Watson, Mark. 1991. "Using Econometric Models to Predict Recessions." Federal Reserve Bank of Chicago *Economic Perspectives* 15, no. 6 (November-December).

READING 6 The Yield Curve as a Predictor of U.S. Recessions

QUESTIONS

1. How do Estrella and Mishkin define the yield curve spread? Do you expect this spread to be positive or negative most of the time? Why?

2. What relationship do Estrella and Mishkin find between the yield curve spread and the probability of recession? Is this relationship plausible? Explain.

3. How do Estrella and Mishkin attempt to ascertain the value of the yield curve spread relative to other possible predictors of recession? What do they conclude about its predictive ability?

READING 7

McCurrencies: Where's The Beef?

Ten years on, *The Economist's* Big Mac index is still going strong. Mad-cow disease notwithstanding, it is time to dish up our annual feast of burgernomics. The Big Mac index was devised as a light-hearted guide to whether currencies are at their "correct" level. It is not intended to be a predictor of exchange-rates, but a tool to make economic theory more digestible.

Burgernomics is based upon the theory of purchasing-power parity (PPP). This argues that, in the long run, the exchange rate between two currencies should move towards the rate that would equalise the prices of an identical basket of goods and services in the two countries. Our basket is a McDonald's Big Mac, which is made to roughly the same recipe in more than 80 countries. The Big Mac PPP is the exchange rate that would make a burger cost the same in America as it does abroad. Comparing this with the actual rate is one test of whether a currency is undervalued or overvalued.

The first column of the table shows the local-currency prices of a Big Mac; the second converts them into dollars. The average price in America (including sales tax) is $2.36. However, bargain hunters should head for China, where a burger costs only $1.15. At the other extreme, the Swiss price of $4.80 is enough to make Big Mac fans choke on their all-beef patties. This implies that the yuan is once again the most undervalued currency, and the Swiss franc the most overvalued.

The third column shows Big Mac PPPs. For example, if you divide the Japanese price of a *Biggu Makku* by the American one, you get a dollar PPP of ¥122. The actual rate on April 22nd was ¥107, implying that the yen was 14% overvalued against the dollar. Similar sums show that the D-mark is overvalued by 37%. In general, the dollar is undervalued against the currencies of most big industrial economies, but overvalued against developing countries' ones.

Thanks partly to the dollar's recovery, the other rich-country currencies look less overvalued than a year ago. Adjustment to PPP can also come from changes in relative prices rather than exchange-rate movements. The most dramatic example of this is Japan where the price of a Big Mac was slashed by more than a quarter late last year. This reduced the yen's over-valuation from 100% to 14%.

The Big Mac index was originally introduced as a bit of fun. Yet it has inspired several serious studies over the past year. Li Lian Ong, an economist at the University of Western Australia, wrote her PhD thesis on

The Economist, April 27, 1996, 82. ©1996 The Economist Newspaper Group, Inc. Reprinted with permission. Further reproduction prohibited.

READING 7   McCurrencies: Where's the Beef?

The hamburger standard

	Big Mac prices In local currency	Big Mac prices In dollars	Implied PPP* of the dollar	Actual $ exchange rate 22/4/96	Local currency under (-)/over(+) valuation,† %
United States‡	**$2.36**	**2.36**	-	-	-
Argentina	Peso3.00	3.00	1.27	1.00	+27
Australia	A$2.50	1.97	1.06	1.27	-17
Austria	Sch36.00	3.40	15.3	10.7	+43
Belgium	Bfr109	3.50	46.2	31.2	+48
Brazil	Real12.95	2.98	1.25	0.99	+26
Britain	£1.79	2.70	1.32††	1.51††	+14
Canada	C$2.86	2.10	1.21	1.36	-11
Chile	Peso950	2.33	403	408	-1
China	Yuan9.60	1.15	4.07	8.35	-51
Czech Republic	CKr51.0	1.85	21.6	27.6	-22
Denmark	DKr 25.75	4.40	10.9	5.85	+87
France	FFr17.5	3.41	7.42	5.13	+46
Germany	DM4.90	3.22	2.08	1.52	+37
Hong Kong	HK$9.90	1.28	4.19	7.74	-46
Hungary	Forint214	1.43	90.7	150	-39
Israel	Shekel9.50	3.00	4.03	3.17	+27
Italy	Lire4,500	2.90	1,907	1,551	+23
Japan	¥288	2.70	122	107	+14
Malaysia	M$3.76	1.51	1.59	2.49	-36
Mexico	Peso14.9	2.02	6.31	7.37	-14
Netherlands	F15.45	3.21	2.31	1.70	+36
New Zealand	NZ$2.95	2.01	1.25	1.47	-15
Poland	Zloty3.80	1.44	1.61	2.64	-39
Russia	Rouble9,500	1.93	4,025	4,918	-18
Singapore	S$3.05	2.16	1.29	1.41	-8
South Africa	Rand7.00	1.64	2.97	4.26	-30
South Korea	Won2,300	2.95	975	779	+25
Spain	Pta365	2.89	155	126	+23
Sweden	SKr26.0	3.87	11.0	6.71	+64

PART II Financial Markets

The hamburger standard

	Big Mac prices		Implied PPP* of the dollar	Actual $ exchange rate 22/4/96	Local currency under (-)/over(+) valuation,† %
	In local currency	In dollars			
Switzerland	SFr5.90	4.80	2.50	1.23	+103
Taiwan	NT$65.0	2.39	27.5	27.2	+1
Thailand	Baht48.0	1.90	20.3	25.3	-20

*Purchasing-power parity: local price divided by price in the United States   †Against dollar
‡Average of New York, Chicago, San Francisco and Atlanta   ††Dollars per pound
Source: McDonald's

the index.* She concludes that "the Big Mac index is surprisingly accurate in tracking exchange rates over the longer term." Another study, by Robert Cumby of Georgetown University in Washington, DC, also found that deviations from "McParity" are usually temporary.**

But a third study, by Michael Pakko and Patricia Pollard of the Federal Reserve Bank of St. Louis, is more sceptical.† It concludes that "The Big Mac does as well—or as poorly—at demonstrating the principles and pitfalls of PPP as more sophisticated measures."

Their study concludes that although Big Mac PPP may hold in the very long run, currencies can deviate from it for lengthy periods. There are several reasons why Big Mac index may be flawed:

• The theory of PPP falsely assumes that there are no barriers to trade. High prices in Europe, Japan and South Korea partly reflect high tariffs on beef. Differences in transport costs also act as a trade barrier: shipping perishable ingredients such as lettuce and beef is dear.

• Prices are distorted by taxes. High rates of value-added tax in countries such as Denmark and Sweden exaggerate the degree to which their currencies are overvalued.

• The Big Mac is not just a basket of commodities: its price must cover rents and the cost of other non-traded inputs. Deviations of PPP may simply reflect differences in such costs.

• Profit margins vary among countries according to the strength of competition. In the United States, the Big Mac has many close substitutes, but in other countries McDonald's is able to charge a premium.

Despite these weaknesses, which *The Economist* has long acknowledged, the Big Mac index still comes up with PPP estimates that are similar to those based on more

READING 7 McCurrencies: Where's the Beef?

sophisticated methods. Burgernomics has its
methodological flaws, but our money is where
our mouths are.

ENDNOTES

*"Burgernomics: The Economics of the Big Mac Standard". University of Western Australia, November 1995.
**"Forecasting Exchange Rates and Relative Prices With the Hamburger Standard: Is What You Want What You Get With McParity?". Georgetown University, July 1995.
†"For Here or To Go? Purchasing Power Parity and the Big Mac". Federal Reserve Bank of St. Louis, January 1996.

QUESTIONS

1. How are Big Mac prices used to calculate an implied purchasing-power parity of the dollar? How is the dollar's PPP value interpreted?

2. What flaws in the Big Mac index are noted?

3. According to the Big Mac index, relative to the dollar the Swiss franc is overvalued 103 percent and the French franc 46 percent. On the other hand, China's yuan is 51 percent undervalued and Poland's zloty 39 percent. How are these figures obtained from the Big Mac index. What predictions for future exchange rate movements do they support?

4. Which two currencies were closest to their implied purchasing power parity exchange rates (as determined by the Big Mac index) on April 22, 1996? What was the exchange rate between these two currencies?

READING 8

Budget Deficit Cuts and the Dollar

Ramon Moreno

Since the spring of this year, policymakers and academics have disagreed on how expected reductions in the U.S. budget deficit will affect the U.S. dollar. Prominent policymakers, including the Federal Reserve Board Chairman, the Bundesbank President, and the Japanese Finance Minister have state publicly that such reductions may lead to a strengthening of the U.S. dollar. Well-known U.S. academics have criticized this view, arguing that budget deficit cuts will lead to a dollar depreciation.

This *Weekly Letter* assesses these conflicting views in the context of standard explanations of the determinants of the exchange rate. A review of these explanations suggests that U.S. academics are focusing on the short-run impact of lower budget deficits on the dollar, whereas policymakers are focusing on medium- and long-run effects.

BUDGET DEFICIT CUTS IN THE SHORT RUN

The simplest way to think of how budget deficits affect the dollar is to use a Keynesian framework where the dollar adjusts to restore equilibrium in the balance of payments. The dollar depreciates if the balance of payments is in deficit, and it appreciates if it is in surplus. So the key to predicting what happens to the dollar when the budget deficit is cut is to see what happens to the balance of payments.

Roughly speaking, the balance of payments is the sum of the trade balance and net capital flows. And part of the ambiguity in the debate is because a cut in the budget deficit affects these two components of the balance of payments differently. It tends to *increase* the trade balance, because it cuts today's income, which reduces the demand for imports; in other words, it can create a balance of payments *surplus*. At the same time, it tends to encourage capital *outflows*, because it tends to lower U.S. interest rates relative to foreign rates—that creates a balance of payments *deficit*.

Which effect is likely to dominate? In the case of a small open economy the answer is clear: A budget deficit cut will push the balance of payments toward a deficit and hence will produce a depreciation of the currency. The reason is that the fall in the domestic interest rate will produce a large

Reprinted from Federal Reserve Bank of San Francisco *Weekly Letter*, no. 95-42, December 15, 1995.

READING 8 Budget Deficit Cuts and the Dollar

incremental capital outflow, because from the point of view of a small economy, the supply of international capital is unlimited.

For a large economy like the U.S., the effects of a budget deficit cut are ambiguous. The supply of international capital is no longer unlimited, so that as domestic income declines, the trade balance increase may exceed the capital outflow associated with the fall in interest rates, causing a balance of payments surplus and dollar *appreciation*. This ambiguity is resolved by (plausibly) assuming that the tendency for budget deficit cuts to result in capital outflows outweighs the effects on the trade balance. Thus, the academics' insistence that a budget deficit cut will tend to lead to a weaker dollar may be motivated by focusing on short-run effects.

BUDGET DEFICIT CUTS AND LONG-RUN EFFECTS

Shifting the focus to the longer-run impacts of budget deficit cuts, we can explore two reasons why such cuts can lead to dollar appreciation.

First, *a budget deficit cut may lead to capital inflows and a balance of payments surplus if the risk premium on domestic interest rates falls by enough*. Suppose investors are worried that the continued accumulation of U.S. government debt may make investors reluctant to hold U.S. treasury securities some time in the future, exposing them to sudden capital losses. In order to bear this risk, investors require a premium, which is reflected in the spread between domestic and foreign interest rates. A budget deficit cut may reassure investors that the future stock of U.S. government debt will not be so large, which would reduce the risk premium. If the reduction is large enough, there may be incipient capital inflows even if the budget deficit cut causes the domestic interest rate to fall. The dollar would then appreciate to restore balance of payments equilibrium.

Second, *a budget deficit reduction may reduce inflationary pressures*. Many international economists believe that in the long run, when prices can adjust, the value of the dollar depends on the relative price of representative baskets of U.S. and foreign goods and therefore on relative money supplies and money demands. This is an implication of the theory of purchasing power parity, and it is known as the monetary approach to the exchange rate. A decline in the budget deficit today may reduce the expected rate of long-run money creation and inflation required to finance current and prospective deficits. The decline in long-run inflationary expectations causes the long-run nominal interest to fall and money demand to rise and the dollar to appreciate in the long-run. Such an expected future appreciation in the dollar from its current expected long-run level will lead to an appreciation in the dollar today, which will offset the tendency towards depreciation in the short-run highlighted earlier.

It is not clear how big a role these reasons are likely to play. For example, Allan Meltzer has point out that historically risk premium effects have been small in the U.S.; however, he notes that they may be rising because private financing of U.S. net debt has been replaced by financing by foreign central banks. In addition, several observers have questioned whether the effect of budget deficit cuts on inflationary expectations is empirically relevant, since the U.S., like other industrial countries, has not monetized its deficits in recent years. However, evidence from other countries suggests that in the absence of credible measures to reduce the budget deficit, the pressure on the central bank to resort to inflationary finance tends to grow.

EFFECTS ON PRODUCTIVITY OR THE COMPOSITION OF DEMAND

While much of the discussion in the financial press focuses on the effects of *deficit reduction* on the dollar, the effect of specific tax and government expenditure policies on sectoral productivity or the composition of demand may have implications for the exchange rate in the long run that are separate from those associated with deficit financing. These policies affect the real, or inflation-adjusted, dollar exchange rate, which, holding monetary factors constant, will affect the nominal exchange rate as well. Some insights into these effects can be gained by assessing how the long-run (real) exchange rate is determined and the possible effects of tax and spending policies.

In what follows, it is useful to think of an economy with two goods, traded and non-traded, and of the real exchange rates as the relative price of traded to non-traded goods. This relative price is widely taken to represent the real exchange rate, because it reflects the relative profitability, or competitiveness of production, in the traded goods sector. A fall in the price of traded goods relative to non-traded U.S. goods means the traded goods sector is relatively less profitable, and represents an appreciation of the dollar.

International economists believe that an important long-run determinant of the real exchange rate is productivity growth. Bela Balassa and Paul Samuelson concluded three decades ago that if productivity grows faster in the traded goods sector than in the non-traded goods sector, then in the long run, the relative price of traded to non-traded goods will fall, which means that the real exchange rate will tend to appreciate. The reason is that an increase in traded goods productivity drives up the demand for workers and their wages. The price of non-traded goods rises in response to the increase in cost, but the price of traded goods does not adjust because it is set in world markets. Richard Marston (1987) provides empirical support for this theory, finding that rising labor productivity differentials between traded and non-traded goods in Japan, in excess of those observed in the U.S., provide a good explanation of the long-run trend real appreciation of the yen against dollar.

These findings suggest that if the budget deficit is cut by reducing spending or altering taxes in a way that increases relative productivity growth in the U.S. traded goods sector, the dollar may appreciate. Unfortunately, the quantitative effects of specific spending or tax policies on aggregate long-run productivity growth are not well understood. For example, it is tempting to argue that past Japanese subsidies to the traded goods sector enhanced that sector's productivity growth and contributed to the trend yen appreciation apparent since the 1960s. However, subsidies to specific sectors in other countries have not necessarily enhanced productivity. Further research on this question would be instructive.

Another factor believed to affect the real value of the dollar is the composition of demand. For example, a budget cut achieved by cutting government spending will cause a dollar depreciation (a fall in the price of U.S. domestic non-traded goods) if government spending is more biased towards domestic non-traded goods. There is some empirical evidence of a connection between government spending and the real exchange rate. In this context, it can be argued that the fiscal factors behind the real appreciation of the dollar in the early 1980s was not so much the result of budget deficits rising as of the increase in government spending that favored domestic goods.

Apart from the composition of government spending, the wealth of consumers is often believed to influence the demand for domestic non-traded goods and therefore the real value of the dollar. In this view, a country incurring a current account surplus accumulates wealth, thus increasing the demand for its own goods and its own money, which results in a real and nominal appreciation of the exchange rate. Thus, fiscal policies that increase the long-run stock of capital or national saving will increase national wealth and the demand for domestic goods, thus causing the dollar to appreciate in the long run. In particular, tax policies that encourage consumers to invest rather than to consume may lead to dollar appreciation.

CONCLUSIONS

The disagreement between policymakers and some academics on the effects of budget deficit reductions on the dollar appears to reflect the former's emphasis on long-run effects and the latter's emphasis on the short-run effects. It is difficult to tell which viewpoint is more credible empirically. As discussed by Kasa (1995), there is no close empirical relationship between macroeconomic fundamentals, such as budget deficits, and short-run exchange rate behavior. Furthermore, while there is some evidence that certain variables (including inflation and productivity growth) affect the exchange rate in the long run, it is difficult to isolate the impact of such long run factors on the behavior of exchange rates in the short run.

It can be argued that if the short-run reduction in the budget deficit is large relative to the planned reductions in the future, short-run effects may dominate and, under plausible conditions, the dollar will depreciate, as argued by academics. If deficit reductions will take place largely in the future, and consumers and investors are mainly worried about the accumulation of government debt, long-run considerations may be dominant. In this case the dollar may appreciate, as suggested by policymakers. In either case, the types of tax or government spending policies that are used to achieve deficit

reduction are likely to affect the path of the
dollar as well.

REFERENCES

Kasa, Kenneth. 1995. "Understanding Trends in Foreign Exchange Rates." *FRBSF Weekly Letter* (June 9).

Marston, Richard. 1987. "Real Exchange Rates and Productivity Growth in the United States and Japan." In *Real Financial Linkages among Open Economies*, S.W. Arndt and J.D. Richardson, eds., pp. 71-96. Cambridge: MIT Press.

Meltzer, Allan H. 1995. "Comment on 'What Do Budget Deficits Do?' by L. Ball and N.G. Mankiw." Delivered at *Budget Deficits and Debt: Issues and Options*, FRB Kansas City Symposium, Jackson Hole, Wyoming.

QUESTIONS

1. How might a cut in the budget deficit affect the dollar in the short run? Can the effect on the dollar be predicted with certainty? Why?

2. Explain the reasoning behind the proposition that a budget deficit cut which reduces inflationary expectations will cause the dollar to appreciate in the long run. Illustrate this proposition using an exchange rate diagram like the ones Mishkin uses in Chapter 8 of the text.

3. According to Moreno, what accounts for the disagreement between academic economists and government policymakers regarding the effect of budget deficit cuts on the dollar? Under what circumstances might each side be correct?

READING 9

The Dollar and the Federal Funds Rate

Charles L. Evans

In early February the Federal Open Market Committee announced a tightening of monetary policy; as of June, this has been reflected in a 125-basis-point increase in the federal funds rate from 3.0% to 4.25%. In light of this action, recent movements in the dollar against the German mark and Japanese yen seem perplexing. From February 4 to June 30, the dollar depreciated by 9.9% against the mark and 10.2% against the yen.

The conventional wisdom would predict that the dollar should strengthen following a tightening of U.S. monetary policy. Yet the dollar depreciated despite central bank interventions in the foreign exchange markets to support it. To take another example, on Wednesday, May 11, the Bundesbank cut its discount and Lombard rates by 50 basis points each. The *Wall Street Journal* characterized this as "an unexpectedly deep" cut.[1] The day before, the dollar had traded at 1.6735 marks; by Wednesday's close in New York, the dollar was trading *lower*—at 1.6695 marks.

This *Chicago Fed Letter* investigates the empirical relationship between the federal funds rate and the yen/dollar and mark/dollar exchange rates in the 1980s and 1990s. The evidence from this period shows that sustained and large increases in the federal funds rate led to an appreciation of the dollar, but it often took two years for these effects to take noticeable hold. The effects of monetary policy actions are difficult to detect initially because exchange rate fluctuations over a one-year period are largely composed of unexplained shocks. Nevertheless, movements in the federal funds rate since the most recent business cycle peak (mid-1990) explain a surprisingly large fraction of the long-term movements in the yen/dollar exchange rate and somewhat less in the mark/dollar rate.

FORECASTING EXCHANGE RATE MOVEMENTS

Accurately forecasting movements in the dollar over short horizons is a difficult exercise. In an influential study, economists Richard Meese and Kenneth Rogoff concluded that sophisticated models of exchange rate determination make poor forecasts.[2] These economists suggested a thought experiment that, in the context of today's foreign exchange markets, could be described as follows: On February 4, Chairman Greenspan

Reprinted from Federal Reserve Bank of Chicago *Chicago Fed Letter*, August 1994.

PART II Financial Markets

announced that "the Federal Open Market Committee decided to increase slightly the degree of pressure on reserve positions." This action sent the federal funds rate to 3.25% from its previous average of 3.0%. Immediately following the announcement, the dollar was trading at 1.752 marks and 109.0 yen. Since the historical pattern of the federal funds rate is to continue rising for some time following an initial upward change in direction, what values of the dollar should a sophisticated analyst forecast for February 4, 1995? Or 1996? Of the models they considered, Meese and Rogoff concluded that the best forecasting model would simply predict *no change*, that is, 1.752 marks and 109.0 yen for 1995 and 1996. Only at horizons of about two or three years can the additional information about the behavior of the economy add forecasting power to these models.

One limitation of standard forecasting models is that they usually identify changes in monetary policy with changes in monetary aggregates such as M1 or M2. A recent study by Eichenbaum and Evans, however, indicates a stronger empirical relationship between the federal funds rate and the dollar.[3] When expansionary (contractionary) changes in monetary policy are measured by unanticipated reductions (increases) in the federal funds rate, the data indicate that the dollar will depreciate (appreciate)—but there is a substantial delay between the policy actions and the maximal effect on the dollar.

ASSESSING THE AVERAGE RELATIONSHIP BETWEEN THE FEDERAL FUNDS RATE AND THE EXCHANGE RATE

For both Germany and Japan, I used a statistical model to analyze three financial variables: the federal funds rate, a short-term interest rate in the foreign country, and the exchange rate. The exchange rate was measured in marks per dollar and yen per dollar. The statistical model was a vector autoregression estimated using weekly data. The German model was estimated for the period March 1979 through June 1994. Because of subtle statistical issues involving trends in the yen/dollar exchange rate, the Japanese model was estimated over the period July 1987 through June 1994. (Estimating the Japanese model over the 1979 to 1994 period would have attributed an even greater explanatory role to the federal funds rate in affecting the yen/dollar exchange rate.) The analysis accounts for changes in U.S. and foreign monetary policies through exogenous changes in the federal funds rate and the foreign short-term interest rate. This *Fed Letter* reports only on the effects that changes in the federal funds rate have on the value of the dollar.[4]

How do unusual movements in the federal funds rate affect the time path of the dollar? I will refer to such unusual movements as FF shocks. These shocks can be interpreted in the following way. Much as bond market traders forecast a value for interest rates each week, the statistical model can generate forecasts of the federal funds rate each week

READING 9 The Dollar and the Federal Funds Rate

on the basis of its past values as well as past values of the foreign interest rate and the exchange rate. Then the new federal funds rate occurs this week. If the forecast is either lower or higher than the actual value, then the forecast is in error and the difference is called an FF shock. When the federal funds rate is unexpectedly high (low), as on February 4, that is a positive (negative) FF shock; this can also be referred to as a contractionary (expansionary) policy shock.

The first column of figure 1 plots the average effect of an FF shock on the federal funds rate (FF) and on the yen/dollar exchange rate (YEN, measured as yen per dollar). An average-sized FF shock causes the federal funds rate to increase approximately 13 basis points during the first six months. So a 25-basis-point shock is a two-standard-deviation shock over the 1987-94 sample period. These shocks are larger over the 1979-94 period. This effect persists for about 18 months and then dampens. The effect of this approximately 13-basis-point FF shock on YEN is initially small, and even perversely negative for about six months. By the end of the first year, however, the dollar has appreciated by about 0.5%, and this appreciation persists through the end of the third year. These estimates imply that a series of FF shocks totalling 125 basis points could increase the value of the dollar by 5% over a two- to three-year period.

Of course, many other things cause exchange rates to fluctuate besides U.S. and foreign monetary policy actions. The statistical model for Japan refers to these as unanticipated changes in the yen/dollar exchange rate (YEN shock) that cannot be accounted for by fluctuations in U.S. or Japanese short-term interest rates. The model has difficulty capturing the effects of irregular phenomena such as fears of a trade war, the toppling of the Berlin Wall, the coup attempt against Gorbachev, or presidential elections, to name only a few. As a result of this difficulty, the model lumps all such nonmonetary effects into what I refer to as the YEN shock for Japan, or the MARK shock for Germany.

The second column of figure 1 displays the effect of the YEN shock on FF and YEN. Unanticipated shocks to the yen/dollar exchange rate are large: An average-sized YEN shock increases the value of the dollar by almost 1.5%. The response patterns of the exchange rate arising from the YEN and FF shocks indicate that over shorter horizons, most of the variation in the yen/dollar exchange rate will be due to factors unrelated to the federal funds rate; it turns out that they are mainly due to YEN shocks. Over longer horizons, more of the variation in the yen/dollar exchange rate will be due to monetary policy factors such as FF shocks.

These results seem consistent with the forecasting results reported by Meese and Rogoff; that is, information about the stance of monetary policy in the U.S. is not very helpful for forecasting future movements in the yen/dollar exchange rate at horizons under two years. The results for Germany are comparable.[5]

PART II Financial Markets

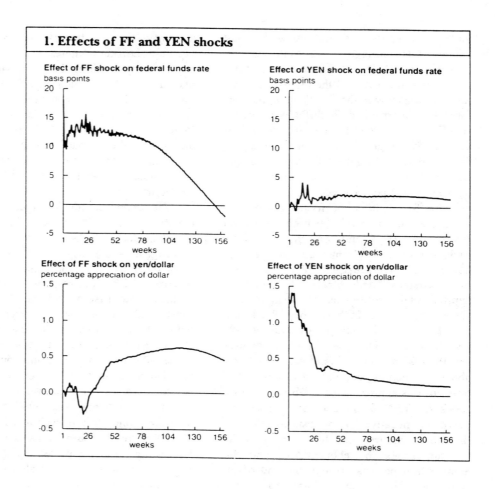

THE YEN/DOLLAR AND MARK/DOLLAR EXPERIENCE, 1987-94

How would the dollar have behaved over the 1987-94 period if the only factors influencing it had been U.S. monetary policy actions? Row 1 of figure 2 suggests an answer for Japan. In the upper left panel, the highly variable blue line is the actual path of the exchange rate from July 1987 through June 1994. The black line is the counterfactual path that the vector

READING 9 The Dollar and the Federal Funds Rate

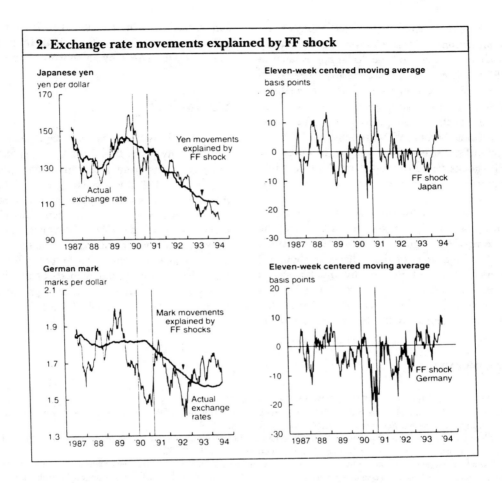

autoregression predicts the exchange rate would have followed if the YEN and Japanese monetary policy shocks had been identical to zero.

The yen/dollar exchange rate path predicted by the FF shocks matches many of the long-term movements in the actual exchange rate over this period. From November 1988 to April 1990, the dollar appreciated 31%; the FF shocks statistically accounted for about 40% of that appreciation. From April 1990 through June 1994, the dollar depreciated by about 60%; the FF shocks captured roughly half of that fall. The upper right panel displays the smoothed FF shocks series, where negative (positive) numbers represent unanticipated policy easing (contraction). The shocks were predominantly positive in 1988, and the dollar appreciated in 1989. The shocks were mostly negative in 1989, and the dollar began to depreciate in 1990. In 1992 and 1993, the shocks were more negative than positive, and the dollar depreciated from 1992 through June 1994. In spite of the reasonably close fit, however, the FF shocks failed to predict much of the high-frequency variability in the yen/dollar exchange rate.

The results for the mark/dollar (MARK) are substantially weaker but still interesting (see row 2 of figure 2). From 1987 to 1989, the average level of the dollar was about 1.8 marks, the level implied by the FF shock; from mid-1992 to the present, the average level of the dollar has been about 1.6 marks, the level implied by the FF shock. As with Japan, however, the forecasted path from the FF shocks misses the high-frequency variability in MARK by an enormous amount.

SUMMARY

Over short horizons, exchange rates can follow many paths that do not correspond to the predictions from recent monetary policy actions. In this sense, the dollar's depreciation against the yen and the mark since February 4 does not seem shocking. Over longer periods, however, these unexplained movements in exchange rates seem to average out. At longer horizons, then, the economic fundamentals of monetary policy seem to provide reasonable predictions for the direction and level of the dollar.

ENDNOTES

1. What's news: Business and finance," *Wall Street Journal*, May 12, 1994, p.1.
2. Richard A. Meese and Kenneth Rogoff, "Empirical exchange rate models of the seventies: Do they fit out of sample?" *Journal of International Economics*, Vol. 14, No. 1/2, 1983, pp. 3-24.
3. Martin Eichenbaum and Charles L. Evans, "Some empirical evidence on the effects of monetary policy shocks on exchange rates," Federal Reserve Bank of Chicago, working paper, No. 92-32.
4. Twenty-six lagged observations for each variable were included in the three-variable vector autoregression. The foreign interest rate variable is a three-month government bill rate. The federal funds shock is an orthogonalized shock from the vector autoregression. For a fuller discussion of the effects of foreign monetary policy shocks on the dollar and a discussion of some technical issues, see Charles L. Evans, "Interest rate shocks and the dollar," *Economic Perspectives*, Vol. 18, No. 5, September/October 1994, forthcoming.
5. These are discussed in Evans, op. cit.

READING 9 The Dollar and the Federal Funds Rate

QUESTIONS

1. Assess Evans's assertion that "the conventional wisdom would predict that the dollar should strengthen following a tightening of U.S. monetary policy." Illustrate with an exchange rate diagram like the ones Mishkin uses in Chapter 8 of the text.

2. What is an FF shock and a YEN or MARK shock? How do these affect the exchange rate for the dollar?

3. The Fed pushed the federal funds rate higher during 1994 and 1995. Based on Evans's evidence, predict what will happen to the value of the dollar, and when.

PART THREE

FINANCIAL INSTITUTIONS

Much of the dynamism associated with the field of money, banking, and financial markets is related to changes in the structure and operations of financial institutions and to the innovation of new financial instruments in response to changes in the economic environment. Part Three of the text develops an economic framework for analyzing financial institutions and uses it to examine such topics as the importance of financial intermediaries as sources of finance for businesses, financial innovation, bank management, banking industry structure, and bank regulatory crisis and reform. Several of these issues are treated in the readings for Part Three. Because this area of the subject changes so rapidly, Part Three is the reader's longest part; the readings here play an important role in keeping the course up to date.

Reading 10, **"A Look at America's Corporate Finance Markets"** by Stephen D. Prowse, surveys the range of financing options available to U.S. firms and provides an explanation for the differences in financing among small, medium, and large firms. This reading supplements Chapter 9's discussion of asymmetric information and financial structure.

Reading 11 is **"Solving the Mystery of High Credit Card Rates"** by Randall J. Pozdena. Pozdena suggests that credit card interest rates have remained high and stable despite significant declines in market interest rates since the early 1980s because credit card debt is unsecured and is subject to moral hazard because the lender cannot closely monitor the borrower's net worth. This reading is suggested for use with Chapter 9's discussion of adverse selection problems.

Reading 12, **"Financial Fragility and the Lender of Last Resort"** by Desiree Schaan and Timothy Cogley, also relates to Chapter 9, specifically to the discussion of financial crises. Schaan and Cogley address asymmetric information problems in the context of financial crises and the advantages and disadvantages of intervention by monetary policymakers when a crisis is at hand.

Reading 13, Joseph G. Haubrich's **"Derivative Mechanics: The CMO,"** describes how collateralized mortgage obligations work, the variety of CMOs that have been innovated, and their advantages and disadvantages for investors and home buyers. It provides a good example of financial innovation discussed in Chapter 10.

Reading 14, **"Small Business Lending and Bank Consolidation: Is There Cause for Concern"** by Philip E. Strahan and James Weston, investigates the separate roles of small and large banks in lending to small businesses and concludes that consolidation in the banking industry need not hurt small businesses. This reading can be used with Chapter 11's treatment of the bank balance sheet and bank lending or used to augment the material on banking industry structure in Chapter 12.

In Reading 15, **"The Rhyme and Reason of Bank Mergers,"** Elizabeth Laderman surveys a variety of reasons which may account for bank merger activity and assesses the results of mergers for banks and their customers. This reading can be used with Chapter 12's discussion of banking industry structure.

Reading 16 is **"Russian Banking"** by Dwight Jaffee and Mark Levonian. This reading describes the private banking system that has developed in Russia since the end of Soviet rule, emphasizing the banking system's structure, the August 1995 crisis it experienced, and the problems that remain to be solved before it can effectively foster development of Russia's economy. It provides international perspective for Chapter 12's discussion of banking industry structure.

Reading 17, **"The Decline of Traditional Banking,"** goes with Chapters 12 and 13. Franklin R. Edwards and Frederic S. Mishkin investigate the causes of the decline and appraise the implications for financial stability and regulatory policy of both the decline and the ways in which banks are responding to it.

Mark Levonian and Fred Furlong describe recent favorable trends in bank risk and the liability of the deposit insurance system in Reading 18, **"Reduced Deposit Insurance Risk."** Levonian and Furlong conclude, based on improved bank capital ratios and reduced deposit insurance liability, that concerns about bank safety ought not constrain policymakers as they consider legal barriers between banking and other activities. This reading is recommended for use with Chapter 13's discussion of bank regulation and the Glass-Steagall Act.

Reading 19, **"Making Sense of Mark to Market"** by Michelle A. Clark, examines the pros and cons of market value accounting in light of the Financial Accounting Standards Board requirement that banks report certain portions of their investment portfolios at market value. This reading goes with Chapter 13's treatment of bank regulation.

In Reading 20, **"Glass-Steagall and the Regulatory Dialectic,"** João Cabral dos Santos describes the process of innovation in banking that results from incongruity between bank regulations and bank incentives. He uses interstate banking and the separation of commercial from investment banking functions as examples. This reading can be used with Chapter 10's discussion of financial innovation or with Chapter 13's discussion of proposed regulatory reforms.

READING 10

A Look At America's Corporate Finance Markets

Stephen D. Prowse

How an economy channels finance from savers—typically individuals—to those with ideas about how to invest productively—the business sector—has always been recognized as important for economic growth. Some recent academic work has emphasized this point. Historians are now attributing a greater role to the development of corporate finance markets in spurring the emergence of the railroads and other heavy industries that were key engines of growth in the industrial revolution. And some recent empirical work suggests that the level of a country's financial development helps predict its future rate of economic growth.[1] Such work has reignited economists' interest in how firms get financed in both the United States and abroad.

This article describes and analyzes the spectrum of finance markets available to U.S. corporations and examines how firms as large as General Motors and as small as the tiniest start-up get financed, with particular attention to the recent dramatic expansion in finance markets for small and medium-sized firms. It explores some reasons for this dramatic expansion. It then examines why U.S. finance markets are structured as they are. Finally, it compares other countries with the United States in terms of how their firms obtain financing and explains why some countries are now trying to emulate the U.S. structure.

HOW FIRMS IN THE U.S. GET FINANCED TODAY

As shown in Chart 1, even after adjusting for inflation, corporate finance markets have grown extremely rapidly over the past 15 years. This expansion has largely been fueled by the rapid growth of nonbank financial institutions, such as pension funds, life insurance companies and mutual funds. In comparison, commercial banks have shown steady though less rapid growth, reflecting in part the regulatory constraints on their activities and the rise of competitors such as finance companies and money market mutual funds. Nonbank financial institutions are now the major suppliers of funds to corporations, and they have helped fashion for the United States the most diverse and rich set of corporate finance markets in the world.

Firms use short-term finance markets for working capital purposes, such as financing inventories or receivables. As shown in Chart

Reprinted from Federal Reserve Bank of Dallas *The Southwest Economy*, Issue 2, 1996.

PART III Financial Institutions

Chart 1
The Growth of Corporate Finance Markets in the United States

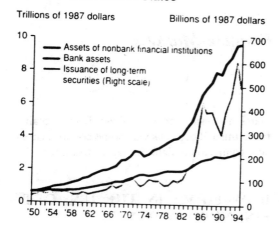

Chart 2
Short-Term Liabilities of Nonfinancial Business, 1994

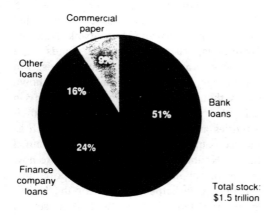

Overall, banks supply over half of all short-term business finance. Finance companies are also important lenders to business, while other intermediaries also make business loans, such as savings institutions and mortgage companies. Issuing commercial paper is typically an option only for larger, more highly rated firms.

Long-term finance markets are used to finance capital expenditures that pay back returns over a long period of time. As shown in Chart 3, issuance of long-term securities so far in the 1990s totaled almost $1.2 trillion. Five markets have contributed to this financing. The most well-known are the public markets for bonds and equity. The public bond market is the largest source of long-term finance because it caters to the biggest firms that have the largest capital needs.

Chart 3
Issuance of Long-Term Securities In the 1990s

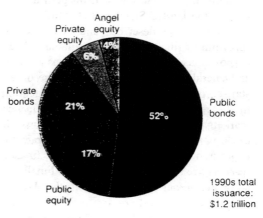

2, in 1994 short-term business liabilities totaled $1.5 trillion, and they came from a number of sources, the most important being loans from banks. Banks are somewhat unique among financial institutions in that they are important lenders to firms of all sizes.

READING 10 A Look at America's Corporate Finance Markets

This article will focus on the three private markets—the private bond, private equity and angel equity markets—because they are the only realistic sources of long-term finance for small and middle-market companies and because they have grown extremely fast in recent years. Despite their importance, relatively little is known about how these markets operate.

The largest of these private markets is the private placement, or private bond, market. It offers long-term debt at fixed interest rates. Primary lenders are life insurance companies. Primary borrowers are middle-market companies with annual revenues between $100 million and $500 million that are generally not large enough to issue public bonds. Although this market receives little attention, it has grown rapidly over the past 15 years and is now quite large. Average annual issuance in recent years is almost five times greater than in the early 1980s, and in some recent years, issuance has actually exceeded that of public bonds, even though individual issue sizes are much smaller than those in the public market. In short, the private placement market is a major source of funds for middle-market firms.[2]

The private equity market consists of equity investments professionally managed by specialized intermediaries, mostly limited partnerships. These limited partnerships are funded by institutional investors such as pension funds, banks, endowments and insurance companies. Although this market is small compared with others, its growth since 1980 has been astronomical, almost 10 times faster than other long-term finance markets. I estimate that the private equity capital stock in 1994 was about $100 billion, almost 25 times larger than in 1980.[3]

One reason for this explosive growth since 1980 has been regulatory and tax changes that encouraged pension fund investment through limited partnerships (LPs). Partnerships have proved to be the most efficient vehicle for investing funds from institutional investors in firms seeking private equity. As shown on the left of Chart 4, most of the growth in the private equity market since 1980 has been through partnerships. Prior to 1980, private equity investments were undertaken mainly by wealthy families, industrial corporations or banks directly investing their own capital. This practice was inefficient because it required all individual investors to bear the costs of managing their own investments. The pooling of funds into one entity—the LP—that does all the management has proved to be a more efficient way of organizing private equity investments.

The right half of Chart 4 shows that in 1980 this market was focused almost exclusively on traditional venture capital targets—small firms, often in high-tech lines of business that have a chance of growing into highly successful large firms. Today, the market has a much wider range of activity, including nonventure investments such as expansion capital for middle-market firms, turnaround capital for firms in financial distress and buyout investments.

Finally, there is the market for angel capital. Angel capital refers to equity investments in small firms by wealthy individuals, often with entrepreneurial backgrounds. Unlike the private equity market, this is a very localized, informal

PART III Financial Institutions

Chart 4
Stock of Private Equity

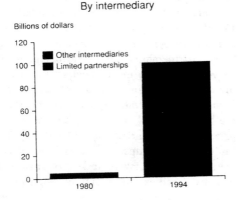

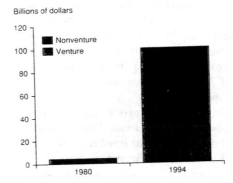

market. Angel capital is targeted at start-up or infant stage firms that cannot attract venture capital because they don't have exciting enough growth prospects. Although it's hard to estimate the size of this market, it is very important for small firms, not least because it's often the only realistic source of capital available to such firms. The most conservative estimates suggest that angels invest about $10 billion in more than 30,000 small firms each year. This market has also likely grown very fast in recent years, in part because the number of wealthy individuals in the economy has grown so fast. For example, after adjusting for inflation, there are roughly six times as many people making $1 million or more a year in the U.S. today than there were in 1980.

Why have the finance markets for small and medium-sized firms expanded so rapidly? First, these firms have become increasingly important in the economy, as illustrated in Chart 5. Per capita new business incorporations have almost doubled since the late '60s, while the share of total employment in small firms has increased sharply since the mid-'70s. The evolution to an information-based economy has probably contributed to small firm growth, since many service and technology-based firms tend to be small or medium-sized. The tendency for large firms to outsource many of their administrative functions to smaller firms (such as payroll, accounting and personnel) may also be a factor. As small and medium-sized firms have increased in importance, so has their demand for capital. Second, there has been an increased interest and ability of institutional investors to supply capital to smaller firms, as illustrated by the previously discussed pension fund involvement in the private equity market.

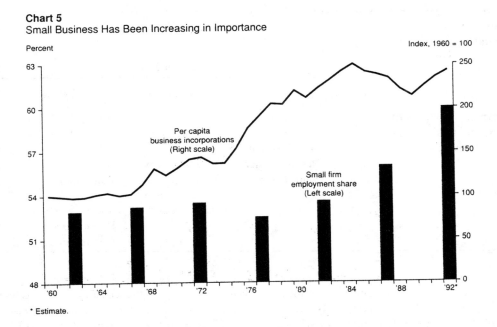

Chart 5
Small Business Has Been Increasing in Importance

* Estimate.

WHY CORPORATE FINANCE MARKETS ARE STRUCTURED AS THEY ARE

Why are corporate finance markets structured as they are in the United States? A partial answer lies in how the finance market has addressed two generic information problems faced by all firms trying to raise capital.

First is the selection problem, which investors face in choosing where to invest. Out of the hundreds of investment proposals investors receive from firms, how do they select the ones most likely to succeed or least likely to fail? A second problem is one of monitoring or governance: how do investors ensure that, after funding, the firm puts funds to the proper uses? These are essentially information problems: they stem from the fact that potential outside investors typically know much less about the firm than the firm's managers. This limitation impairs investors' ability both to assess which firms are the best investments and to know exactly what the firm is doing with the money made available to it.

Information problems tend to be worse for small firms, which do not produce very detailed information about themselves and are often too young to have a track record about which they can boast. Medium-sized firms, being typically somewhat more mature than small firms, have a more solid track record

PART III Financial Institutions

Table 1
Capital Sources for Firms

	Firm Size		
	Small	Medium	Large
Information availability:	Low	More	High
Selection/monitoring problems:	High	Less	Low
Capital sources:	Angel capital		
	Private equity	Private equity	
	Bank loans	Bank loans	Bank loans
		Private bonds	
		Public equity	Public equity
			Public bonds
			Commercial paper

and tend to produce more information about their activities. They consequently suffer somewhat less from the handicap of the unknown. Large public firms make available detailed information about their activities and usually have long track records. They suffer least from such problems.

However, just as firms differ in the extent of the information problems they pose to outside investors, corporate finance markets differ in the extent to which they can deal with these shortcomings. As shown in Table 1, small firms are forced to raise funds in markets for angel capital, private equity and bank loans. Medium-sized firms may be able to tap the private bond market, while some of the larger or more promising middle-market firms may also be able to issue public equity. Large firms that suffer least from information problems gravitate toward the markets that have the fewest such safeguards and where, in general, capital is the cheapest, such as the public bond and commercial paper markets.

What type of safeguards have markets developed? Two phenomena are common in the bank loan, private placement, private equity and angel capital markets. First, as a general practice, investors in these markets have the expertise and resources to obtain information about the firms who solicit them for money. These investors report selecting about 1 percent of the hundreds of investment proposals they receive per year. Proposals are usually from firms about which there is little or no publicly available information. Thus, banks, life insurance companies and limited partnerships have staff capable of producing information about the firm from scratch and analyzing that information intelligently. These resources help mitigate the selection problem.

READING 10 A Look at America's Corporate Finance Markets

Second, investors use their direct influence or other control mechanisms to ensure that the firm makes proper use of invested funds. Such influence helps mitigate the monitoring problem. Tight covenants in bank loans and private placements, for example, give the firm little leeway to stray from the straight and narrow path.

Private equity investors and angels also use a number of mechanisms to gain management influence. Representation on the firm's board and a majority voting right position are common examples. In addition, investors typically hold the purse strings for subsequent capital. Fast-growing firms depend crucially on the initial investors to either provide subsequent capital themselves or find other investors to do so. Initial investors will be unwilling to do either task if they believe the management team has not performed up to par. And management almost always has a significant level of stock ownership in the firm, so that management's incentives are more aligned with those of the outside investors.

Chart 6 shows how this structure of financial markets works in reality, using the financing history of Dell Computer as an illustration. Dell, based in Austin, is currently the world's fifth largest personal computer maker, with annual revenues of almost $3.5 billion. Twelve years ago, Dell was merely an idea in its founder's head. In 1984, Michael Dell started making and selling IBM PC clones through the mail from his college dorm. As with almost every start-up, his first source of financing was his own personal savings. Since the company had some inventory and sales to which it could point, for the next three years Dell tapped bank lines of credit secured by inventories and receivables.

By 1987, the company had grown so fast that it had exhausted its debt capacity. Given the company's size and youth, the only realistic source of funds was private equity venture capital. That year Dell convinced a group of venture capitalists to invest $20 million in the company. As is typical in venture financings, the investors wanted some control over the company in return for their money—in this case the lead venture capitalist took the positions of president and chief operating officer. The infusion of equity proved crucial to subsequent expansion, and by 1988 Dell had become large enough to raise $28 million from the public equity markets through an initial public offering (IPO).

Dell continued to grow fast, and in 1991 returned to the public equity market for $120 million. Although Dell was a successful, fast-growing company, its relatively small size, youth and potentially volatile line of business meant that it still could not tap the public bond market. After obtaining a $200 million bank line of credit in early 1993, Dell had enough of a track record to be acceptable to public bond investors and issued $100 million of public bonds in August 1993. Thus, in 12 years, and with the aid of a variety of corporate finance markets, Dell Computer went from a one-man operation housed in a college dormitory to a multinational company that employs over 7,500 people.

PART III Financial Institutions

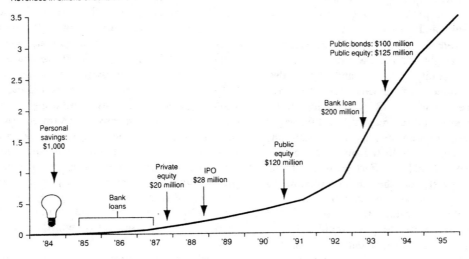

Chart 6
From an Idea to a $3.5 Billion Company in 12 Years...
Dell Computer's Financing History

INTERNATIONAL COMPARISONS

In Japan and Germany, the corporate finance system is very different from that of the United States. Firms in these countries, large and small, typically have relied much more on bank financing than have U.S. firms. The primary reason for this reliance lies in the heavily regulated nature of German and Japanese securities markets, which has severely stunted their growth. Their public securities markets are extremely small compared with those of the United States, and their small firm finance markets are even more undeveloped. For example, many medium-sized European firms are now finding it easier to do IPOs on the U.S. NASDAQ exchange rather than raise capital domestically.

Although the bank-centered systems may have had some advantages in the past, there is an increasing feeling that such systems may not provide adequately for the credit needs of small and medium-sized firms that are the engine of future economic growth and innovation. This may be one reason many of the success stories in the past 15 years have come predominately from the United States, while there have been few Dell's or Microsoft's in Japan or Germany. Recognizing this, policy-makers in these countries recently have deregulated their securities markets in an effort to emulate the U.S. system of corporate finance.

CONCLUSION

A recent *Business Week* cover article celebrated America's access to the public equity markets and the positive effect the recent boom in IPOs had for innovation and growth. The magazine called this phenomenon "IPO capitalism."[4] This article argues that the story is really a much bigger and broader one. Dell is a success story about the capacity of U.S. capital markets to provide funds to firms at *all* stages in their life, not just the IPO stage.

This is not to say that all deserving firms get the type of access that Dell enjoyed, nor that our capital markets could not be improved. Nor is it meant to imply that it is now easy for small firms to raise capital. Raising capital for small firms is not easy and probably never will be because of the severe information problems that small firms pose to outside investors. But the rapid expansion of markets devoted to solving these problems has made raising capital easier than it was in the past. And today there are thousands of firms of all sizes in America that are benefiting from the unique scope and breadth of U.S. corporate finance markets. Such access to capital deserves a somewhat more encompassing term than just "IPO capitalism."

As Joseph Schumpeter once put it, "Credit creation is the monetary complement to innovation." For every underlying type of "real" economy—agricultural, industrial and so forth—there are a unique set of financing problems for firms and an optimal way of addressing those problems. As American innovation moves us beyond the agrarian and manufacturing eras and into the service and information age, our capital markets must evolve also, else economic growth will surely slow. The rapid expansion of the corporate finance markets for small and medium-sized firms documented in this article is one sign that this evolution is already taking place. Indeed, U.S. corporate finance markets today appear to have become the best in the world at funding "entrepreneurial capitalism," whatever the source of that entrepreneurial spirit.

ENDNOTES

1. See R.G. King and R. Levine, "Finance and Growth: Schumpeter Might Be Right," *Quarterly Journal of Economics* 108 (August 1993): 717-37.
2. See M. Carey, S. Prowse, J. Rea and G. Udell, "The Economics of the Private Placement Market," Federal Reserve Board Staff Study, no. 166, 1993.
3. See G. Fenn, N. Liang and S. Prowse, "The Economics of the Private Equity Market," Federal Reserve Board Staff Study, no. 168, 1995.
4. See *Business Week*, December 18, 1995.

PART III   Financial Institutions

QUESTIONS

1. How is the growth of corporate finance markets in the U.S. adjusted for inflation in Chart 1?

2. Describe the participants (lenders and borrowers) in the private bond, private equity, and angel equity markets.

3. Why have finance markets for small businesses experienced rapid growth?

4. What types of asymmetric information problems does the reading identify? How do these problems vary with firm size? How are they overcome in the private bond and equity and angel equity markets?

READING 11

Solving the Mystery of High Credit Card Rates

Randall J. Pozdena

The behavior of credit card interest rates has befuddled many observers. The rates seem high, relative to other interest rates, currently averaging about 12 percentage points above the Treasury bill rate. In addition, whereas market interest rates have declined significantly since the early 1980s, credit card rates have not moved down significantly. Indeed, the spread between the Treasury bill rate and credit card rates has doubled in that time.

The credit card industry has not offered a good explanation of the behavior of credit card rates. In light of the high level of credit card rates, therefore, about half the states have imposed usury limits on credit card rates. While credit card issuers have been able to avoid these restrictions in many cases by moving their activities to other states, other policy makers recently have proposed national rate caps. It is important to know whether such usury laws are justified.

The purpose of this *Weekly Letter* is to present a simple view of credit card rate-setting that produces the high and insensitive rate structure observed. The model is used to reproduce the actual historical performance of credit card rates. The conclusion is that high and invariant credit card rates are not necessarily evidence of a failure of competition in the credit card market. This calls into question the advisability of usury restrictions.

THE CREDIT CARD MARKET

Credit cards are both payment and credit devices. Cardholders can use them in lieu of cash for a variety of retail transactions. At any given time, a bit fewer than half of all cardholders also use them to access a revolving credit line of a preset amount. The use of credit cards as a payments device is growing at the rate of about 10 percent per year. The amount of credit card debt outstanding is growing at about a 6 percent annual rate and represents about 30 percent of all consumer installment credit.

Providers of "interchange" services (such as MasterCard and Visa) transmit payment information between the cardholder's and the merchant's banks. However, the issuing institution sets the card's terms, including the interest rate, the grace period, annual fees, penalties, and most other card features. While

Reprinted from Federal Reserve Bank of San Francisco *Weekly Letter*, November 29, 1991.

PART III   Financial Institutions

there are relatively few suppliers of interchange services, according to the Nilson Report there are at least 5,000 credit card issuers in the United States (excluding private label variations of these cards). In addition, entry into the business is relatively easy, with individual retailers and other commercial entities of even modest size offering credit card plans.

RESOLVING A CONUNDRUM

The existence of this many suppliers normally would be expected to lead to aggressive price competition. Yet, credit card rates appear to be very sticky, responding sluggishly, if at all, to trends and fluctuations in other market interest rates. The volatility of credit card rates is less than one-fifth that of Treasury Bill rates, for example, and the correlation between the two interest rates over the past 10 years has been less than 0.1.

In addition, as pointed out by Ausubel (1991) and the Board of Governors (1991), the rate of return to banks on credit card assets appears to be high relative to the return observed for other bank assets. Yet actual loss (charge-off) rates do not appear to be very high, averaging below 3 percent for most of the past decade—seemingly too little to justify a 12 percent premium over riskless rates.

All of this evidence is seen as being consistent with abnormally high profits in credit card lending, in sharp contrast to what would be expected given the structure of the industry.

To resolve this conundrum, it is necessary to focus on the nature of the debt created by using the revolving credit feature of a credit card. In particular, credit card debt is unsecured debt; when a customer uses a credit card in a purchase and does not pay off the balance within the grace period, the issuing bank acquires an unsecured loan. That is, neither the merchandise purchased, nor any other asset of the cardholder, may be repossessed easily by the lender to ensure payment.

The obvious reason for this feature is that for small transactions, the additional contractual steps involved in establishing title as part of the loan agreement would be costly. (Such steps do make sense, on the other hand, for larger denomination installment credit, such as auto loans or home equity lines.)

The only avenue open to the lender to obtain repayment from delinquent cardholders is to proceed in court against the general assets or income of the cardholder and to report the delinquency to credit rating agencies. In the former case, the transactions costs conceivably could be large relative to outstanding balances, which average only about $1,200 per card in 1990 (using data from the market for credit card-backed securities). The threat of impaired credit ratings serves to discipline the user against excessive use of the card, but does not actually assist in recovery of outstanding balances.

MODELING CREDIT CARD DEBT

Finance theory provides a way of pricing risky debt using options pricing theory, by recognizing that the default potential of a loan essentially implies the existence of a financial option. Using such models, it can be shown that the value (to the lender) of such a loan depends on more than just the market interest rate; in particular, the loan value declines with increases in the riskiness of the cardholder's net worth (which provide the ultimate security of the loan) and with decreases in collateralization.

If the issuing bank can predict the risk accurately, of course, it can charge a higher initial interest rate on the credit to compensate for the additional risk. However, even if the bank knows the risk beforehand, its ability to control the riskiness of the borrower, once the borrower has the credit, is limited. Indeed, once the borrower has the funds at an agreed price, he has a strong incentive to use it under conditions that are most favorable to him—namely, when his net worth is impaired. The issuing bank has limited ability to identify when these conditions prevail and to exercise control over its exposure.

Banks can (and do) impose limits on credit card credit as a means of controlling exposure. In addition, credit card companies try to identify consumer segments that pose lower risks of default (and these selective issuers charge lower rates). But within any consumer segment, the lender can never be certain how leveraged the borrower has become because of other obligations, and because of the lack of collateralization, must assume "worst case" exposure within each segment.

IMPLICATIONS

The primary, practical solutions to this so-called "moral hazard of lending" dilemma are (1) to collateralize the loan (a possibility likely foreclosed because of the title cost considerations expressed above), or (2) to price the loan assuming maximum risk exposure. That is, credit card debt interest rate must be set very high in order to compensate the issuer for the fact that users will adjust their risk in response to the price of the credit.

Indeed, if there were no way to limit the moral hazard problem, no rate would be high enough. (As a practical matter, of course, the reputational costs associated with a bad credit rating help cap extreme behavior of borrowers.) The result is that under conditions of poor collateralization, lenders must charge considerably higher credit card rates than when lending is secured, even to "creditworthy" segments. (In addition, it can be shown theoretically that the rate on a poorly collateralized loan is insensitive to variations in riskless rates.)

The resultant use of high rates implies that credit card debt will be "overpriced" for households that pose low risks of default. These households will tend not to use the revolving credit features of their cards, but rather to use them mainly as transactions devices. (In practice, slightly more than half of all cardholders use the cards without running credit balances.) They will be

PART III   Financial Institutions

primarily sensitive to annual fees and the grace period, an implication consistent with observations of credit card marketers cited by Ausubel.

"Riskier" households, on the other hand, will self-select into using the credit feature of their cards because, for them, the rate premium is attractive given the costs to them of alternative credit. Although the charge-off rate for these borrowers will be accordingly high, the average across all outstanding balances is reduced by those who choose to pay at the end of the grace period, partly explaining the low, actual charge-off rates.

SIMULATING CREDIT CARD PRICING

The options pricing model described above can be stated mathematically, and its parameters estimated by varying them until they best fit the historical experience of credit card rates. Through such an exercise, we can determine (1) if it is possible for the model to match actual credit card pricing and (2) if the parameters are consistent with the assumptions of the nature of credit card debt. In particular, we can see whether it is priced assuming a low level of collateralization and high marginal risk.

The author performed this exercise, using a simple Black-Scholes type representation of collateralized debt. Actual short-term interest rates were used, with all other parameters of the model selected using an optimization technique to find the best fit of the modeled rates to actual credit card rates. The results,

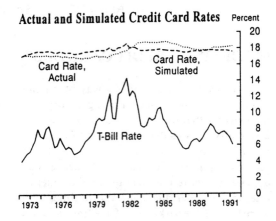

Actual and Simulated Credit Card Rates

present in the Chart, show that it was easy to fit the options-based model to the actual data, even if it is assumed that the risk exposure of the lender has not varied over this time period. (In addition, there is no attempt to control for the removal of interstate usury controls in 1982.)

More importantly, however, the parameters of the underlying model are consistent with the representation of credit card debt as costly-to-service, unsecured credit extended to relatively high-risk borrowers. Specifically, the loan seems to be priced as if the lender perceived the debt as poorly collateralized or costly to service, and the variance of the borrower's net worth as high. (As a point of reference, the implied variance is similar to the variance in the S&P 500 returns.) As a check on the internal consistency of the simulation exercise, the term of the credit card debt was also estimated, rather than assumed, as a part of the empirical exercise. The implied term of the credit card debt in the model is about four years, in the range of the terms implied in secondary market sales of credit card debt.

CONCLUSION

In Ausubel's very thorough study of the credit card market, he concludes that cardholders were "irrational," acquiring the cards with no intention of ever using them, but ending up incurring large credit card balances and debt service costs. The implication of the analysis here is that no such irrationality need be invoked. Rather, the high, and insensitive, credit card rates are consistent with the pricing of risky credits in an atmosphere of moral hazard and costly collateralization or service. The fact that credit card issuers that do offer lower rates do so only to more carefully selected consumer segments also is consistent with the risk management model employed here.

This alone, of course, does not prove that the credit card market is as competitive as it should be. However, the current performance of credit card rates is completely consistent with the model used in this *Letter*. This suggests that attempts to reduce credit card rates through usury legislation will have the effect of exposing banks to increased risk, and reducing the availability of consumer credit. This is a curious policy direction in an economy already plagued by weak financial institutions and sluggish credit growth.

REFERENCES

Ausubel, L. 1991. "The Failure of Competition in the Credit Card Market." *American Economic Review* (March) pp. 50-81.
Board of Governors of the Federal Reserve System. 1991. "Profitability of Credit Card Plans: Second Annual Report to Congress."

PART III Financial Institutions

QUESTIONS

1. What is Pozdena's explanation for high credit card rates?

2. How do the high credit card rates affect low risk and high risk households? Does this represent an adverse selection problem?

3. Pozdena claims that usury limits on credit card rates will expose banks to more risk and reduce the availability of consumer credit. Is this the result you would expect from asymmetric information problems? Explain.

READING 12

Financial Fragility and the Lender of Last Resort

Desiree Schaan & Timothy Cogley

Financial crises, such as banking panics and stock market crashes, were a common occurrence in the U.S. economy before World War II. Since then, financial crises have been less common. However, events of the past decade have led to renewed concerns about financial instability and about the proper role of monetary policy in reacting to financial turbulence.

This *Weekly Letter* provides some background on the nature of financial crises, and it discusses whether and how policymakers should intervene. Our discussion borrows heavily from papers by Frederic Mishkin (1991, 1994). Because there are costs to inappropriate intervention, Mishkin suggests that the central bank should intervene only when certain informational problems make it difficult for financial markets to efficiently channel funds to productive investment opportunities. A conceptual framework is needed in order to determine when these informational problems arise. This *Letter* discusses a framework that is based upon theories of asymmetrical information, and it describes the trade-offs that policymakers face.

THEORIES OF FINANCIAL CRISES

The traditional theory of financial crises focuses on the effects of bank runs on the money supply. Other things equal, bank runs tend to reduce the money supply by increasing the public's desire to hold currency and banks' desire to hold reserves. Unless the central bank reacts by increasing the supply of currency and reserves, the money supply would fall and interest rates would rise, thus reducing the public's spending on goods and services. For example, Milton Friedman and Anna Schwartz (1963) argue that the Federal Reserve's inaction during the banking panics of the early 1930s helped turn an ordinary recession into the Great Depression. They argue that the Federal Reserve should intervene in a banking panic in order to prevent a contraction in the money supply.

In addition to this effect, modern theories of financial crises focus on the consequences of asymmetrical information between borrowers and lenders. Borrowers generally know more about their investment projects than lenders, and this can lead to problems related to adverse selection and moral hazard.

Reprinted from Federal Reserve Bank of San Francisco *Weekly Letter*, May 26, 1995.

Adverse selection occurs when events cause low-risk borrowers to drop out of credit markets. Borrowers invest in projects that involve various payoffs and degrees of risk. High-risk projects also tend to have high expected returns. If lenders do not have enough information to assess the risk-return tradeoffs of particular projects, they must extend credit at an interest rate that reflects the average risk of the market. The average interest rate is too high for projects with low risk and expected return, and it is too low for high-risk, high-return projects. Thus asymmetrical information tends to push low-risk borrowers out of credit markets, leaving only the high-risk borrowers.

Asymmetrical information can also give rise to moral hazard. Once a borrower has received credit, he may have an incentive to undertake activities which raise his own expected return but which also increase the probability of default. This is especially problematic when credit takes the form of a debt contract that allows for bankruptcy and when lenders have difficulty monitoring the borrower's activities.

To mitigate adverse selection and moral hazard problems, Stiglitz and Weiss (1981) show that lenders might prefer to ration credit rather than to raise interest rates when credit demand or uncertainty increases. If lenders were to raise interest rates when credit demands or uncertainty increased, low-risk, low-return borrowers would drop out of the credit market, and high-risk, high-return borrowers would remain. Thus, if creditors were to increase interest rates, the riskiness of the pool of borrowers would increase. Therefore, lenders may choose not to raise interest rates and may instead choose to supply less credit than borrowers demand at the going interest rate. Thus, borrowers who have profitable investment opportunities may be unable to find credit.

Mishkin defines a financial crisis as a situation in which adverse selection and moral hazard problems become much worse, so that financial markets are unable to channel credit to borrowers with profitable investment opportunities. Clearly, this definition does not apply to markets in which creditors can easily evaluate the riskiness of projects and monitor the behavior of investors. But in markets where information is asymmetrical, financial crises are costly, because they reduce economic efficiency and because they may lead to a sharp reduction in investment and aggregate demand. Finally, note that a market crash does not by itself constitute a crisis. A crash could reflect a sharp, adverse turn in fundamentals, as in May 1940 when the U.S. stock market crashed after the fall of France.

SYMPTOMS OF FINANCIAL CRISIS

To identify a crisis, policymakers must determine whether adverse selection or moral hazard problems have become critical. Mishkin lists a number of symptoms. One is a sharp increase in interest rates. This tends to push low-risk borrowers out of credit markets and may lead to credit rationing.

Another symptom is a sharp, unexpected decline in stock prices or inflation. This exacerbates asymmetrical information problems because it reduces the net worth of firms that seek credit. Bernanke and Gertler (1989) show how a large decline in borrower net worth can increase adverse selection and moral hazard problems. A firm's net worth performs a role that is similar to collateral, since a lender can take title to a firm's assets in case of default. Collateral mitigates adverse selection and moral hazard problems because it reduces the lender's losses if the borrower defaults. A decline in net worth implicitly reduces the value of a firm's collateral and may tighten credit rationing.

A third symptom is a banking panic or the failure of other financial institutions. Banks specialize in processing information about borrowers and in monitoring their activities. For example, they usually engage in long-term relationships with their customers, and can monitor their customers' behavior by overseeing their checking account or credit line activity. Bank services are valuable because they reduce the degree of information asymmetry between borrowers and individual savers, who are the ultimate lenders. During a panic, bank failures increase the degree of information asymmetry. Furthermore, banks that remain in business seek to protect themselves by increasing reserves relative to deposits, and this also results in a reduction of lending.

A fourth symptom is an increase in the spread between interest rates on high- and low-quality bonds. This spread reflects the difference in default risk on well-known, high-quality borrowers (such as the U.S. Treasury) and lesser-known, lower-quality borrowers. Hence, this interest rate spread tends to widen when asymmetrical information problems become severe. Historically, this has proven to be a relatively reliable indicator.

IMPLICATIONS FOR MONETARY POLICY

The classical policy prescription in the event of a financial panic is for the central bank to act as a lender of last resort. In a narrow sense, this can be justified on monetarist principles. Bank failures are contractionary because they reduce the stock of money. Thus, during a banking panic, the central bank should lend through the discount window or engage in open-market purchases in order to prevent a contraction in the supply of money.

The asymmetrical information theory suggests a broader perspective. There may also be occasions when the central bank may need to provide lender-of-last-resort services to nonbanking firms as well. This can be done through the discount window, but other policy actions also may have a role. For example, in June 1970, when Penn Central defaulted on more than $200 million in commercial paper, the Federal Reserve became concerned that at a time when financial markets were already unsettled, the liquidity of the commercial paper market might be impaired and the pressures arising in that market might spill over to other short-term credit markets. The Federal Reserve moved to suspend the maximum interest rate ceilings on large-denomination time deposits with maturities of 30 to 89 days imposed by Regulation Q. This made it easier for private

PART III   Financial Institutions

banks to serve as intermediaries. Investors reluctant to lend to the commercial paper market now provided additional funds to the private banking sector, and borrowers unable to roll over their commercial paper were provided with this new source of credit. The Fed also increased liquidity in the commercial paper market by allowing banks to borrow at its discount window (see Board of Governors, 1971).

The stock market crash of 1987 provides another example of a successful intervention and illustrates the value of lender-of-last-resort activity. On Monday, October 19th, the Dow Jones Industrial Average fell by 22 percent. The day after the crash, many securities firms and exchange specialists needed credit to finance inventories of stocks whose value had fallen sharply. Also, many investors were asked to provide more collateral for securities bought on credit. These demands, known as margin calls, occur when the value of equities in an investor's account fall below a set minimum. Since the value of collateral had fallen sharply, banks were increasingly reluctant to lend. The interest rate spread between junk bonds and Treasury bills jumped by 130 basis points during the week of the crash and rose by another 60 basis points over the following two weeks. The presence of both the stock market crash and the increase in the spread of interest rates between high- and low-quality bonds indicates that asymmetrical information may have increased in the securities sector.

The Federal Reserve became concerned about a possible systemic breakdown in the market's clearing and settlement systems, and it announced a readiness to "serve as a source of liquidity to support the economic and financial system." The Federal Reserve then proceeded to accommodate the increase in demand for liquidity in the economy by buying government securities on the open market. This provided banks with the extra reserves they needed to extend credit to the securities dealers. The Fed also tried to maintain a high level of visibility in the financial markets to help calm fears of a potential crisis. The Fed placed examiners in major banking institutions to monitor banking developments, and also closely monitored securities firms' demands for credit (Greenspan 1988).

While lender-of-last-resort activity may help protect against financial crises, there is a cost. If depositors know that the central bank will bail private banks out if their loans go bad, they may have less incentive to monitor the riskiness of the banks' portfolios. Likewise, if nonbanking institutions know that the central bank will step in during a financial crisis, they might take on more risks that are associated with an economy-wide financial crisis. Because of these costs, lender-of-last-resort activity should probably be used sparingly.

CONCLUSION

Theories based on asymmetrical information suggest that financial markets can be fragile, since lenders may opt out of the market when credit demands increase or when uncertainty is especially great. By serving as a lender of last resort, central banks can play an important role in reducing financial panics, as they can ensure that credit markets remain liquid in the event of a crisis. However, this literature suggests that central banks should intervene sparingly, as too much involvement may cause market participants to assume more risk.

REFERENCES

Bernanke, Ben, and Mark Gertler. 1989. "Agency Costs, Net Worth, and Business Fluctuations." *American Economic Review* 79, pp. 14-31.
Board of Governors of the Federal Reserve System. 1971. *Annual Report*, 1970.
Friedman, Milton, and Anna Schwartz. 1963. *A Monetary History of the United States.* Princeton: Princeton University Press.
Greenspan, Alan. 1988. "Statement before the Committee on Banking, Housing, and Urban Affairs, February 2, 1988." Reprinted in the *Federal Reserve Bulletin* (April), pp. 217-225.
Mishkin, Frederic S. 1991. "Asymmetric Information and Financial Crises: A Historical Perspective." In *Financial Markets and Financial Crises, A National Bureau of Economic Research Project Report*, ed. R. Glenn Hubbard, pp. 69-108. Chicago: University of Chicago Press.
_____. 1994. "Preventing Financial Crises: An International Perspective." NBER Working Paper No. 4636.
Stiglitz, Joseph, and Andrew Weiss. 19891. "Credit Rationing in Markets with Imperfect Information." *American Economic Review* 71, pp. 393-410.

QUESTIONS

1. Describe the traditional and modern theories of financial crises and their economic effects.

2. How are adverse selection and moral hazard problems worsened during a financial crisis? What signals that these problems are worsening can policymakers look for?

3. Why did the Fed intervene in the financial system following the 1970 Penn Central default and the 1987 stock market crash? Is there a drawback to such intervention? Explain.

READING 13

Derivative Mechanics: The CMO

Joseph G. Haubrich

The current interest in financial derivatives sometimes appears to be driven by the same tastes that support police and doctor dramas on television: many crashes and a lot of blood. Though undeniably exciting, such shows do not teach you how to drive safely or how to administer first aid. Likewise, a concentration on the blowups of financial derivatives slights the more basic information needed for policy decisions or corporate risk management.

This *Economic Commentary* looks under the hood of one particularly important type of financial derivative, the Collateralized Mortgage Obligation or CMO (sometimes known as a REMIC, or Real Estate Mortgage Investment Conduit[1]). CMOs have prominence both because of their wide use ($650 billion in 1994) and because of their role in a series of major financial setbacks. Wall Street professionals, including the investment bank of Kidder Peabody and mortgage guru Lew Ranieri's Hyperion Capital Management, lost money investing in CMOs. So did small towns and counties (some as close to home as Sandusky County and Jackson, Ohio), colleges, and even an Indian reservation.[2] To understand what went wrong, it is necessary to understand how CMOs work. This, too, has its own rewards, at least for those whose taste runs more toward the dazzle of gleaming machinery and the challenge of complexity.

MORTGAGE-BACKED SECURITIES

The story begins as ordinary mortgages become securitized, or bundled into a pool and then sold. It's a bit ironic that some of the most sophisticated financial derivatives ultimately depend on a very common, even mundane, instrument—the homeowner's mortgage. These mortgages provide the underlying collateral backing up the security.

The first type of mortgage-backed security, still quite common, is the "pass-through." Investors get a pro rata share of payments—some fraction of the monthly mortgage payments made by the myriad homeowners in the pool. Since each monthly payment includes both principal and interest, investors get a mixture of those elements "passed through" from the homeowners. This presents a problem in that the security has a

Reprinted from Federal Reserve Bank of Cleveland *Economic Commentary*, September 1, 1995.

READING 13 Derivative Mechanics: The CMO

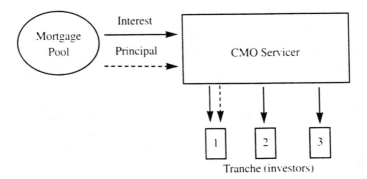

SOURCE: Frank J. Fabozzi, ed., *The Handbook of Mortgage-Backed Securities* (footnote 3).

very long maturity—it takes years until the last homeowner completely pays off the last mortgage and returns the full value of the principal. Since homeowners have the option to pre-pay their mortgages, pass-throughs also face the risk that payments may arrive on a different schedule than investors initially expected.

In the summer of 1983, market participants developed the CMO to solve these problems. CMOs break the mortgage-backed security into a series of bonds known as "tranches" (French for trench). Each tranche gets its share of interest payments, but the principal is repaid sequentially. That is, principal payments go exclusively to the first tranche until it is paid off, then to the second tranche until it is paid off, and so forth. This breaks the security into several shorter bonds (see figure 1). For example, an investor holding $10 million of a $100 million pass-through would not get all of his principal back until every mortgage had been paid off. The holder of a $10 million first tranche, by contrast, would get his principal back from the first $10 million paid. This structure makes CMOs *derivatives*: Their value depends on, or derives from, the value of the underlying mortgage pool.[3]

RISK REMAINS

The standard CMO still exhibits two types of risk. Interest-rate risk exists because market rates can change, making the present value of the payment stream worth different amounts. Pre-payment risk still exists, and it continues to make the maturity of the bond uncertain. For example, as interest rates fall, more people pre-pay their mortgages, so each tranche has a shorter maturity. As interest rates rise, fewer people pre-pay their mortgages, so each tranche has a longer maturity.

Why do people care about pre-payment risk? On the simplest level, slow pre-payments mean that the investor does not get his money back as quickly, and the value of the bond declines. When interest rates rise, even ordinary bonds drop in price as the present discounted value of their payments falls. CMO tranches take another hit, because now their payments also come later as pre-payment rates fall. Market participants refer to this as extension risk.

Extension risk has two additional downsides. One is that it subjects investors to reinvestment risk. Normally, investors holding a bond want interest rates to drop because it gives them a capital gain: The present discounted value of the cash stream is worth more. Bond prices rise as interest rates fall. But the pre-payment effect makes CMOs work somewhat differently. When interest rates rise, the CMO extends at exactly the wrong time, that is, when interest rates are high and investors would like to reinvest at the higher rate. When rates fall, the CMO tranche pays off quickly, again at the wrong time. The investor receives more principal today, when interest rates are down, and so must trade the high interest on the original CMO for lower interest on something else. This reinvestment risk offsets, and may dominate, the capital gain or loss stemming from a change in interest rates.

Furthermore, the extended (or shortened) bond now has a new, different sensitivity to risk, with a five-year bond behaving differently from a two-year or 10-year bond. With a change in pre-payments, investors now hold a bond that reacts to interest rates in a manner unlike the original, so it may be less useful for hedging liabilities or fitting into their portfolio.

FANCY CMOs

To mitigate these risks, market participants created a new type of tranche—the accrual bond, or Z-bond. This bond gets neither principal nor interest until all previous tranches are paid off. The interest due accrues, and like a zero-coupon bond, it initially makes no interest payment. The Z-bond acts as a stabilizing influence on the other tranches. The interest that would otherwise go to the Z-bond tranche (recall that standard CMOs pay interest to all tranches) instead goes to the other tranches and counts as a principal payment. This constant flow of payments has a steadying effect, offsetting some of the variability from pre-payment. As pre-payments rise, the tranches pay off ahead of schedule and the Z-bond starts making payments earlier than originally anticipated. Because it is the last tranche, however, pre-payment fluctuations often average out by the time the Z-bond comes due.

Some investors wanted even more certainty about their bonds, so the market responded with PACS and TACS: Planned Amortization Classes and Targeted Amortization Classes, two fancier tranches. PACs provide principal payments according to a pre-specified schedule. They stick to this schedule as long as pre-payments stay in some broad range (for example, 50 to 350 percent PSA [see box]). Furthermore, the PAC is exempt from the serial paydown pattern of the tranches, so that other tranches may receive

READING 13 Derivative Mechanics: The CMO

> **Measuring Pre-Payment Speed**
> Market participants measure pre-payment speed as a percentage of PSA, the Public Securities Association pre-payment model. The model assumes that pre-payments start at zero at the beginning of the mortgage and rise linearly to 6 percent at 30 months (see figure 2), where they remain constant until the end at 360 months. 150 percent PSA means that pre-payments rise to 9 percent at 30 months (150 percent of 6 percent = 9 percent), remaining constant thereafter, and 50 percent PSA means that pre-payments rise to 3 percent at 30 months, remaining constant thereafter. Some investors have developed their own, more complicated models.

principal payments at the same time as the PAC. In effect, the PAC has priority over the other tranches through having first claim on the money available. For example, if PAC investors are scheduled to receive $1 million each month and the underlying mortgages produce $2 million, then $1 million can go to the "companion" tranche. If pre-payments fall so that the mortgages generate only $1.25 million, the companion tranche gets only $250,000. If pre-payments fall even more so that the mortgages generate only $800,000, even the PAC winds up short, although it receives the entire $800,000.

How, then does a PAC provide protection against both high and low pre-payment? The issuer calculates the available cash flows in the protected range (known as the collar) and

SOURCE: Author's calculations.

restricts PAC payments to that spread. Thus, to continue the above example, the 50 to 350 percent PSA range may have allowed for payments of between $800,000 and $4 million for the month in question, so the planned payment should fall within that range.[4]

It is important to note that although PACS are fairly safe bonds, the process of creating them necessarily shoves more risk into the other tranches. Companion bonds, which receive payments only after the PAC schedule is met, are particularly risky.

TACs offer a similar sort of protection, but only against pre-payments rising. The TAC has priority over other tranches and hence can keep to its schedule if pre-payments increase. If they drop off, however, the TAC has no protection. It is effectively a PAC with one side of the collar at the expected pre-payment rate, that is, 100 to 350 percent or 125 to 350 percent.

CMOs entail a second type of risk—default risk—because some people will not (or cannot) make their mortgage payments. To compensate, issuers over-collateralize CMOs. For instance, a CMO with a face value of $10 million may have mortgages backing it worth $11 million, for a 10 percent overcapitalization rate. This means that investors will get their money even if some homeowners default. What happens to this extra collateral if people do not default? Known as equity in the CMO, or the residual, it too can be bought and sold. Per usual in the mortgage-backed market, variations have developed, and it is now possible to invest in bullish, bearish, humped, stable, *De Minimus*, and smile residuals.

EXOTIC CMOs

Once market participants got the idea of splitting up the cash flows from a pool of mortgages, there was no stopping them. One innovation quickly spawned others, just as PACs and TACs spawned the companion classes that made them possible.

The market created IOs, or interest-only bonds, in which investors get interest payments as long as the underlying tranche gets principal payments. POs are the inverse, paying principal only.

Fancier still are the floaters, bonds whose coupon (interest payment) is linked to some interest-rate index, such as LIBOR or the 11th District Cost of Funds.[5] A standard floater may be quoted at something like LIBOR+1, meaning that the interest payment is 12 percent if LIBOR is 11 percent, and so forth. A superfloater responds to the index with a multiple greater than one. Thus, when the LIBOR rate moves from 10 percent to 11 to 12 percent, the interest rate on the bond moves from 10 percent to 12 percent to 14 percent. (Of course, the reverse is also true: A 2 percent drop in LIBOR sends the rate down 4 percent.) With an inverse floater, an increase in the index decreases the rate on the bond. And, yes, you can have a super inverse floater.

Z-bonds have also gotten more complicated. One innovation is the jump Z. That's were a Z tranche can jump to the head of the tranche line. For example, the Z tranche is last in line unless interest rates rise above 10 percent, at which point it moves up and becomes the tranche getting the principal payments. We have a sticky jump Z if the Z stays in that position. We have a non-sticky jump Z if the Z moves back to the end of the line when interest rates fall below 10 percent. And the market has adopted even more complicated Z-bonds, such as the toggle Z.

Exotic CMO constructs can make it easier for the unwary to get into trouble. As with any interest-rate-sensitive financial instrument, if an investor does not properly hedge, changes in interest rates will imply big changes in asset value. Exotics only make these changes happen faster. Thus, when interest rates fall, interest received by superfloaters falls even more, and their value (and corresponding resale price) drops. In the past, some investors consciously took an exposed position, knowing the consequences if their interest-rate predictions proved wrong. Others did not realize how fast or how far CMO prices could change. Still others failed to account for the complicated effects of pre-payment risk. Of course, guessing wrong and not understanding your investment are two classic ways to lose money.

CONCLUSION

This brief overview perhaps paints the CMO market as one vast poker game, so it is particularly important to point out the social benefits of CMOs. Mortgage-backed securities, by bringing investors into the mortgage market reduce housing costs for all mortgage holders. The major innovations in the market have allowed investors to reduce their risk, decreasing the chance of bankruptcy and further lowering costs to homeowners.

Initially, investors who wished to buy mortgage-backed securities faced a variety of problems. A pure pass-through security had a longer maturity than many investors liked. All mortgaged-backed securities entailed not only interest-rate risk and default risk, but pre-payment risk as well. A sequence of ingenious innovations helped investors both protect against and speculate in these risks.

Readers need not plan on adding sticky jump Zs to their portfolio, but looking under the hood of CMOs may help investors understand—and later avoid—financial crashes.

ENDNOTES

1. A provision of the Tax Reform Act of 1986 created REMICs. The provision changed the tax liability of particular types of CMOs issued by private firms, as apposed to those issued by public agencies such as the Government National Mortgage Association, or Ginnie Mae. For more details, see Robert Gerber, "Adjustable-Rate Mortgages: Products, Markets, and Valuation," in Frank J. Fabozzi, ed., *The Handbook of Mortgage-Backed Securities*, 3d ed., Chicago: Probus Publishing Co., 1992, pp. 155-96.
2. For interesting journalistic accounts of these episodes, along with some additional information on the mortgage-backed securities market, see Michael Carroll and Alyssa A. Lappen, "Mortgage-Backed Mayhem," *Institutional Investor*, vol. 28, no. 7 (July 1994), pp. 81-96. See also Lillian Chew, "Backing Down," *Risk*, vol. 8, no. 1 (January 1995), pp. 20-25.

PART III Financial Institutions

3. This article makes no attempt to offer investment advice. For more details on the CMO market and bonds, consult Frank J. Fabozzi, ed., *The Handbook of Mortgage-Backed Securities*, 3d ed., Chicago: Probus Publishing Co., 1992.
4. For other months, the payments will differ. For high pre-payment rates, a lot of money will be available early on, then less in later months when most people have already paid off their mortgages. The reverse is true for low pre-payment rates.
5. LIBOR is the London Interbank Offered Rate, or the rate that large international banks charge each other for short-term loans. The 11th District cost of Funds is an index produced by the 11th Federal Home Loan Bank District. Adjustable-rate mortgages are often tied to this index.

QUESTIONS

1. What is a pass-through? How does it differ from a CMO?

2. Describe the various types of risk associated with standard CMOs.

3. Do innovations in CMOs fit Mishkin's model of financial innovation?

4. Does Haubrich view CMOs and the risks they involve as dangerous or harmful for society? Why does he hold this view?

READING 14

Small Business Lending and Bank Consolidation: Is There Cause for Concern?

Philip E. Strahan and James Weston

In May 1995, Texas became the first state to opt out of the interstate branching provision of the Riegle-Neal Interstate Banking and Branching Act of 1994. In Texas, foes of interstate banking and branching voiced a concern over how consolidation might affect small business lending and community development. If small banks are increasingly acquired by large, superregional banking companies, they argued, consolidation will have a negative effect on the availability of credit to small businesses and communities. Proponents countered by arguing that despite consolidation, the need for independent community banks will remain, leaving an important niche for the small banker to fill.

Who's right? The answer's implications go well beyond the welfare of one state. We can probably anticipate further consolidation in the banking system nationwide as bank holding companies (BHCs) continue to purchase banks and as banks themselves continue to merge. In this edition of *Current Issues*, we use recent information to analyze the likely consequence of that consolidation for small business lending. The preponderance of our evidence suggests that consolidation will not adversely affect credit availability to small businesses and communities.

LENDING PATTERNS OF SMALL AND LARGE BANKS

Small banks are a primary source of credit for small businesses. Unlike large, publicly traded firms, which have access to capital markets, small businesses rely heavily on banks.[1] These businesses often concentrate their borrowing at institutions with which they have long-term relationships—relationships that prove mutually beneficial: They enable banks to collect information about the borrower's ability to repay, reducing the cost of providing credit. Borrowers, in turn, enjoy better access to credit and lower borrowing costs. Small banks make more of these "relationship" loans than do large banks, which are more likely to make generic loans based on financial ratios and credit checks.[2]

Large banks may have an advantage in lending to large businesses because they typically offer a wider array of the products

---

Reprinted from Federal Reserve Bank of New York *Current Issues in Economics and Finance*, March 1996.

and services demanded by their large clients. For instance, large banks can provide more transaction-based services than small banks can. Moreover, large banks are less likely to be constrained by regulatory lending limits.[3] Even absent explicit lending limits, small banks generally avoid very large loans in order to preserve adequate diversification.

With these considerations in mind, we ask whether consolidation in banking will reduce relationship lending and therefore small business lending. According to one view, relationship loans require tighter control and oversight over loan officers by senior management than do loans based on simple ratio analyses or credit scoring models. As a consequence, the complexity of large banks makes relationship loans infeasible (or at least more difficult). Since senior management of small banks can monitor lending decisions closely, they can authorize more non-standard, relationship loans. Therefore, critics of interstate banking and consolidation argue, as small banks disappear no one will be willing to engage in relationship loans upon which small businesses depend.

Others argue, however, that relationship lending will survive bank consolidation because it will continue to be profitable. As large banks acquire smaller banks, they will have a financial incentive to continue to make relationship loans to small businesses. Moreover, if small banks have a cost advantage in providing relationship loans to small businesses, consolidation will *not* lead to the disappearance of small banks; they will continue to play a vital role at the small end of the lending market.

A PROFILE OF SMALL BUSINESS LENDING

In June 1993, the federal banking agencies began collecting data on small business loans. This information appears annually in the June *Report of Condition and Income* (the Call Report) filed by all commercial banks. The data are collected for three size categories of loans: those whose "original amounts" are $100,000 or less, $100,001 to $250,000, and $250,001 to $1,000,000. For our analysis, we refer to all commercial and industrial (C&I) loans under $1 million as small business loans. The loan's original amount provides a measure of the total amount of credit extended to the borrower and therefore provides a good proxy for borrower size.[4]

The Call Report data for 1995 enable us to compare the recent small business lending activity of large and small banks.[5] Large banks make a substantial contribution—35 percent—to the market for loans to small businesses, although this share falls well below their 82 percent share of the large C&I loan market (Table 1, panel A).[6] In contrast, small banks focus primarily on small business lending. Banks with assets under $300 million hold less than 2 percent of the large C&I loan market but hold about 35 percent of the small business loan market.

Despite their size difference, small banks can accomplish the same volume of small business lending as large banks because they focus almost completely at this end of the market. The smallest banks held almost 97 percent of their total C&I loans in small business loans in 1995 (Table 1, panel B).

READING 14 Small Business Lending and Bank Consolidation

TABLE 1
PROFILE OF SMALL BUSINESS LENDING BY BANK SIZE

Panel A: Market Shares of C&I Loans[a]

Banks by Asset Size	Small C&I Loans	Large C&I Loans
Less Than $100 million	16.3	0.3
$100 million-$300 million	18.3	1.5
$300 million-$1 billion	13.4	3.7
$1 billion-$5 billion	16.5	12.7
Greater than $5 billion	35.4	81.9
Totals	100.0	100.0

Panel B: Portfolio Shares of Small C&I Loans[b]

Banks by Asset Size	Small C&I Loans/ Total C&I Loans	Small C&I Loans/ Total Assets
Less than $100 million	96.7	8.9
$100 million-$300 million	85.2	8.8
$300 million-$1 billion	63.2	6.9
$1 billion-$5 billion	37.8	4.9
Greater than $5 billion	16.9	2.9

Source: June 1995 *Report of Condition and Income*.
Notes: All Figures are in percent. Data for small C&I loans (those under $1 million) are based on the original amounts. For large C&I loans, the figures are computed by subtracting the original amount for small C&I loans from the book value of all C&I loans.
[a]Market shares equal the sum of all small (large) C&I loans held by banks in that size category divided by the sum of all small (large) C&I loans made by all banks.
[b]Portfolio shares equal the sum of all small C&I loans held by banks in that size category divided by all C&I loans (assets) held by banks in that size category. These figures are equivalent to weighted averages of the small C&I loans to total C&I loans (assets) ratio, weighted by total C&I loans (assets).

This portfolio share declines as bank size increases; the largest banks devote only about 17 percent of total C&I lending to small businesses. The share of total assets devoted to small business loans also falls as bank size increases.[7]

These portfolio shares seem to be the main force propelling the foes of interstate banking and bank consolidation. If the portfolio shares remain fixed as the size distribution evolves toward one dominated by large banks, the total availability of small business loans will indeed fall. To see why, imagine shifting $100 million in banking assets from the smallest to the largest end of the size distribution (which would occur if a $10 billion bank bought a $100 million bank). Taking $100 million in assets away from the smallest banks would lower small business lending by $8.9 million (8.9 percent times $100 million). Adding that $100 million to the largest end of the size distribution would raise small business lending by only $2.9 million. The net loss would be $6 million.[8]

Note, however, that this experiment does not take into account the dynamic responses of the marketplace to changes in loan availability. Two types of adjustments are likely. First, if small businesses are not being served because small banks have been acquired, large banks will have a strong profit motive to expand their small business lending. Second, if it turns out that small banks have a cost advantage in providing credit to small businesses (because of their ability to originate and monitor relationship loans), small banking will remain profitable. If this is the case, we should expect that a significant number of small banks will remain viable in the long run and that surviving small banks will increase their emphasis on small business lending. In fact, we see some evidence of this kind of dynamic market adjustment. Between 1993 and 1995, a period of rapid consolidation, the share of total assets invested in small business loans rose by about 5 percent for banks with assets under $100 million (from 8.5 percent to 8.9 percent of total assets).

BANK CONSOLIDATION AND SMALL BUSINESS LENDING

To determine whether consolidation will reduce the availability of small business lending, we consider whether the size and location of bank holding companies affect the propensity of their subsidiary banks to hold small business loans. We also consider whether bank mergers have reduced small business lending.

BHC Ownership and Small Business Lending

The acquisition of banks by large BHCs may reduce small business lending, at least when small banks are acquired by large BHCs. As Table 2 shows, banks with under $1 billion in assets hold fewer small business loans when owned by large BHCs. For instance, the typical independent bank with assets under $100 million holds 8.7 percent of assets in small business loans, compared with only 6.2 percent for the typical small bank owned by a large BHC. By contrast, banks with more than $1 billion in assets hold more small business loans when owned by large BHCs.[9]

Whether a bank is owned by an out-of-state or an in-state BHC does not substantially affect the extent of its small business lending. In four of the five bank asset size categories, banks owned by out-of-state BHCs held fewer

TABLE 2
SMALL BUSINESS LOANS AS A PERCENTAGE OF TOTAL ASSETS BY BHC AFFILIATION AND LOCATION

Banks by Asset Size	Independent Banks and Banks Owned by Small BHCs	Banks Owned by Large BHCs	Difference (T-statistic)	Banks Owned by In-State BHCs	Banks Owned by Out-of-State BHCs	Difference (T-statistic)
Less than $100 million	8.66	6.15	2.52 (9.79)[a]	6.38	5.83	0.55 (1.11)
$100 million-$300 million	9.27	7.38	1.89 (6.97)[a]	7.20	7.62	-0.42 (-0.91)
$300 million-$1 billion	7.94	6.25	1.69 (4.44)[a]	6.50	5.96	0.53 (1.02)
$1 billion-$5 billion	3.64	5.61	-1.96 (-2.88)[a]	5.97	5.15	0.82 (1.64)
Greater than $5 billion	2.89	3.51	-0.62 (-0.68)	3.78	3.12	0.67 (1.62)

Source: June 1995 *Report of Condition and Income.*
Notes: This table presents the simple (unweighted) average share of total assets invested in small business loans for banks in different size categories. All figures are in percent. Data for small business loans (those under $1 million) are based on the original amounts for C&I loans. T-statistics in columns 3 and 6 test the null hypothesis that the means in each of the preceding two columns are equal. Large BHCs are defined as bank holding companies with assets greater than $1 billion.
[a]Statistically significant at the 1 percent level.

small business loans. Nevertheless, the difference between the average ratio of small business loans to assets for the two groups of banks is not statistically significant in any of those cases. Overall, it appears that small banks may make fewer small business loans when owned by large banking companies, although the location of the owner relative to the bank seems to have little bearing on small business lending.[10]

Bank Mergers and Small Business Lending

To analyze the effects of consolidation through mergers, we construct a sample of 180 bank mergers that occurred between June 1993 and June 1994. Since only the newly merged bank is observable in 1994 or 1995, we construct a pro forma bank for each merger by summing the assets and liabilities of the acquiring and target banks in June 1993 (before the merger actually occurred). This pro forma bank provides the benchmark to which we compare the percentage of total assets devoted to small business lending before and after the merger.[11] A simple before-and-after comparison of small business lending, however, could be misleading because aggregate trends in demand for credit by small borrowers will affect changes in the ratio of small business loans to assets for all banks, apart from the effects of mergers. To isolate these effects, we compare changes in this ratio for the merger sample with a sample of nonmerged banks (the control group). For each merger, we randomly select one nonmerging bank with the same total assets as the pro forma bank in 1993.

Overall Changes After Mergers. The top panel of Table 3 compares the average change in the ratio of small business loans to assets at banks involved in a merger between June 1993 and June 1994 with the change for the control group. The changes for banks involved in mergers represent the average difference between the pro forma bank's ratio of small business loans to assets in June 1993 and the newly merged bank's actual ratio of small business loans to assets in June 1995.[12] The ratio of small business loans to assets for the pro forma bank in 1993 is a measure of the expected amount of small business lending for the newly merged bank *provided that no change occurs in the target bank's propensity to engage in small business lending*. If the new management of the target bank reduces its small business lending following the merger, the ratio of small business loans to assets will decline from 1993 to 1995; if management increases small business lending, we should see an increase in that ratio.

As shown, the average ratio of small business loans to assets rose from 8.3 percent in June 1993 for the pro forma banks to 8.5 percent in June 1995 for the newly merged banks. By contrast, the average ratio *fell* from 7.4 percent to 6.9 percent for banks not involved in mergers.[13]

The same test was performed using three different size classifications for the pro forma bank. Here we found a significant increase in small business lending for small mergers, and no significant difference between the newly merged banks and the control group for medium-size and large mergers.[14]

Changes By Merger Type. Although our evidence suggests that bank mergers do not

TABLE 3
BANK MERGERS AND SMALL BUSINESS LENDING

Panel A: Comparison of Small-Loans-to-Assets Ratio for Newly Merged Banks and Control Group by Size of Pro Forma Bank

Pro Forma Bank Asset Size	Number of Banks	1993 Small-Loans-to-Assets			1995 Small-Loans-to-Assets		1993-95 Change in Small-Loans-to-Assets		T-statistic
		Pro Forma Banks	Merged Banks	Control Banks	Merged Banks	Control Banks	Merged Banks	Control Banks	
Less than $300 million	102	9.12		8.15	10.12	8.20	1.00	0.05	1.90[a]
$300 million-$1 billion	39	9.10		8.03	7.64	6.66	-1.46	-1.38	-0.10
Greater than $1 billion	39	5.25		4.70	5.13	3.19	-0.11	-0.78	2.23
All Banks	180	8.28		7.38	8.50	6.94	0.22	-0.44	1.82[a]

Panel B: Changes in Small-Loans-to-Assets Ratio for Newly Merged Banks Relative to Control Group by Size of Target and Acquiring Banks

Target Bank	Acquiring Bank is Small	Acquiring Bank is Medium-Size	Acquiring Bank is Large
Small	2.17 (2.17)[a] [53]	0.06 (0.09) [52]	-0.13 (-0.33) [14]
Medium-Size	NA	-0.50 (-0.29) [15]	1.09 (0.85) [7]

Source: June 1993-95 *Reports of Condition and Income*.
Notes: All figures are in percent. Differences are percentage point differences (not percentage changes). In panel B, medium-size banks have total assets between $100 million and $1 billion, and large banks have assets above $1 billion. The average percentage point change in the ratio of small business loans to assets relative to the control group is presented first; the T-statistic testing that the average change equals zero appears in parentheses and the number of observations appears in brackets.
[a] Statistically significant at the 10 percent level.

reduce small business lending on average, certain types of mergers may work to reduce banks' propensity to serve the credit needs of small businesses. For instance, when two medium-size banks combine to form one large bank, the new bank may be so large and complex that relationship loans become more costly. The new, large bank may therefore provide less credit to small borrowers than the two medium-size banks did.

The bottom panel of Table 3 reports changes in the ratio of small business loans to assets (relative to the control group) for our sample of mergers broken down by the size of the target and acquiring banks.[15] For instance, the first column presents changes in the ratio of small business loans to assets from 1993 (pro forma) to 1995 when the acquiring bank is small. When two small banks merge, we find significant increases in small business lending; otherwise, we find no significant change.[16]

Overall, our research provides no support for the idea that consolidation from bank mergers reduces the portfolio share of a bank's small business loans. If anything, mergers seem to *increase* banks' propensity to hold these loans. Even when a marked change in the size of the target bank occurs post-merger (for example, when a large bank buys a small one or when two medium-size banks merge), we see no significant decline in the share of resources devoted to small business lending.

CONCLUSIONS

The availability of small business loans has recently received considerable attention in political and academic spheres. The new Call Report data show that small businesses receive credit from banks of all sizes. Both large and small banks are responsible for small business lending, although small banks' C&I lending is almost completely devoted to small businesses.

Looking ahead, we can probably anticipate further consolidation in the banking industry. Can we conclude that a decline in the presence of independently owned, small banks would have an adverse impact on the credit available to small businesses? The preponderance of our evidence suggests no. Although small banks hold more small business loans as a percentage of total assets than do large banks, the largest banks currently hold more than one-third of all small business loans. Evidently, some large banks find small business lending profitable. We also find that the share of small banks' assets invested in small business loans has risen over the past two years, at least partially offsetting the decline in the number of small banks.

We do find, however, that small banks owned by large banking companies hold fewer small business loans than do independent banks. This may mean that the costs of providing credit to small borrowers are lowest in small banking companies. If so, we would expect at least some small banking companies to survive the wave of consolidation and continue to serve the credit needs of small businesses. Finally, banks involved in mergers, on average, hold more small business loans two years after the merger.

READING 14 Small Business Lending and Bank Consolidation

Since small business loan data only became available in June 1993, this merger analysis is necessarily limited. As more data become available, the long-run effects of bank mergers on small business loans will likely become clearer.

ENDNOTES

1. According to the 1993 National Survey of Small Business Finances, commercial banks are the most important single source of credit to small firms (Cole and Wolken 1995).
2. Following Berger and Udell (1996), we use the term relationship loan to refer to loans that require borrowers to have established a relationship with the lender before receiving credit. By contrast, standard loans do not require such a relationship. Non-relationship borrowers can be approved if they pass a formal set of criteria based, for instance, on financial ratios, appraisals, and credit scores. See Peterson and Rajan (1994) for evidence on the importance of relationship lending. See Berger and Udell (1996) for evidence that small banks engage in more relationship lending than do large banks.
3. Nationally chartered banks are restricted from making loans greater than 15 percent of capital to a single borrower. State-chartered banks face similar lending limits, although these vary somewhat based on state regulations (Spong 1994).
4. We define small business loans by the loan's original amount, rather than by actual borrower size, since this is how the data are collected. The original amount is defined under the following guidelines: For loans drawn under commitment, the original amount is the size of the line of credit or loan commitment when the line of credit or loan commitment was most recently approved, extended, or renewed before the report date. If the amount outstanding as of the report date exceeds this size, however, the original amount is the amount currently outstanding on the report date. For loan participations and syndications, the original amount is the entire amount of credit originated by the lead lender. For all other loans, the original amount is the total amount of the loan at origination or the amount outstanding as of the report date, whichever is larger.
5. The figures reported for June 1995 in Table 1 are representative of those that prevailed in June 1993 and June 1994.
6. The original amounts for large C&I loans (that is, loans greater than $1 million) are not collected in the June *Report of Condition and Income*. The figures in Tables 1-3 using large C&I loans are computed by subtracting the original amount of small C&I loans from the book value of all C&I loans. Moreover, we do not have original amounts for banks that report that "all or substantially all" of their loans are below $100,000. For these banks, we use the book value of their C&I loans and assume that 100 percent of these loans are small.
7. Levonian and Soller (1996) also find that small banks concentrate on small business lending but large banks hold a significant share of the small business loan market.
8. Berger, Kashyap, and Scalise (1995) simulate the impact of future consolidation on small business lending holding bank portfolio shares constant. They find a large decline in small business lending, but this simulation experiment does not account for the dynamic market adjustments described in the text.
9. Keeton (1995) finds that multi-office banking companies hold fewer small business loans than single-office banking companies.
10. Whalen (1995) also finds no adverse effects of out-of-state ownership on small business lending by banks in Illinois, Kentucky, and Montana.
11. We construct a sample of 180 mergers completed between June 1993 and June 1994 from the Federal Reserve System's National Information Center transformation table (a summary of structural changes in the banking industry). We exclude mergers of banks held by the same BHC.
12. We consider the two-year change to allow enough time for significant changes to have been made in the new, merged bank's focus on small business lending. We can look only at two-year changes because we only have small business loan

PART III Financial Institutions

data available in 1993, 1994, and 1995. Note that the amount of time that has passed from the time of the merger to June 1995 can range from a maximum of two years (if the merger occurred on June 30, 1993) to a minimum of one year (if the merger occurred on June 30, 1994).

13. Peek and Rosengren (1996), however, find that small lending falls following mergers, based on a small sample of mergers that occurred in New England during 1993-94. They do not compare the change in small business lending with a control group, nor do they present statistical tests of their findings.

14. We also compared the average change in the ratio of small business loans to assets for the merger sample with a second control group of banks that began the period with similar assets and grew at roughly the same rate over the next two years. We compared the behavior of the merged banks with this second control group because the typical bank involved in a merger may also be a rapidly growing bank. If rapidly growing banks differ systematically from other banks, the comparison of the merged banks with the control group in Table 3 may be misleading. After controlling for asset growth following the merger, however, we found even stronger evidence that mergers increase small business lending.

15. Note that Table 3, panel B, includes only mergers in which the acquiring bank merged with a single target bank during the 1993-94 period.

16. The results in Table 3 were also computed using $300 million in assets as the cutoff for the definition of a small bank. These results are almost identical to those presented in Table 3.

REFERENCES

Berger, Allen N., and Gregory Udell. 1996. "Universal Banking and the Future of Small Business Lending." In Anthony Saunders and Ingo Walter, eds., *Universal Banking: Financial System Design Reconsidered*. Burr Ridge, Illinois: Irwin Publishing (forthcoming).

Berger, Allen N., Anil K. Kashyap, and Joseph M. Scalise. 1995. "The Transformation of the U.S. Banking Industry: What a Long Strange Trip It's Been." *Brookings Papers on Economic Activity* 2.

Cole, Rebel, and John D. Wolken. 1995. "Financial Services Used by Small Businesses: Evidence from the 1993 National Survey of Small Business Finances." *Federal Reserve Bulletin* 81: 629-67.

Keeton, William R. 1995. "Multi-Office Bank Lending to Small Businesses: Some New Evidence." *Federal Reserve Bank of Kansas City Economic Review* 80(2): 45-57.

Levonian, Mark, and Jennifer Soller. 1996. "Small Banks, Small Loans, Small Business." *FRBSF Weekly Letter* no. 96-02.

Peek, Joe, and Eric S. Rosengren. 1996. "Small Business Credit Availability: How Important Is the Size of the Lender?" In Anthony Saunders and Ingo Walter, eds., *Universal Banking: Financial System Design Reconsidered*. Burr Ridge, Illinois: Irwin Publishing (forthcoming).

Petersen, Mitchell A., and Raghuram G. Rajan. 1994. "The Benefits of Lending Relationships: Evidence from the Small Business Data." *Journal of Finance* 49: 3-37.

Spong, Kenneth. 1994. *Banking Regulation: Its Purposes, Implementation and Effects*. Federal Reserve Bank of Kansas City.

Whalen, Gary. 1995. "Out-of-State Holding Company Affiliation and Small Business Lending." Comptroller of the Currency Economic & Policy Analysis Working Paper no. 95-4.

READING 14 Small Business Lending and Bank Consolidation

QUESTIONS

1. What is the distinction between a "relationship" loan and a standard or non-relationship one? What size business firms depend most heavily on the former? Why?

2. What are the main opposing views regarding the effect banking consolidation will have on small business lending? What arguments support each view?

3. Large banks devote a smaller share of their assets to small business loans than smaller banks do. Does this imply that consolidation which shifts assets from small to large banks will cause the total amount of small business lending to decline? Why?

4. What tests do Strahan and Weston perform to determine how bank holding company affiliation and location and bank mergers affect small business lending? What do they conclude?

READING 15

The Rhyme and Reason of Bank Mergers

Elizabeth Laderman

Lately it seems that not a week goes by without a major bank merger announcement: Chemical will merge with Chase Manhattan, First Union with First Fidelity, Fleet Financial with Shawmut. Although the pace of bank mergers and acquisitions this year is running somewhat behind last year (156 versus 218 in the first half of each year), this year's crop has been much better publicized, because they often involve much bigger partners—according to SNL Securities, average target bank assets equaled $751.9 million in the first half of 1995, compared to $239.4 million in the first half of 1994.

Is this pace of consolidation a good thing? In the past, some analysts have been skeptical of the merger phenomenon, citing results showing that, in general, bank mergers do not increase efficiency. However, research in this area continues and banks' regulatory and technological circumstances are changing. In this *Weekly Letter*, I discuss what past and current research tells us about the likely reasons for and results of bank mergers in this changing environment.

THE EFFICIENCY OF BANK MERGERS

One reason banks may merge is to improve efficiency. Efficiency can be measured by the cost of producing a given amount of a given product. When efficiency improves, the cost per unit of output falls, thereby increasing the firm's profits. An increase in efficiency also benefits society, because it frees up resources for other uses.

Bank mergers *might* increase efficiency simply by making banks larger. Economists say that the production of a certain good or service is subject to "economies of scale" if unit costs decrease as the scale of production increases. This may happen if, for example, production over a range of output requires using a fixed amount of a certain input. In the case of banking, the delivery of certain services requires that the bank build a branch. That branch could provide facilities for serving anywhere from, say, one to one thousand customers. But, the cost of building and maintaining the branch would be the same, no matter how many customers were served. Clearly, then, branch costs per customer would decrease as the number of customers increased, at least up to some point.

Reprinted from Federal Reserve Bank of San Francisco *Weekly Letter* no. 95-39, November 17, 1995.

Of course, banks produce many products and services, some of which are very difficult to measure, and this substantially complicates any assessment of whether banking is subject to economies of scale. Nevertheless, some observers maintain that banks must grow larger to survive and that recent technological changes have only made this more true. For example, technological improvements have encouraged the growth of areas that favor larger banks, such as credit enhancement, mutual funds, and derivative products. In addition, the introduction of automated teller machines and other forms of electronic delivery means that one branch can serve many more customers than in the past, thereby increasing the range of production over which economies of scale apply to branch costs.

If larger banks are more efficient, last year's interstate branching legislation may have been the catalyst for some recent mergers. The Riegle-Neal Interstate Banking and Branching Efficiency Act of 1994 permits a bank in one state to acquire a bank in another state and then turn the acquired institution's offices into branches, beginning on June 1, 1997. Bank holding companies that already own separately capitalized banks in more than one state may consolidate them into one bank with branches in more than one state at that time. It may be the case that certain banking activities are subject to economies of scale, but only if the organization is consolidated under one bank. For many banking organizations, it may be too expensive to run operations in each state under a separately capitalized bank. If this is the case, bank holding companies may currently be acquiring banks in other states in anticipation of being able to consolidate them in 1997.

DECREASING RISK

Banks may merge to decrease risk rather than to increase expected profits. (Of course, the two motivations are not mutually exclusive.) For any firm, profits vary, and investors generally prefer less variability to more, for a given level of expected profits. Regulators, and therefore taxpayers, also prefer less variability, because it means less chance that the bank fails.

One way to decrease variability, or risk, may be to diversify earnings. In some cases, a bank can reduce risk by merging with a bank from another geographic area. This can happen, if, for example, the bank's new area tends to experience a relatively strong economy whenever the home area experiences a relatively weak economy, and vice versa. The combined earnings stream from these two areas would then be smoother than the earnings stream from either one alone. (See Levonian (1994), who found that, on average, if all Twelfth District banks became fully diversified across the nine District states, the variability of the return on assets would decline.) In addition to geographic diversification, product diversification also may provide opportunities to reduce risk. For example, the combination of certain fee-based activities with interest-sensitive activities may help to smooth earnings.

The 1994 interstate banking and branching legislation may have spurred some banks to merge to gain risk reduction benefits. Again, bank holding companies that previously may not have acquired out-of-state banks despite possible risk-reducing benefits may now find that such benefits do justify interstate acquisitions that soon can be consolidated. In addition, relaxation of certain product restrictions, such as those involving mutual funds and securities underwriting, may have introduced new risk reduction opportunities. Some banks may have found that taking full advantage of such opportunities required mergers rather than just expansion of their own activities into new areas.

RESEARCH FINDINGS

Economists have conducted numerous studies aimed at determining whether bank mergers increase efficiency. Generally, these studies compare the expense ratios of merged banks to those of the pre-merger component banks, using non-merging banks as a control group. Both bank mergers and bank holding company acquisitions of banks have been studied, using, for example, total expenses to assets and noninterest expenses to assets for the cost ratios.

To date, most of the studies find that bank mergers do not, on average, decrease cost ratios. Moreover, such results hold even when banks with overlapping branch networks merge and close branches. In addition, even more sophisticated studies that take into account the cost effects of changes in the output mix generally come to the same conclusion. These findings also are consistent with the results of much of the research on economies of scale in banking, which tend to show that the minimum average cost point of production is below the size of many post-merger consolidated banks.

We have only indirect evidence on whether, in general, bank mergers reduce risk. Boyd and Graham (1991) found that, between 1971 and 1988, banks with $1 billion or more in assets failed at roughly twice the rate of banks with less than $1 billion in assets. It is possible, then, that even though larger banks may have available greater risk reducing opportunities through diversification, they may not, in practice, take advantage of these opportunities. An alternative interpretation is that large banks' high failure rate was due to their lower capital ratios and says little regarding these banks' operating risk.

ALTERNATIVE HYPOTHESES

The efficiency and risk-reduction hypotheses will continue to be tested as new data reflecting banks' current technological and regulatory circumstances become available. Meanwhile, economists have considered alternative hypotheses regarding the motivations for bank mergers and the likely benefits or costs to society.

Some economists have suggested that banks may merge to take better advantage of an implicit "too-big-to-fail" regulatory policy. In 1984, the Comptroller of the Currency suggested that the very largest banks were too big for the government to allow to fail. To the degree that banks believe that they have a greater chance of the government rescuing them from bankruptcy if they are larger, the too-big-to-fail policy may be encouraging more bank mergers than is socially optimal. However, some recent research by Benston, Hunter, and Wall (1995) suggests that this is not the case. The same motivation that might prompt banks to try to increase in size in order to take advantage of an implicit government guarantee also would likely encourage them to increase risk to get the most out of any such guarantee. These authors find that, contrary to this hypothesis, acquiring banks do not pay more for riskier banks than less risky banks.

Another hypothesis is that banks merge to gain market share and thereby market power. The "structure-conduct-performance" paradigm hypothesizes that markets in which the share of output is concentrated in a few large firms are less competitive than markets in which there are numerous smaller firms with roughly equal market shares. The decrease in competition means that firms can make higher profits by holding prices above socially optimal levels. In one of the few studies of the market power hypothesis, Berger (1991) suggests that many within-market mergers may result in minor increases in market power for the consolidated firms.

REVENUE EFFECTS

While many within-market mergers may increase market power for the merged banks, the average size of this effect likely is small. Moreover, such an effect would not motivate the many inter-market mergers that we see. About half of the 75 largest bank and thrift acquisitions announced in the first half of 1995 were inter-state transactions, and this likely understates the proportion of inter-market mergers.

A more likely source of overall merger benefits may stem from changes in the bundle of products and services that banks produce. Although sophisticated cost studies take into account the effect on costs of changes in the product mix, they do not generally take into account the effect on revenues. If a bank can increase revenues by changing the collection of goods and services it produces, without generating an offsetting increase in costs, its profits will increase. So, too, will the net benefits to society, as more highly valued goods and services replace less valued goods and services.

In a recent overview of the literature, Berger, Hunter, and Timme (1993) pointed out that a few studies do find efficiency gains from bank mergers, and that all of these studies include revenue effects. In contrast, they said, studies that do not find efficiencies generally use only cost data. These authors suggest that a bank merger may help the consolidated bank better achieve a higher-revenue output bundle through, say, improved marketing or product innovation. Indeed, Benston, et al., find that acquiring banks pay relatively more for smaller banks than larger banks. One interpretation these authors give is that a smaller bank offers greater opportunities for the acquirer to offer new products that the smaller bank is not already producing.

As many observers have emphasized, banking is changing rapidly, with new electronic banking and off-balance sheet financial management products partially replacing traditional deposit-taking and lending activities. Although it is unclear why mergers would be necessary to carry out such changes, they may help facilitate them. For example, mergers may replace relatively ineffective managers with managers that are better able to carry out a shift in product mix.

CONCLUSION

The rapid pace of bank mergers continues to draw the attention of the public and the economics profession. While there still is much to learn about why banks merge and what it means, economic research has revealed several general conclusions. First, up until the recent past, at least, bank mergers have not, on average, increased efficiency by decreasing unit costs. Second, while risk reducing, risk increasing, and market power motivations have not been extensively investigated, available research indicates that these likely do not play major roles in the merger phenomenon. And, third, whether banks merge in order to facilitate shifts in product mix remains an intriguing and very open question.

REFERENCES

Benston, George J., William C. Hunter, and Larry D. Wall. 1995. "Motivations for Bank Mergers and Acquisitions: Enhancing the Deposit Insurance Put Option versus Earnings Diversification." *Journal of Money, Credit, and Banking* 27, pp. 777-788.

Berger, Allen N. 1991. "The Profit-Concentration Relationship in Banking." *Finance and Economics Discussion Series* 176, Board of Governors of the Federal Reserve System.

Berger, Allen N., William C. Hunter, and Stephen G. Timme. 1993. "The Efficiency of Financial Institutions: A Review and Preview of Research Past, Present, and Future." *Journal of Banking and Finance* 17, pp. 221-249.

Boyd, John H., and Stanley L. Graham. 1991. "Investigating the Banking Consolidation Trend." *FRB Minneapolis Quarterly Review* (Spring), pp. 3-15.

Levonian, Mark E. 1994. "Interstate Banking and Risk." *FRBSF Weekly Letter* 94-26.

READING 15 The Rhyme and Reason of Bank Mergers

QUESTIONS

1. How might a merger of two banks increase efficiency and reduce risk? Have researchers found that bank mergers actually have these effects?

2. How might the "too-big-to-fail" policy, desire to increase market share, and desire to produce a higher-revenue output bundle motivate banks to merge? Which of these incentives would provide the clearest benefit to society? Explain.

READING 16

Russian Banking

Dwight Jaffee and Mark Levonian

On the last day of 1991 the Soviet Union vanished, and the various countries of the former USSR accelerated their ongoing political and economic transformation. One result is that the title of this *Weekly Letter* is no longer an oxymoron. Indeed, the Russian banking system stands out among sectors of the Russian economy for its high degree of privatization, its market orientation, and its rapid adoption of Western technology and management methods.

But partly because of its rapid development, the Russian banking sector is fragile. This point was emphasized during August 1995 when the Russian interbank credit and payments system froze, precipitating calls for central bank intervention and government action. This *Letter* describes the emergence of a private banking system in Russia, provides insight into banking's current state, and discusses the critical issues Russian banking still faces.

A BRIEF HISTORY

During the Soviet era the Russian banking system, such as it was, consisted of branches of the central bank (the Gosbank), and functioned primarily as an accounting network for the annual central plan. Credits were transferred on the books of the Gosbank to account for flows of physical production and inputs between state-owned enterprises. Firms paid wages in cash provided by the Gosbank; workers paid cash for purchases and deposited the excess "under the mattress" or in the Gosbank's savings bank section, called Sberbank. In 1987, under *perestroika*, the Gosbank was split into several specialized banks for different sectors of the economy, with each bank still centrally controlled. Beginning in 1988, a few commercial banks began operating, although their legal foundation remained vague.

Formal banking legislation was passed in late 1990, and a licensing and regulatory process was put in place. After the breakup of the Soviet Union, the former specialized banks were partially or totally privatized through the issuance of shares to the public, although in some cases (notably Sberbank) the government retained some degree of control. What remained of the old Gosbank within Russia became the new Central Bank of the Russian Federation (or CBR).

Reprinted from Federal Reserve Bank of San Francisco *Weekly Letter*, no. 95-35, October 20, 1995.

INDUSTRY STRUCTURE

Establishment of new banks has been rapid; there are now more than 2500 commercial banks in Russia. Sberbank is in a category by itself; its branch network is immense (roughly 30,000 offices, compared to about 5500 for the rest of the banking system), and it is by far the largest holder of personal deposits. The rest of the Russian commercial banking industry divides into three segments. One segment arose early in the transition process: Large industrial enterprises, needing a mechanism to make and receive payments and needing access to credit, established their own banks. Since these banks are owned and controlled by their one major customer, they are like treasury departments of the associated industrial firms. A second segment of the industry sprang up when the specialized arms of the former Gosbank were privatized. Many regional branches of the specialized banks have themselves become independent commercial banks, about 750 in all. The third segment of the industry consists of a large number of completely new commercial banks, some quite small, including many of the most progressive. It is hard to get precise figures on the various types of banks, but this third segment probably accounts for about two-thirds of the total number.

A small number of U.S. and other foreign banks now operate in Russia, although primarily to service their existing international clients. In the other direction, Russian banks are just starting to apply for entry into U.S. banking markets.

SUPERVISION AND REGULATION

A new central banking law, signed by President Yeltsin in April 1995, specifies the duties of the CBR as Russia's bank supervisor. The CBR licenses new banks, supervises existing banks, and can impose penalties or revoke banking licenses when appropriate.

The CBR has been criticized as lax in its efforts to close troubled banks; many poorly capitalized and even insolvent banks remain open. Following some clarification of the CBR's powers, the pace of closures has increased: 65 banks were closed in 1994, and an additional 71 during the first six months of 1995. However, some observers believe that many more Russian banks are insolvent. Part of the problem is simply knowing which banks are the bad ones. The CBR has been hiring and training examiners, or inspectors as they are called in Russia, but real competency will come only with time.

Russian banks must meet various regulatory standards: liquid liabilities cannot exceed liquid assets, large credit exposures cannot exceed 25 percent of a bank's capital, and loans to shareholders of the bank cannot exceed 20 percent of capital. Currently, banks must have capital of at least 1 million ECU (roughly $800,000 at current exchange rates); recent increases in this minimum should help weed out some of the worst banks, and the requirement is due to rise further, to 5 million ECU by 1999. In addition, the CBR measures capital adequacy using standards similar to those developed by the Bank for International Settlements; a bank's equity must equal at least 4 percent of its risk-weighted assets, rising to 8 percent by 1999.

Russia has no formal deposit insurance system. The Russian Federation explicitly guarantees deposits in the Sberbank. Deposits in other commercial banks have been uninsured since the discontinuation of a guarantee fund maintained by the CBR, although several versions of a deposit insurance act have drifted through parts of the Russian legislative system.

THE BUSINESS OF BANKING IN RUSSIA

The activities of an institution called a "bank" in Russia differ from those of a typical U.S. bank. Intermediation, or the transformation of deposits into loans, is much less important. A sizable part of the lending Russian banks do is to each other: over 25 percent of aggregate bank assets are plowed into the interbank market. Loans to non-bank customers have increased recently, to about 45 percent of total bank assets, but are still far less than the 60 percent figure typical for the U.S. These loans predominantly finance inventories and receivables, and are very short term; loans for capital investment or housing are virtually nonexistent. Deposits amount to only 35 percent of assets on average, compared to 60 percent in the U.S., and (outside of Sberbank) most are business deposits; in fact, the new Central Bank Law requires that total personal deposits not exceed a bank's own capital.

Banks are heavily involved in foreign currency dealings, both as brokers to earn fees, and as traders to attempt to earn speculative profits from exchange rate movements. They also provide payments services for business enterprises, although there are not checking accounts in Russia. Russian enterprises use third party transfers, carried out by commercial banks, to make inter-firm payments. It takes an inordinate amount of time to clear these transfers, although new private and central bank electronic clearing systems now are being introduced.

Beyond these activities, banks are active investors in real estate and nonbank securities, including common shares. Thus, Russian banks are "universal banks," with powers more like those of European banks than those of U.S. banks. Until recently a certain amount of centrally directed credit also flowed through the banking system, primarily to former state-owned enterprises, and banks earned a fixed spread for acting as the conduit. However, such credit programs appear to have ceased.

CRISIS AND AFTERMATH

The August 1995 paralysis of the banking system was caused largely by the practices of Russian bankers, likely aggravated by a change in monetary policy in early 1995. Previously, monetary policy had a "stop-go" character, with slow monetary growth and low inflation during the first half of each year, followed by rapid monetary growth and high inflation in the second half. Annual inflation rates in excess of 1000 percent had two effects on banking. One was that credit analysis was not emphasized: the real value of loans became so small so fast that principal repayments was irrelevant, as along as borrowers continued to pay interest. The second effect of rapid inflation was that banks with foreign exchange licenses profited by positioning against the ruble, betting correctly that the currency would depreciate against foreign currencies.

But significant monetary tightening was introduced in early 1995. Banks' reserve requirements went up and money growth slowed; annualized inflation fell from 700 percent in January to 70 percent in August, and the ruble began to appreciate on exchange markets. As welcome as these developments were to the Russian economy, many banks suffered. Previously profitable foreign currency positions became losers, higher required reserves meant forgone interest, and default by marginal borrowers became likely as loan principal no longer was trivialized by inflation. With no sign of the usual monetary policy reversal, suspicions grew that the condition of some banks was tenuous. A lack of truthful, publicly available financial information made it impossible to tell strong banks from weak. The banks themselves became nervous about their large exposures in the interbank market; the crisis erupted as banks, with no good way to judge counterparty risk, reacted to mild signs of illiquidity by simply refusing to transact.

The banking crisis may stimulate two changes for the better. First, banks may be pushed to abandon speculation and take up the hard work of analyzing credit risk and making loans. Currently, the banking sector is stunted: the ratio of banking industry assets to GDP is only 0.17 in Russia, compared to 1.3 in the EC (or 0.75 in the United States). With powers like those of banks in the EC, Russian banks may eventually play a similar role in the economy, and assets may reach a similar relationship to GDP. Russia desperately needs the investment finance that a deeper, more mature banking sector could supply.

A second positive result of the crisis may be consolidation. Russia has too little banking, but also too many banks: the 2500 banks currently average only about $20 million in assets, compared to $300 million in the U.S. or $3 billion in the EC. Similar banking crises in other transitional economies have been followed by consolidation, which may increase the efficiency of the banking system. If a "fully banked" Russia had the same 1.3 ratio of banking sector assets to GDP found in the EC, it could support 150 EC-sized or 1500 U.S.-sized banks.

DEEPER PROBLEMS

But while the immediate crisis may be the catalyst for such changes, it will not solve deeper problems that are retarding the development of a healthy banking system. Russia lacks the "financial infrastructure" that would let its banks provide credit effectively. One problem is information: unreliable or false financial information raises the risks facing lenders and obstructs the flow of capital through the banking system. A second, perhaps more significant problem is contract enforcement. Property rights are ill-defined, the legal status of collateral is unclear, and Russia still does not have laws governing such things as the order of claims in bankruptcies. Traditional banking is difficult under these handicaps.

Of course, if disclosure problems and a hazy legal structure make banking difficult, they make corporate governance through market mechanisms nearly impossible. With some basic improvements in the financial infrastructure, large universal banks might be the ideal way to resolve the conflicts that arise between debtholders and shareholders, or between insiders and outsiders, in the wildly imperfect Russian capital markets. An offsetting concern is that it might be hard to make large universal banks smaller and narrower at some later stage of Russia's financial development.

CONCLUSION

An efficient, well-functioning banking system is crucial for a peaceful transition to a new order in Russia. Four years ago, Russia had no bankers, at least in the Western sense of the word. Today, Russians are eagerly adopting many Western practices, but cultural change is slow.

One danger is that attempts to "solve" the August crisis in the banking system might reverse the macroeconomic gains Russia has made recently. Over the near term, consolidation in the banking system may lead to fewer and larger Russian banks, but more fundamental improvements to laws governing contract enforcement and information disclosure will be far more important. Without changes in the financial infrastructure, banks will continue to be restricted in their ability to help the Russian economy grow.

READING 16 Russian Banking

QUESTIONS

1. What agency supervises Russian banks and what regulations must they follow?

2. How do the activities of Russian banks compare with those of U.S. banks?

3. What causes contributed to Russia's August 1995 banking crisis? How might that crisis work in the long run to strengthen Russia's banking system?

4. How do information and contract enforcement problems affect the ability of Russia's banking system to finance economic growth? Why do these problems have this effect?

READING 17

The Decline of Traditional Banking: Implications for Financial Stability and Regulatory Policy

Franklin R. Edwards and Frederic S. Mishkin[1]

The traditional banking business has been to make long-term loans and fund them by issuing short-dated deposits, a process that is commonly described as "borrowing short and lending long." In recent years, fundamental economic forces have undercut the traditional role of banks in financial intermediation. As a source of funds for financial intermediaries, deposits have steadily diminished in importance. In addition, the profitability of traditional banking activities such as business lending has diminished in recent years. As a result, banks have increasingly turned to new, nontraditional financial activities as a way of maintaining their position as financial intermediaries.[2]

This article has two objectives: to examine the forces responsible for the declining role of traditional banking in the United States as well as in other countries, and to explore the implications of this decline and banks' responses to it for financial stability and regulatory policy. A key policy issue is whether the decline of banking threatens to make the financial system more fragile. If nothing else, the prospect of a mass exodus from the banking industry (possibly via increased failures) could cause instability in the financial system. Of greater concern is that declining profitability could tip the incentives of bank managers toward assuming greater risk in an effort to maintain former profit levels. For example, banks might make loans to less creditworthy borrowers or engage in nontraditional financial activities that promise higher returns but carry greater risk. A new activity that has generated particular concern recently is the expanding role of banks as dealers in derivatives products. There is a fear that in seeking new sources of revenue in derivatives, banks may be taking risks that could ultimately undermine their solvency and possibly the stability of the banking system.

The challenge posed by the decline of traditional banking is twofold: we need to maintain the soundness of the banking system while restructuring the banking industry to achieve long-term financial stability. A sound regulatory policy can encourage an orderly shrinkage of traditional banking while strengthening the competitive position of banks, possibly by allowing them to expand into more profitable, nontraditional activities.

Reprinted from Federal Reserve Bank of New York *Economic Policy Review*, July 1995, 27-45.

READING 17 The Decline of Traditional Banking

In the transitional period, of course, regulators would have to continue to guard against excessive risk taking that could threaten financial stability.

The first part of our article documents the declining financial intermediation role of traditional banks in the United States. We discuss the economic forces driving this decline, in both the United States and foreign countries, and describe how banks have responded to these pressures. Included in this discussion is an examination of banks' activities in derivatives markets, a particularly fast-growing area of their off-balance-sheet activities. Finally, we examine the implications of the changing nature of banking for financial fragility and regulatory policy.

THE DECLINE OF TRADITIONAL BANKING IN THE UNITED STATES

In the United States, the importance of commercial banks as a source of funds to nonfinancial borrowers has shrunk dramatically. In 1974 banks provided 35 percent of these funds; today they provide around 22 percent (Chart 1). Thrift institutions (savings and loans, mutual savings banks, and credit unions), which can be viewed as specialized banking institutions, have also suffered a decline in market share, from more than 20 percent in the late 1970s to below 10 percent in the 1990s (Chart 2).

Another way of viewing the declining role of banking in traditional financial intermediation is to look at the size of banks'

Chart 1

COMMERCIAL BANKS' SHARE OF TOTAL NONFINANCIAL BORROWING
1960-94

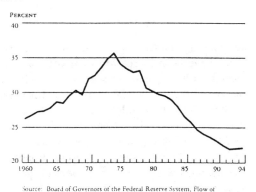

Source: Board of Governors of the Federal Reserve System, Flow of Funds Accounts.

Chart 2

THRIFTS' SHARE OF TOTAL NONFINANCIAL BORROWING
1960-94

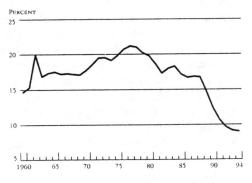

Source: Board of Governors of the Federal Reserve System, Flow of Funds Accounts.

PART III Financial Institutions

Table 1
RELATIVE SHARES OF TOTAL FINANCIAL INTERMEDIARY ASSETS, 1960-94
Percent

	1960	1970	1980	1990	1994
Insurance companies					
Life insurance	19.6	15.3	11.5	12.5	13.0
Property and casualty	4.4	3.8	4.5	4.9	4.6
Pension funds					
Private	6.4	8.4	12.5	14.9	16.2
Public (state and local government)	3.3	4.6	4.9	6.7	8.4
Finance companies	4.7	4.9	5.1	5.6	5.3
Mutual funds					
Stock and bond	2.9	3.6	1.7	5.9	10.8
Money market	0.0	0.0	1.9	4.6	4.2
Depository institutions (banks)					
Commercial banks	38.6	38.5	37.2	30.4	28.6
Savings and loans and mutual savings	19.0	19.4	19.6	12.5	7.0
Credit unions	1.1	1.4	1.6	2.0	2.0
Total	100.0	100.0	100.0	100.0	100.0

Source: Board of Governors of the Federal Reserve System, Flow of Funds Accounts.

balance-sheet assets relative to those of other financial intermediaries (Table 1). Commercial banks' share of total financial intermediary assets fell from around the 40 percent range in the 1960-80 period to below 30 percent by the end of 1994. Similarly, the share of total financial intermediary assets held by thrift institutions declined from around 20 percent in the 1960-80 period to below 10 percent by 1994.[3]

Boyd and Gertler (1994) and Kaufman and Mote (1994) correctly point out that the decline in the share of total financial intermediary assets held by banking institutions does not necessarily indicate that the banking industry is in decline. Because banks have been increasing their off-balance-sheet activities (an issue we discuss below), we may understate their role in financial markets if we look solely at the on-balance-sheet activities. However, the decline in *traditional* banking, which is reflected in the decline in banks' share of total financial intermediary assets, raises important policy issues that are the focus of this article.

There is also evidence of an erosion in traditional banking profitability. Nevertheless, standard measures of commercial bank profitability such as pretax rates of return on assets and equity (shown in Chart 3) do not

READING 17 The Decline of Traditional Banking

Chart 3

RETURN ON ASSETS AND EQUITY FOR COMMERCIAL BANKS
1960-94

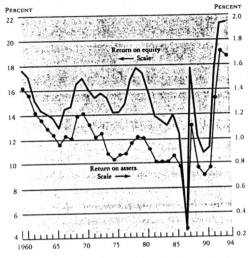

Sources: Federal Deposit Insurance Corporation, *Statistics on Banking* and *Quarterly Banking Profile*.

Chart 4

SHARE OF NONINTEREST INCOME IN TOTAL INCOME FOR COMMERCIAL BANKS
1960-94

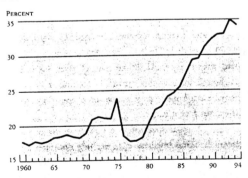

Sources: Federal Deposit Insurance Corporation, *Statistics on Banking* and *Quarterly Banking Profile*.

provide a clear picture of the trend in bank profitability. Although banks' before-tax rate of return on equity declined from an average of 15 percent in the 1970-84 period to below 12 percent in the 1985-91 period, bank profits improved sharply beginning in 1992, and 1994 was a record year for bank profits.

Overall bank profitability, however, is not a good indicator of the profitability of traditional banking because it includes the increasingly important nontraditional businesses of banks. As a share of total bank income, noninterest income derived from off-balance-sheet activities, such as fee and trading income, averaged 19 percent in the 1960-80 period (Chart 4). By 1994, this source of income had grown to about 35 percent of total bank income. Although some of this growth in fee and trading income may be attributable to an expansion of traditional fee activities, much of it is not.

A crude measure of the profitability of the traditional banking business is to exclude noninterest income from total earnings, since much of this income comes from nontraditional activities. By this measure, the pretax return on equity fell from *more than* 10 percent in 1960 to levels that approached *negative* 10 percent in the late 1980s and early 1990s (Chart 5). This measure, however, does not adjust for the expenses associated with generating noninterest income and therefore overstates the decline in the profitability of traditional banking. Another indicator of the decline in the profitability of traditional banking is the fall in the ratio of market value to book value of bank capital from the mid-1960s to the early 1980s. As noted by Keeley (1990), this fall indicates that

PART III   Financial Institutions

Chart 5

RETURN ON ASSETS AND EQUITY FOR COMMERCIAL BANKS EXCLUDING NONINTEREST INCOME
1960-94

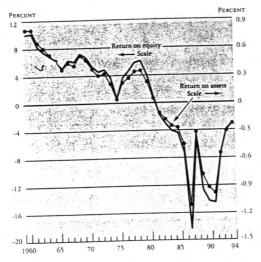

Sources: Federal Deposit Insurance Corporation, *Statistics on Banking* and *Quarterly Banking Profile*.

Chart 6

EQUITY-TO-ASSET RATIOS, MARKET VALUE VS. BOOK VALUE
1960-93

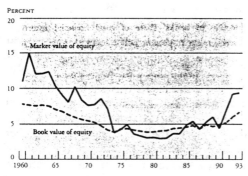

Source: Standard and Poor's Compustat.

Note: Chart presents equity-to-asset ratios for the top twenty-five bank holding companies in each year.

bank charters were becoming less valuable in this period (Chart 6). The decline in the value of bank charters in the years preceding the sharp increase in nontraditional activities supports the view that there was a substantial decline in the profitability of traditional banking. Only with the rise in nontraditional activities that begins in the early 1980s (Chart 4) does the market value of banks begin to rise.

WHY IS TRADITIONAL BANKING IN DECLINE?

Fundamental economic forces have led to financial innovations that have increased competition in financial markets. Greater competition in turn has diminished the cost advantage banks have had in acquiring funds and has undercut their position in loan markets. As a result, traditional banking has lost profitability, and banks have begun to diversify into new activities that bring higher returns.

Diminished Advantage in Acquiring Funds (Liabilities)

Until 1980, deposits were a cheap source of funds for U.S. banking institutions (commercial banks, savings and loans, mutual savings banks, and credit unions). Deposit rate ceilings prevented banks from paying interest on checkable deposits, and Regulation Q limited them to paying specified interest rate ceilings on savings and time deposits.

For many years, these restrictions worked to the advantage of banks because a major source of bank funds was checkable deposits (in 1960 and earlier years, these deposits constituted more than 60 percent of total bank deposits). The zero interest cost on these deposits resulted in banks having a low average cost of funds.

This cost advantage did not last. The rise in inflation beginning in the late 1960s led to higher interest rates and made investors more sensitive to yield differentials on different assets. The result was the so-called disintermediation process, in which depositors took their money out of banks paying low interest rates on both checkable and time deposits and purchased higher yielding assets. In addition, restrictive bank regulations created an opportunity for nonbank financial institutions to invent new ways to offer bank depositors higher rates. Nonbank competitors were not subject to deposit rate ceilings and did not have the costs associated with having to hold non-interest-bearing reserves and paying deposit insurance premiums. A key development was the creation of money market mutual funds, which put banks at a competitive disadvantage because money market mutual fund shareholders (or depositors) could obtain check-writing services while earning a higher interest rate on their funds. Not surprisingly, as a source of funds for banks, low-cost checkable deposits declined dramatically, falling from 60 percent of bank liabilities in 1960 to under 20 percent today.

The growing disadvantage of banks in raising funds led to their supporting legislation in the 1980s to eliminate Regulation Q ceilings on time deposits and to allow checkable deposits that paid interest (NOW accounts). Although the ensuing changes helped to make banks more competitive in the quest for funds, the banks' cost of funds rose substantially, reducing the cost advantage they enjoyed.

Diminished Income (Or Loan) Advantages

Banks have also experienced a deterioration in the income advantages they once enjoyed on the asset side of their balance sheets. The growth of the commercial paper and junk bond markets and the increased securitization of assets have undercut banks' traditional advantage in providing credit.

Improvements in information technology, which have made it easier for households, corporations, and financial institutions to evaluate the quality of securities, have made it easier for business firms to borrow directly from the public by issuing securities. In particular, instead of going to banks to finance short-term credit needs, many business customers now borrow through the commercial paper market. Total nonfinancial commercial paper outstanding as a percentage of commercial and industrial bank loans has risen from 5 percent in 1970 to more than 20 percent today.

The rise of money market mutual funds has also indirectly undercut banks by supporting the expansion of competing finance companies. The growth of assets in money market mutual funds to more than $500 billion created a ready market for commercial paper because money market mutual funds must hold liquid, high-quality, short-term assets.

Further, the growth in the commercial paper market has enabled finance companies, which depend on issuing commercial paper for much of their funding, to expand their lending at the expense of banks. Finance companies provide credit to many of the same businesses that banks have traditionally served. In 1980, finance company loans to businesses amounted to about 30 percent of banks' commercial and industrial loans; today these loans constitute more than 60 percent of banks' commercial and industrial loans.

The junk bond market has also taken business away from banks. In the past, only Fortune 500 companies were able to raise funds by selling their bonds directly to the public, bypassing banks. Now, even lower quality corporate borrowers can readily raise funds through access to the junk bond market. Despite predictions of the demise of the junk bond market after the Michael Milken embarrassment, it is clear that the junk bond market is here to stay. Although sales of new junk bonds slid to $2.9 billion by 1990, they rebounded to $16.9 billion in 1991, $42 billion in 1992, and $60 billion in 1993.

The ability to securitize assets has made nonbank financial institutions even more formidable competitors for banks. Advances in information and data processing technology have enabled nonbank competitors to originate loans, transform these into marketable securities, and sell them to obtain more funding with which to make more loans. Computer technology has eroded the competitive advantage of banks by lowering transactions costs and enabling nonbank financial institutions to evaluate credit risk efficiently through the use of statistical methods. When credit risk can be evaluated using statistical techniques, as in the case of consumer and mortgage lending, banks no longer have an advantage in making loans.[4] An effort is being made in the United States to develop a market for securitized small business loans as well.

U.S. banks have also been beset by increased foreign competition, particularly from Japanese and European banks. The success of the Japanese economy and Japan's high savings rate gave Japanese banks access to cheaper funds than were available to American banks. This cost advantage permitted Japanese banks to seek out loan business in the United States more aggressively, eroding U.S. banks' market share. In addition, banks from all major countries followed their corporate customers to the United States and often enjoyed a competitive advantage because of less burdensome regulation in their own countries. Before 1980, two U.S. banks, Citicorp and BankAmerica Corporation, were the largest banks in the world. In the 1990s, neither of these banks ranks among the top twenty. Although some of this loss in market share may be due to the depreciation of the dollar, most of it is not.

Similar forces are working to undermine the traditional role of banks in other countries. The U.S. banks are not alone in losing their monopoly power over depositors. Financial innovation and deregulation are occurring worldwide and have created attractive alternatives for both depositors and borrowers. In Japan, for example, deregulation has opened a wide array of new financial instruments to the public, causing a

READING 17 The Decline of Traditional Banking

disintermediation process similar to the one that has taken place in the United States. In European countries, innovations have steadily eroded the barriers that have traditionally protected banks from competition.

In other countries, banks have also faced increased competition from the expansion of securities markets. Both financial deregulation and fundamental economic forces abroad have improved the availability of information in securities markets, making it easier and less costly for business firms to finance their activities by issuing securities rather than going to banks. Further, even in countries where securities markets have not grown, banks have still lost loan business because their best corporate customers have had increasing access to foreign and offshore capital markets such as the Eurobond market. In smaller economies, such as Australia, which still do not have well-developed corporate bond or commercial paper markets, banks have lost loan business to international securities markets. In addition, the same forces that drove the securitization process in the United States are at work in other countries and will undercut the profitability of traditional banking there. Thus, although the decline of traditional banking has occurred earlier in the United States than in other countries, we can expect a diminished role for traditional banking in these countries as well.

HOW HAVE BANKS RESPONDED?

In any industry, a decline in profitability usually results in exit from the industry (often by widespread bankruptcies) and a shrinkage of market share. This occurred in the banking industry in the United States during the 1980s through consolidations and bank failures. From 1960 to 1980, bank failures in the United States averaged less than ten per year, but during the 1980s, bank failures soared, rising to more than 200 a year in the late 1980s (Chart 7).

To survive and maintain adequate profit levels, many U.S. banks are facing two alternatives. First, they can attempt to maintain their traditional lending activity by expanding into new, riskier areas of lending.

Chart 7

BANK FAILURES
1960-94

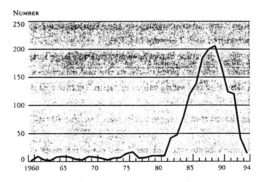

Sources: Federal Deposit Insurance Corporation, *1993 Annual Report* and *Quarterly Banking Profile*.

PART III Financial Institutions

Chart 8

COMMERCIAL REAL ESTATE LOANS AS A PERCENTAGE OF TOTAL COMMERCIAL BANK ASSETS
1960-94

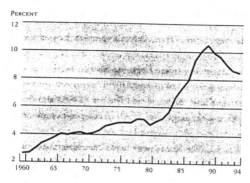

Sources: Board of Governors of the Federal Reserve System, *Federal Reserve Bulletin* and Flow of Funds Accounts.

Chart 9

LOAN LOSS PROVISIONS RELATIVE TO ASSETS FOR COMMERCIAL BANKS
1960-94

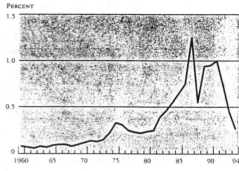

Sources: Federal Deposit Insurance Corporation, *Statistics on Banking* and *Quarterly Banking Profile*.

For example, U.S. banks have increased their risk taking by placing a greater percentage of their total funds in commercial real estate loans, traditionally a riskier type of loan (Chart 8). In addition, they have increased lending for corporate takeovers and leveraged buyouts, which are highly leveraged transactions. There is evidence that banks have in fact increased their lending to less creditworthy borrowers. During the 1980s, banks' loan loss provisions relative to assets climbed substantially, reaching a peak of 1.25 percent in 1987. Only with the strong economy in 1994 have loan loss provisions fallen to levels found in the worst years of the 1970s (Chart 9). Recent evidence suggests that large banks have taken even more risk than have smaller banks: large banks have suffered the largest loan losses (Boyd and Gertler 1993). Thus, banks appear to have maintained their profitability (and their net interest margins—interest income minus interest expense divided by total assets) by taking greater risk (Chart 10).[5] Using stock market measures of risk, Demsetz and Strahan (1995) also find that before 1991 large bank holding companies took on more systematic risk than smaller bank holding companies.

The second way banks have sought to maintain former profit levels is to pursue new, off-balance-sheet activities that are more profitable. As Chart 4 shows, U.S. commercial banks did this during the early 1980s, doubling the share of their income coming from off-balance-sheet, noninterest-income activities.[6] This strategy, however, has generated concerns about what activities are proper for banks and whether nontraditional activities might be riskier and result in banks' taking excessive risk.

READING 17 The Decline of Traditional Banking

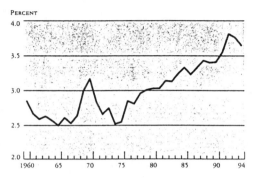

Chart 10

NET INTEREST MARGINS FOR COMMERCIAL BANKS
1960-94

Sources: Federal Deposit Insurance Corporation, *Statistics on Banking* and *Quarterly Banking Profile.*

Although banks have increased fee-based activities, the area of expanding activities in nontraditional banking that has raised the greatest concern is banks' derivatives activities. Great controversy surrounds the issue of whether banks should be permitted to engage in unlimited derivatives activities, including serving as off-exchange or over-the-counter (OTC) derivatives dealers. Some feel that such activities are riskier than traditional banking and could threaten the stability of the entire banking system. (We discuss this issue more fully later in the paper.)

The United States is not the only country to experience increased risk taking by banks. Large losses and bank failures have occurred in other countries. Banks in Norway, Sweden, and Finland responded to deregulation by dramatically increasing their real estate lending, a move followed by a boom and bust in real estate sectors that resulted in the insolvency of many large banking institutions. Indeed, banks' loan losses in these countries as a fraction of GNP exceeded losses in both the banking and the savings and loans industries in the United States. The International Monetary Fund (1993) reports that government (or taxpayer) support to shore up the banking system in Scandinavian countries is estimated to range from 2.8 to 4.0 percent of GDP. This support is comparable to the savings and loan bailout in the United States, which amounted to 3.2 percent of GDP.

Japanese banks have also suffered large losses from riskier lending, particularly to the real estate sector. The collapse of real estate values in Japan left many banks with huge losses. Ministry of Finance estimates in June 1995 indicated that Japanese banks were holding 40 trillion yen ($470 billion) of nonperforming loans—loans on which interest payments had not been made for more than six months—but many private analysts think that the actual amount of nonperforming loans may be substantially larger.

French and British banks suffered from the worldwide collapse of real estate prices and from major failures of risky real estate projects funded by banks. Olympia and York's collapse is a prominent example. The loan-loss provisions of British and French banks, like those of U.S. banks, have risen in the 1990s. One result has been the massive bailout of Credit Lyonnais by the French government in March 1995. Even in countries with healthy banking systems, such as Switzerland and Germany, some banks have run into trouble. Regional banks in Switzerland failed, and Germany's BFG Bank

PART III Financial Institutions

Table 2
DERIVATIVES CONTRACTS
December 31, 1994

	Trading ($ Billions)	Percentage of Total	Asset/Liability Management ($ Billions)	Percentage of Total	Total ($ Billions)
BankAmerica	1,333	95	68	5	1,401
Bank One	0	0	45	100	45
Bankers Trust	1,982	98	44	2	2,026
Chase	1,293	95	67	5	1,360
Chemical	3,069	97	109	3	3,178
Citicorp	2,449	92	216	8	2,665
J.P. Morgan	2,180	88	292	12	2,472
NationsBank	485	95	26	5	511
Total/average[a]	12,791	94	867	6	13,658

Sources: Annual reports for 1994.

[a] Totals, expressed in billions of dollars, appear in columns 1, 3, and 5. Averages, expressed as percentages, appear in columns 2 and 4.

suffered huge losses (DM 1.1 billion) in 1992 and needed a capital infusion from its parent company, Credit Lyonnais. Thus, fundamental forces not limited to the United States have caused a decline in the profitability of traditional banking throughout the world and have created an incentive for banks to expand into new activities and take additional risks.

BANKS' OFF-BALANCE-SHEET DERIVATIVES ACTIVITIES

Much of the controversy surrounding banks' efforts to diversify into off-balance-sheet activities has centered on the increasing role of banks in derivatives markets. Large banks, in particular, have moved aggressively to become worldwide dealers in off-exchange or OTC derivatives, such as swaps.[7] Their motivation, clearly, has been to replace some of their lost "banking" revenue with the attractive returns that can be earned in derivatives markets.

Banks have increased their participation in derivatives markets dramatically in the last few years. In 1994, U.S. banks held derivatives contracts totaling more than $16 trillion in notional value.[8] Of these contracts, 63 percent were interest rate derivatives, 35 percent were foreign exchange derivatives, and the remainder were equity and commodity derivatives.[9] In addition, most of these derivatives were held by large banks, and were held primarily to facilitate the banks' dealer and trading operations (Table 2).[10] In

READING 17 The Decline of Traditional Banking

Table 3
NOTIONAL/CONTRACT DERIVATIVES AMOUNTS OF FIFTEEN MAJOR U.S. OVER-THE-COUNTER DERIVATIVES DEALERS
Millions of Dollars

Banks	
Chemical Banking Corporation	3,177,600
Citicorp	2,664,600
J.P. Morgan & Co., Inc.	2,472,500
Bankers Trust New York Corporation	2,025,736
BankAmerica Corporation	1,400,707
The Chase Manhattan Corporation	1,360,000
First Chicago Corporation	622,100
Securities firms	
Salomon, Inc.	1,509,000
Merrill Lynch & Co., Inc.	1,326,000
Lehman Brothers, Inc.	1,143,091
The Goldman Sachs Group, L.P.	995,275
Morgan Stanley Group, Inc.	843,000
Insurance companies	
American International Group, Inc.	376,869
General Re Corporation	306,159
The Prudential Insurance Co. of America	102,102
Total	17,852,239

Sources: Annual reports for 1994.

Table 4
CONTRIBUTION OF DERIVATIVES TRADING TO TOTAL TRADING INCOME

	1994 ($ Millions)	Percent	1993 ($ Millions)	Percent
Chase	108	15	201	28
Chemical	391	61	453	42
Citicorp	400	29	800	27
J.P. Morgan	663	65	797	39
Total/average[a]	1,562	42	2,251	34

Sources: Company annual reports.

[a] Totals, expressed in millions of dollars, appear in columns 1 and 3. Averages, expressed as percentages, appear in columns 2 and 4.

PART III Financial Institutions

1994, the seven largest U.S.-bank derivatives dealers accounted for more than 90 percent of the notional value of all derivatives contracts held by U.S. banks (Table 3).[11] The profitability of derivatives activities has clearly encouraged banks to step up their involvement: in 1994, derivatives accounted for between 15 and 65 percent of the total trading income of four of the largest bank dealers (Table 4).[12]

The increased participation of banks in derivatives markets has been a concern to both regulators and legislators because they fear that derivatives may enable banks to take more risk than is prudent. There can be little doubt that derivatives can be used to increase risk substantially, and can potentially be quite dangerous.[13] In the last year, many banks sustained substantial losses on interest rate derivatives instruments when interest rates continued to rise. Because of the leverage that is possible, derivatives enable banks to place sizable "bets" on interest rate and currency movements, which—if wrong—can result in sizable losses. In addition, as dealers in OTC derivatives markets, banks may be exposed to substantial counterparty credit risk. Unlike organized futures exchanges, the OTC market offers no clearinghouse guarantee to mitigate the credit risk involved in derivatives trading. Finally, because derivatives are often complex instruments, sophisticated risk-control systems may be necessary to measure and track a bank's potential exposure. Questions have been raised about whether banks are currently capable of managing these risks.

Concern about the growing participation of banks in derivatives markets is exemplified by the remarks of Representative Henry Gonzalez, Chairman of the Banking Committee of the House of Representatives:

> I have long believed that growing bank involvement in derivative products is, as I say and repeat, like a tinderbox waiting to explode. In the case of many market innovations, regulation lags behind until the crisis comes, as it has happened in our case with S&L's and banks . . .
>
> We must work to avoid a crisis related to derivative products before, once again, . . . the taxpayer is left holding the bag.[14]

In May 1994, Representative Gonzalez and Representative Jim Leach introduced the Derivatives Safety and Soundness Act of 1994. This bill directs the federal banking agencies to establish common principles and standards for capital, accounting, disclosure, and examination of financial institutions using derivatives. In addition, the bill requires the Federal Reserve and the U.S. Comptroller of the Currency to work with other central banks to develop comparable international supervisory standards for financial institutions using derivatives. In discussing the need for derivatives legislation, Representative Leach said, "one of the ironies of the development of [derivatives markets] is that while [individual firm] risk can be reduced . . . systematic risk can be increased." A second problem, Leach noted, is that in many cases derivatives instruments "are too sophisticated for financial managers."[15] A further indication of these concerns is the plethora of recent studies that have examined the activities of financial institutions in derivatives markets. Studies have been conducted by the Bank for International Settlements (the "Promisel Report"), the Bank of England, the Group of Thirty, the Office of the U.S. Comptroller of the Currency, the Commodity Futures Trading Commission, and, most recently, the U.S. Government Accounting Office (GAO).

The GAO released its report, "Financial Derivatives: Actions Needed to Protect the Financial System," in May 1994. The report concluded that there is some reason to believe that derivatives do pose a threat to financial stability. It raises the prospect that a default by a major OTC derivatives dealer—and in particular by a major bank—could result in spillover effects that could "close down" OTC derivatives markets, with potentially serious ramifications for the entire financial system. The GAO recommends that a number of measures be taken to strengthen government regulation and supervision of all participants in OTC derivatives markets, including banks.

The fear of a major bank failure because of OTC derivatives activities appears to stem from two sources. First, the sheer size of banks' OTC derivatives activities suggests that they may be exposed to substantial market and credit risk because of their derivatives positions. In particular, there is concern that as OTC derivatives dealers, banks may be exposed to sizable counterparty credit risk. This concern has been heightened in recent months by the near-bankruptcy of Metallgesellschaft, Germany's fourteenth largest firm and a major end-user and counterparty in the swap market. Second, many fear that regulation, as well as managerial sophistication, has lagged developments in the derivatives area, and as a consequence, banks may be taking more risk than is prudent (and more than they even realize).

How Risky Are Banks' OTC Derivatives Activities?

Much of the concern about banks' activities in derivatives markets has centered on their central position as major dealers in the swap market. At year-end 1994, the notional value of all swap contracts outstanding was $7.1 trillion (Table 5).[16] Interest rate swaps represented 82 percent of this amount, with currency swaps making up most of the remaining contracts (Table 6). Although detailed information about the nature of these swap agreements is not available, the bulk of them are probably "plain vanilla" swaps—an exchange of fixed for floating rates. As such, these contracts are similar to "strips" of forward or futures contracts (for example, Eurodollar futures strips). Swaps are attractive to end-users because of their customized nature, low cost, and longer maturities.

As major dealers in the swap market, banks have extensive counterparty obligations and may be exposed to substantial market and counterparty credit risk. The notional or principal amount of the swap contracts that banks hold, however, is not a good measure of the magnitude of their credit exposure. Unlike credit instruments such as loans and bonds, swaps and other derivatives transactions do not involve payments of principal amounts. Derivatives contracts require periodic payments based on notional amounts but not payments of the notional

PART III Financial Institutions

Table 5
NOTIONAL/CONTRACT AMOUNTS FOR DERIVATIVES WORLDWIDE BY INDIVIDUAL PRODUCT TYPE AS OF THE END OF FISCAL YEARS 1990-93

Type of Derivative	1990 ($ Billions)	1991 ($ Billions)	1992 ($ Billions)	1993 ($ Billions)	Percentage of Total 1993	Percentage Increase from 1990 to 1993
Forwards						
Forward rate agreements	1,156	1,533	1,807	2,522		
Foreign exchange forwards[a]	3,277	4,531	5,510	6,232		
Total forwards	4,433	6,064	7,317	8,754	35	97
Futures						
Interest rate futures	1,454	2,157	2,902	4,960		
Currency futures	16	18	25	30		
Equity index futures	70	77	81	119		
Total futures	1,540	2,252	3,008	5,109	20	231
Options						
Exchange-traded interest rate options	600	1,073	1,385	2,362		
Over-the-counter interest rate options	561	577	634	1,398		
Exchange-traded currency options	56	61	80	81		
Exchange-traded equity index options	96	137	168	286		
Total options	1,313	1,848	2,267	4,127	17	214
Swaps						
Interest rate swaps	2,312	3,065	3,851	6,177		
Currency swaps	578	807	860	900		
Total swaps	2,890	3,872	4,711	7,077	28	145
Total derivatives[b]	10,176	14,036	17,303	25,067	100	146
Total derivatives[c]	6,899	9,505	11,893	18,835		

Sources: Bank for International Settlements; U.S. Government Accounting Office; International Swaps and Derivatives Association; Federal Reserve Bank of New York.

[a] Estimates for foreign exchange forward contracts are from U.S. Government Accounting Office 1994 (GAO report), Table IV.5. These also include an unknown amount of over-the-counter foreign exchange options.

[b] Does not include complete data on physical commodity derivatives and equity options on the common stock of individual companies. Table IV.2 of the GAO report shows that seven of the databases contain equity and commodity derivatives that ranged from 1.1 to 3.4 percent of total derivatives' notional/contract amounts.

[c] Before including GAO estimates for foreign exchange forwards and over-the-counter options.

Table 6
NOTIONAL PRINCIPAL OF INTEREST RATE AND CURRENCY SWAPS WRITTEN ANNUALLY BY UNDERLYING AND OUTSTANDING
Billions of U.S. Dollars

Type of Swap	1987	1990	1991	1992	1993
Interest rate swaps					
U.S. dollar	287	676	926	1,336	1,546
Deutsche mark	22	106	103	237	399
Yen	32	137	194	428	789
Others	47	345	397	821	1,370
Subtotal	388	1,264	1,622	2,822	4,104
Currency swaps					
Dollar	38	65	122	106	109
Nondollar	48	148	206	196	186
Subtotal	86	213	328	302	295
Total swaps written	474	1,477	1,950	2,124	4,399
Total swaps outstanding (at year-end)	867	2,890	3,872	4,711	7,077

Source: International Swaps and Derivatives Association.

amounts themselves. For example, a swap of a variable interest rate for a 7 percent fixed rate on a $10 million principal (notional) amount commits the swap parties to annual payments to each other on the order of $700,000, with differences in future payments depending on how interest rates move in the future. A party's credit exposure, therefore, is not the notional value of the contract, as it is for a loan, but the "replacement cost" of the contract.[17] Thus, the typical derivatives transaction involves a credit exposure that is only a fraction of its notional principal.

The GAO report closely examined fourteen major OTC derivatives dealers. Together, these dealers held derivative contracts with a notional principal of $6.5 trillion as of year-end 1992. The "gross" credit exposure (or replacement cost) on these derivatives, however, was far less. The GAO estimated the replacement cost to be only $114 billion, or about 1.8 percent of the dealers' $6.5 trillion of notional outstandings.[18]

In addition, this figure does not take into account the various risk-management mechanisms that banks use to limit counterparty exposure. Bilateral contractual netting provisions, which allow banks to offset losses with gains from other contracts outstanding with a defaulting party and its corporate affiliates, are common. Moreover, when swaps are undertaken with lower quality parties, such counterparties are usually required to post collateral on a mark-to-market basis. After taking these risk-reducing mechanisms into account, the GAO report

PART III Financial Institutions

estimated the "net" credit exposure of the fourteen dealers to be only $68 billion, or about 1 percent of the notional value of their outstanding derivatives contracts.

This credit exposure is managed by banks in a variety of ways. Internal credit limits are commonly used to diversify credit risk and to restrict the size of exposures to individual counterparties, industries, and countries. Most counterparties in swap transactions are required to have investment grade ratings,[19] and credit "triggers" frequently require the automatic termination of a swap agreement if the credit rating of either party falls below a prespecified threshold (such as a single A rating).

To put banks' derivatives credit exposures in perspective, the derivatives exposures of bank derivatives dealers can be compared with credit exposures that the same banks face as a consequence of their loan portfolios.[20] For the seven largest U.S.-bank derivatives dealers, derivatives-related gross credit exposures as a percentage of bank equity were generally less than a fourth of their loan exposures (Chart 11). Only Bankers Trust New York Corporation, which is probably the most active bank in derivatives markets, and J.P. Morgan had a gross derivatives credit exposure far in excess of their loan exposure. Although it is true that banks' credit exposure to derivatives is substantial—it exceeds 100 percent of the equity of all of the surveyed banks—a bank's capital would be wiped out by derivatives losses only if *all* counterparties were to default, there were no offsetting netting agreements or other risk-reduction mechanisms in force, and actual counterparty losses were identical to total credit exposures.

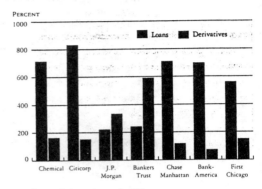

Chart 11

CREDIT EXPOSURES FROM DERIVATIVES AND LOANS OF SEVEN U.S. BANKS AS A PERCENTAGE OF EQUITY, 1994

Sources: Bank annual reports for 1994.

Such assumptions are extreme, for loan defaults as well as for derivatives-related exposures.

Properly measured, therefore, banks' credit-risk exposures associated with their OTC derivatives activities do not seem out of proportion to their other credit exposures, such as the exposure they have to defaults on their loan portfolio. Banks also appear to be managing these derivatives-related exposures reasonably well. Indeed, the GAO reported that actual losses incurred by derivatives dealers as a result of counterparty defaults have been quite small: 0.2 percent of their combined gross credit exposure.[21]

Finally, derivatives activities can clearly be used by banks to increase their exposure to changes in interest rates and exchange rates—that is, to increase their market risk. This kind of risk, however, is hardly new to banks. Banks have always been exposed to such risks because of their holdings of fixed-rate, long-term loans and securities, and because of their foreign operations and foreign currency positions. Derivatives can be used either to increase or decrease these risks. Consequently, like all other transactions that pose market risk, derivatives contracts must be managed prudently.

Regulation Of Banks' Derivatives Activities

There has also been concern that banks may be taking excessive risk in their derivatives activities.[22] Indeed, the GAO report suggests that there may be an intrinsic regulatory problem associated with banks' dealing in OTC derivatives:

> The regulation of banks is essential, because they have deposit insurance and direct access to the Federal Reserve's discount window. At the same time, however, this combination of deposit insurance and access also can result in potential problems because it may induce the banks and their customers to inappropriately rely on such backing. Therefore, banks may be willing to run greater risks in their trading activities—in relation to their capital—than otherwise would be the case. In addition, market participants may prefer using banks for derivatives and related trading activities simply because banks are perceived to be safer counterparties. In the past, similar concerns caused us to recommend that nontraditional banking activities, such as those associated with underwriting and dealing in corporate debt and equity securities, be conducted only by well-managed and well-capitalized banks in separate subsidiaries of the bank holding company. Whether derivatives should be placed in this category depends on regulators' determinations on how they are being used by individual banks.[23]

An important question, therefore, is whether banks' derivatives activities are so different from other bank activities that they cannot be effectively regulated. Is there something special about derivatives that makes prudential regulation to protect the federal deposit insurance fund and taxpayers more difficult or even impossible? A key issue is whether bank capital requirements, the central component of prudential regulation, can be successfully applied to banks' derivatives activities. If not, there may be an argument for either prohibiting derivatives activities (or possibly dealer activities) or segregating them into separately capitalized bank affiliates.[24]

Banks' derivatives activities are already subject to extensive prudential regulation. Both U.S. and Basle Accord capital requirements apply to U.S. banks' derivatives activities. U.S. banks are required to comply with two different types of capital requirements—a risk-based requirement and a leverage ratio requirement. The risk-based requirement applies to the credit risk associated with derivatives contracts or activities. The leverage ratio requires banks to hold capital as a cushion against losses arising from other risks associated with derivatives positions, such as operations risk. Not surprisingly, there is considerable controversy about whether these capital requirements are too low or too high.

The more important question, however, is whether *any* capital requirements on derivatives activities can successfully control banks' risk taking. Some argue that derivatives are so complex and so nontransparent that it is difficult for regulators to devise capital regulations to control banks' risk taking (or, for that matter, for the market to monitor banks' derivatives activities).

We are skeptical about this view. Although some derivatives instruments are undoubtedly complex, exposure to derivatives risk does not seem much different from exposure to many other bank activities, such as credit risk in a loan portfolio or interest rate risk in a variety of fixed-income securities. Banks can achieve high leverage in a number of ways other than through derivatives and can quickly change (or increase) their risk exposure in many different ways. While it is not clear how much capital should be required for a given derivatives risk exposure, these implementation problems are not unique to derivatives activities. All new bank activities are likely to present similar problems.

Thus, banks' recent push into derivatives activities raises all of the questions commonly raised when banks engage in new off-balance-sheet activities. Are these activities too risky for banks? Do banks have the managerial capacity to engage in these activities in a safe way? Can these activities be effectively regulated? The challenges posed by these questions are no different for derivatives than they are for other banking activities.

IMPLICATIONS FOR POLICY

The decline of traditional banking presents a challenge to regulators and policymakers. On the one hand, banks may respond to their shrinking intermediary role and diminished profitability by taking greater risk, which, if unchecked, could undermine the stability of the banking system. There is some evidence that banks have in fact increased their risk taking, either by pursuing riskier strategies in their traditional business lines or by seeking out new and riskier activities. On the other hand, long-run financial stability would benefit from a restructuring of the banking industry that strengthens the competitive position of banks. Achieving this goal may require eliminating unnecessary (nonprudential) regulations and permitting banks to enter new markets and to engage in new activities.

One approach to achieving these dual objectives is to couple adequate capital requirements for banks with early corrective action by regulators to prevent capital from falling below specified levels.[25] Requiring banks to hold adequate capital promotes financial stability in two ways. First, it provides a greater cushion with which banks can absorb losses, lessening the likelihood of failure. Second, with more capital at risk, banks have less incentive to take excessive risk—they have more to lose if their bets go wrong. To ensure that banks hold the requisite amount of capital and do not engage in either excessively risky or illegal activities, supervision and field examinations of banks would continue to be necessary.[26] Requiring early corrective action by regulators to recapitalize a bank that has suffered an erosion in its capital promotes stability in three ways. First, it provides predictability for banks and bank shareholders. Certain regulatory actions predictably follow certain economic events. Second, it prevents a bank's capital from falling to levels that threaten losses to the bank insurance fund. In addition, by requiring banks to maintain a positive net worth, it mitigates the moral hazard problem—banks will have something to lose by taking excessive risk. Lastly, early corrective action mitigates the regulatory forbearance problem by preventing regulators from using their discretion about whether or not to take action.[27]

A benefit of this regulatory strategy is that regulation need no longer restrict banks' activities. As long as banks must hold sufficient capital against whatever activities they engage in, taxpayers will be protected and banks will have an incentive to avoid excessive risk taking. Further, freedom to offer additional products and services will better enable banks to compete with nonbank competitors and with foreign banks, and will make banks less susceptible to failure because they will be better diversified. (An example of such diversification benefits is casualty insurance, where losses are due principally to acts of god and have a very low correlation with the losses that banks typically incur, which are due primarily to adverse economic events.)

A key component of this approach is that bank risk exposures need to be measured accurately and capital requirements be set high enough to deter excessive risk taking. This requires, among other things, the adoption of market-value accounting principles for valuing bank assets and liabilities. Historical-cost accounting principles do not ensure that changes in the economic value of a bank's assets and liabilities will be reflected in its true net worth. It is the market value of a bank's assets and liabilities, together with the market value of its equity capital, that determines a bank's economic solvency. Further, the market value of a bank's net worth is what the bank risks when it takes additional risk.

Objections to market-value-based capital requirements center on the difficulty of making accurate market-value estimates of assets and liabilities. Historical-cost accounting has an important advantage in that it is easier to value assets and liabilities. Market-value accounting, in contrast, requires estimates and approximations that are harder to justify and are often more expensive to obtain. Despite these difficulties, market-value accounting may still be able to provide a more accurate picture of a bank's economic condition. Clearly, an important research topic for regulatory authorities is the feasibility of applying market-value accounting principles to banking institutions.

Adoption of market-value accounting would have the additional advantage of making a bank's condition more transparent and therefore making regulators and politicians more accountable. Regulators and politicians are subject to a principal-agent problem: they often have an incentive to hide potential problems, even though taxpayers would be better off if these problems were dealt with sooner rather than later (or not at all). Market-value accounting would make it easier for taxpayers to monitor the actions of regulators and politicians, and would make it more difficult for regulators to engage in policies of forbearance.

Another important component of a regulatory strategy to maintain bank soundness is supervisory monitoring. Regulation must be able to keep banks from changing their risk exposure after capital requirements are determined. Both this element of regulatory supervision and the need for early intervention have increased in importance of late because of the emergence of derivatives markets that make it easier for banks to quickly take large bets on interest rate and other asset price movements. As we have learned from the recent collapse of Barings, regulators must also ensure that adequate internal controls are in place with regard to asset quality and risk management procedures.

Finally, public disclosure of banks' risk exposures would increase market efficiency and bolster market discipline. Banks should provide a meaningful depiction of the risks associated with their trading activities, both in derivatives and in on-balance-sheet securities, and of their ability to manage these risks. More public information about the risks incurred by banks will better enable stockholders, creditors, and depositors to evaluate and monitor banks, and will act as a deterrent to excessive risk taking. This view is consistent with a recent discussion paper issued by the Euro-currency Standing Committee of the G-10 Central Banks (1994), which goes so far as to recommend that estimates of financial risk generated by firms' own internal risk management systems be adapted for public disclosure purposes.[28] Such information would supplement disclosures based on traditional accounting conventions by providing information about risk exposures and risk management that is not normally included in conventional balance sheet and income-statement reports.

CONCLUSION

The decline of traditional banking entails a risk to the financial system only if regulators fail to adapt their policies to the new financial environment that is emerging. A constructive regulatory approach is to adopt a system of structured bank capital requirements together with early corrective action by regulators. An important element of this system is the adoption of market-value accounting principles for all financial institutions. In addition, supervisory monitoring and greater public disclosure by all financial institutions of the risks associated with their trading activities would be beneficial. Lastly, to enhance the competitiveness and efficiency of financial markets, banks could be permitted to engage in a diversified array of both bank and nonbank products and services. This general regulatory strategy, we believe, can successfully keep in check excessive risk taking by banks while providing the flexibility for both banks and regulators to restructure the banking system to achieve greater long-term stability. Finally, we do not view banks' off-balance-sheet activities, including their derivatives activities, as a threat to financial stability. Properly used and regulated, derivatives can facilitate the management of risk and increase the long-term viability of banks and the financial system.

ENDNOTES

1. Franklin R. Edwards is Arthur Burns Professor of Finance and Economics at the Graduate School of Business, Columbia University and Visiting Scholar at the American Enterprise Institute. Frederic S. Mishkin is Executive Vice President and Director of Research at the Federal Reserve Bank of New York, Research Associate at the National Bureau of Economic Research, and A. Barton Hepburn Professor of Finance and Economics at the Graduate School of Business, Columbia University. An earlier version of this article appeared in Spanish in the June 1995 issue of *Moneda y Credito* as part of the proceedings of the Symposium on Financial Instability. The research is part of the National Bureau of Economic Research's programs in Monetary Economics and Economic Fluctuations. Any opinions expressed are those of the authors and not those of Columbia University, the National Bureau of Economic Research, the American Enterprise Institute, the Federal Reserve Bank of New York, or the Federal Reserve System.

   The authors thank Atturo Estrella, Charles Goodhart, Stavros Peristiani, Eli Remolona, Philip Strahan, and Betsy White for their comments and William Bassett for research assistance. Discussants at the Symposium on Financial Instability and participants in a workshop at the Federal Reserve Bank of New York also provided helpful comments.

2. Although many banks may be able to maintain their relative position as financial intermediaries by engaging in nontraditional banking activities, for policy purposes it is important to focus on the economic forces that have undercut the role of banking. Indeed, an important question is whether substantive public policy issues are raised by banks having to transform themselves into financial intermediaries that look more like nonbank financial intermediaries.

3. See also Edwards (1993).

4. Banks have also been engaged in the securitization process and, with the advent of higher bank capital requirements, have had greater incentives to move loans off balance sheet by securitizing them. Banks' involvement in the securitization process has been another contributing factor to the growth in their off-balance-sheet activities. Nevertheless, the basic point still stands: computer technology that can be used by nonbanking institutions to securitize assets has diminished the banks' competitive position.

5. U.S. banks have an incentive to take additional risk because of federal deposit insurance. Insured depositors have little incentive to monitor banks and to penalize them for taking too much risk. This moral hazard problem was compounded by our de facto "too-big-to-fail" policy for large banks. Although the 1991 Federal Deposit Insurance Corporation Improvement Act (FDICIA) has a least-cost resolution provision that makes it harder to bail out large depositors, there is an exception to the provision whereby a bank would be in effect declared too big to fail so that all depositors would be fully protected if a two-thirds majority of both the Board of Governors of the Federal Reserve System and the Directors of the Federal Deposit Insurance Corporation as well as the secretary of the Treasury agreed. Thus, the moral hazard problem created by the too-big-to-fail policy has been reduced but not entirely eliminated by the 1991 FDICIA legislation.

6. Note that some off-balance-sheet activities that produce fee income, such as loan commitments and letters of credit, can be classified as traditional banking business. The data in Chart 4 overstate somewhat nontraditional banking business.

7. As of the third quarter, 1993, all insured commercial banks held interest rate swaps contracts with a notional value of $2.79 trillion. See Bank Administration Institute and McKinsey & Company, Inc. (1994, p. 5).

8. Federal Reserve call report (RC-L) data for U.S. banks for the first quarter of 1992. See also U.S. General Accounting Office (1994, p. 182).

9. U.S General Accounting Office (1994).

10. Salomon Brothers (1994, p. 8). Qualitative statements in the banks' annual reports suggest that much of their derivatives trading is customer-driven.

11. U.S. General Accounting Office (1994, p. 188, Appendix V, and p. 182, Appendix IV).

12. Salomon Brothers (1994, p. 9, Chart 5).

13. See Franklin R. Edwards (1994).

14. Remarks made on the floor of the House of Representatives, Congressional Record, June 18, 1993, H. 3322.

15. Mark Kollar (1994, p. 1, col. 2).

PART III Financial Institutions

16. This amount includes interest rate and currency swaps plus caps, floors, collars, and swaptions outstanding. Equity, commodity, and multi-asset derivatives are not included. The latter totaled $131 billion at year-end 1992, relative to a total of $4.7 trillion of swap contracts at year-end 1992. See Group of Thirty (1993, p. 58).

17. Measured at any point in time, credit risk exists only for counterparties with profitable positions. A losing counterparty has no credit risk. For example, assume that under an interest rate swap agreement, a firm receives fixed-interest payments and pays floating rates. At the inception of this swap, the market value of the firm's position in the swap may be zero. If, subsequently, interest rates decline substantially, the firm will receive more than it will pay, so the firm will have a valuable or profitable position in the swap. This value, created by the change in interest rates, is the firm's replacement cost for the swap, and represents the credit risk to which it is exposed. If its counterparty defaults on future swap payments, the replacement cost is the cost to the firm of replacing the swap on the same favorable terms.

18. These include both swaps and forward contracts.

19. U.S. General Accounting Office (1994, p. 59, Table 3.1).

20. U.S. General Accounting Office (1994, pp. 54-55).

21. U.S. General Accounting Office (1994, p. 55).

22. For a review of the current regulation of banks' derivatives activities, see U.S. General Accounting Office (1994, pp. 69-84).

23. U.S. General Accounting Office (1994, p. 125).

24. Alternatively, there may be an argument for some form of "narrow banking," where the deposit-taking function of the bank is separated from other bank activities, such as derivatives activities.

25. This approach is discussed extensively in Benston and Kaufman (1988), elements of which are in the 1991 FDICIA act.

26. As Gorton and Rosen 1994) point out, corporate control (agency) issues may also contribute to excessive risk taking when traditional banking business declines. Thus, steps to control this agency problem may also be needed to control risk taking. What form these steps should take requires additional research and is beyond the scope of this paper.

27. As capital declined below certain "trigger" levels, for example, regulatory authorities would be required to take specific actions, such as restricting the ability of the bank to expand and preventing the bank from paying dividends and interest on subordinated debentures.

28. See also the Federal Reserve Bank of New York (1994), which is a companion piece to the Euro-currency Standing Committee's report.

REFERENCES

Bank Administration Institute and McKinsey & Company, Inc. 1994. "Banking Off the Balance Sheet."

Benston, George J., and George G. Kaufman. 1988. "Rick and Solvency Regulation of Depository Institutions: Past Policies and Current Options." New York University, Salomon Center for Graduate School of Business, Monograph Series in Finance and Economics, no. 1.

Boyd, John H., and Mark Gertler. 1993. "U.S. Commercial Banking Trends, Cycles, and Policy." In Olivier Blanchard and Stanley Fischer, eds., NATIONAL BUREAU OF ECONOMIC RESEARCH MACROECONOMICS ANNUAL.

———. 1994. "Are Banks Dead? Or, Are the Reports Greatly Exaggerated?" In THE DECLINING ROLE OF BANKING, pp. 85-117. Federal Reserve Bank of Chicago, May.

Demsetz, Rebecca, and Philip Strahan. 1995. "Historical Patterns and Recent Changes in the Relationship Between Bank Holding Company Size and Risk." FEDERAL RESERVE BANK OF NEW YORK ECONOMIC POLICY REVIEW 1, no. 2 (July): 13-26.

READING 17 The Decline of Traditional Banking

Edwards, Franklin R. 1993. "Financial Markets in Transition—or the Decline of Commercial Banking." In CHANGING CAPITAL MARKETS: IMPLICATIONS FOR MONETARY POLICY, pp. 5-62. Federal Reserve Bank of Kansas City, 1993.
_____. 1994. "Are Derivatives Hazardous to Your Health? The Case of Metallgesellschaft." Mimeo.
Euro-currency Standing Committee of Central Banks of Group of Ten Countries (Fisher Group). 1994. "Public Disclosure of Markets and Credit Risks by Financial Intermediaries." Discussion paper, September.
Federal Reserve Bank of New York. 1994. "Public Disclosure of Risks Related to Market Activity." Discussion paper, September.
Gorton, Gary and Richard Rosen. 1994. "Corporate Control, Portfolio Choice and the Decline of Banking." University of Pennsylvania, July. Mimeo.
Group of Thirty. 1993. "Derivatives: Practices and Principles," July, p. 58, Table 6.
International Monetary Fund. 1993. "The Deterioration of Bank Balance Sheets." Part II of INTERNATIONAL CAPITAL MARKETS, pp. 2-22. August.
Kaufman, George. 1994. "FDICIA: The Early Evidence." CHALLENGE MAGAZINE, July-August: 53-57.
Kaufman, George G., and Larry R. Mote. 1994. "Is Banking a Declining Industry? A Historical Perspective." FEDERAL RESERVE BANK OF CHICAGO ECONOMIC PERSPECTIVES, May-June: 2-21.
Keeley, Michael C. 1990. "Deposit Insurance, Risk, and Market Power in Banking." AMERICAN ECONOMIC REVIEW 80 (December): 1183-1200.
Kollar, Mark. 1994. "Congressman Sees Need for Safety Net." KNIGHT-RIDDER FINANCIAL PRODUCTS & NEWS, July-August, p. 1, col. 2.
Salomon Brothers. 1994. "Derivatives: New Disclosures Still Fall Short," May 16.
U.S. General Accounting Office. 1994. "Financial Derivatives: Actions Needed to Protect the Financial System." Report to Congressional Requestors, GAO/GGD-94-133, May.

QUESTIONS

1. What do Edwards and Mishkin mean by the "traditional role" of banks? What evidence do they present that this role is declining?

2. What advantages in acquiring and lending funds did banks have? Why did they lose them?

3. How have banks responded to the decline of their traditional role and what policy concerns have their responses raised?

4. What regulatory policy changes do Edwards and Mishkin suggest to deal with the changes in banking activities they discuss? Why do they believe each change is needed, and how would it help?

READING 18

Reduced Deposit Insurance Risk

Mark E. Levonian and Fred Furlong

Public policy toward financial liberalization has often been cautious. This year is not likely to be an exception, as the Congress considers proposals to remove long-standing barriers separating commercial banking from investment banking, insurance activities, and even nonfinancial activities.

One key issue that has made policymakers take a cautious approach is concern that expanded bank powers may add to the strains on the federal deposit insurance funds. Fortunately, several developments in recent years have worked to reduce bank risk and the liability of the deposit insurance system substantially. Most prominent among these is the improvement in capital positions of banks.

This *Letter* analyzes trends in bank risk over the past several years and the implications for the deposit insurance system. The analysis suggests that, while the risk associated with bank assets and activities has increased, bank capital positions have soared, pushing down estimates of the federal deposit insurance liability to relatively moderate levels. In the public policy debate, the improvement in the health of banks and of the deposit system should allow more weight to be given to the potential gains in efficiency from further removing the barriers separating banks from other financial institutions.

DEPOSIT INSURANCE RISK

Public policy concern over the risk exposure of the federal deposit insurance system is not surprising in light of the sizeable tab taxpayers picked up in the thrift crisis and the heavy losses to the FDIC from bank failures in recent years. These events have focused attention on the moral hazard problems that can stem from deposit insurance. Moral hazard arises when the existence of insurance severs the connection between a bank's risk-taking and its cost of financing, thereby removing a natural check on risk-taking. Without the proper safeguards, banks may then take excessive risks.

Two broad types of banking risk can be affected by moral hazard. The first is operating risk, which can be measured most directly in terms of the volatility of the rate of return on a bank's assets. All else equal, a bank with a higher volatility of returns is more likely to fail, and if it fails it is more

Reprinted from Federal Reserve Bank of San Francisco *Weekly Letter*, February 24, 1995.

likely to impose a larger loss on the insurance fund. The second broad type of risk is leverage or financial risk, which depends inversely on a bank's capital ratio (the ratio of capital to total assets). For a given level of asset volatility, a bank with a lower capital ratio is more likely to fail.

ADDRESSING THE PROBLEM

In recent years, several legislative and regulatory measures have been implemented to deal with risk in banking and the exposure of the deposit insurance system. One element they have in common is the goal of putting the consequences of bank decision making, the downside and the upside, on the shoulders of the banks and some of their liability holders. These measures include Prompt Corrective Action for troubled banks, rules that make uninsured depositors and other creditors regularly bear losses when banks fail, explicit accounting for changes in the market value of some bank assets and liabilities, and deposit insurance premiums that depend on bank risk.

The most far-reaching change, though, has been the recapitalization of banking. The capital position of the banking industry today is far stronger than it was just three years ago. Banks have responded to regulatory efforts and market pressure by issuing equity and longer-term debt and using retained earnings to rebuild capital ratios. In addition, strengthened balance sheets and an improved outlook for banking have been reflected in the rise in bank stock prices from the depressed levels of the early 1990s. The effect has been a marked turnaround in bank capitalization that has muted the effects of a rise in bank operating risk and has increased tremendously the buffer between potential private losses in banking and the deposit insurance system.

ASSESSING RISK

We can evaluate the net impact of the changes in the two broad types of bank risk—operating risk and financial risk—on the deposit insurance system's liability by using analytical tools that incorporate information from financial market data. Market prices succinctly capture a huge amount of diverse information, reflecting consensus opinions of many market participants. Financial models have been created to use this market information to gauge the condition of banks. In particular, models have been developed to infer the market value of capital and assets (financial risk) and the volatility of returns (operating risk), by working backwards from the stock prices of banks. These models are based on "contingent claim" analysis: The level and volatility of bank stock prices are used to divine bank capital ratios and the standard deviation of the rate of return on assets as well as to filter out any effects deposit insurance might have on stock prices.

Contingent claim analysis was applied to about 300 U.S. bank holding companies, using data from January 1989 through September 1994. These firms tend to be larger than the industry average, and thus may not be completely representative. However, they give direct information about an important segment of the industry, and probably serve as a barometer for U.S. banking as a whole.

PART III Financial Institutions

Market capital ratios and the volatility of returns were computed quarterly for each bank; results for each date were then averaged, with individual bank results weighted by bank asset size. Financial risk rises if the average market capital ratio falls; operating risk goes up if average volatility increases. The estimated capital ratios and volatilities of returns also were combined to examine the net effect of the two basic types of risk on the deposit insurance liability. (The deposit insurance contract is in effect another contingent claim, the value of which can be estimated from asset volatility and capital ratios.) For further discussion of the computation of the three measures, see Furlong (1988).

TRENDS IN OPERATING RISK AND FINANCIAL RISK

Figure 1 shows the evolution of bank operating risk during the 1990s. The most striking feature of these estimates is the sharp rise in the industry's operating risk from mid-1990 to mid-1991. This jump roughly coincides with the recession. However, during the subsequent recovery, the estimates show a decline in average operating risk that has only partially reversed the initial jump. This suggests the possibility of a longer-lasting shift in bank operating risk. In fact, viewed over the entire period, the risk in the 1990s roughly matches the rate of increase Furlong (1988) and Levonian (1991) find for 1981-1989.

Figure 1
Average Standard Deviation of Return on Bank Assets

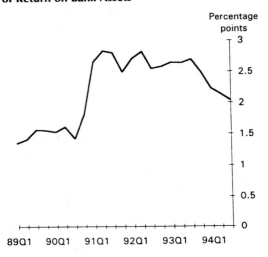

Figure 2 shows the weighted-average market capital ratio. The low point in bank capital ratios—and hence the high point in financial risk—coincides with the beginning of the sharp rise in operating risk in 1990. However, as asset volatility rose, market capital ratios began a sustained increase that continued even after operating risk stabilized. The average market-value capital ratio for this sample of banks rose nearly fivefold from the third quarter of 1990 to early 1993. Since then, the average capital ratio has receded some, but is still high relative to the extremely low level in the early 1990s.

Since the early part of the 1990s, then, trends in the two broad measures of bank risk have pushed the deposit insurance liability in opposite directions. Operating risk generally has increased the liability, while the decline in

Figure 2
Average Market Equity Capital Ratio

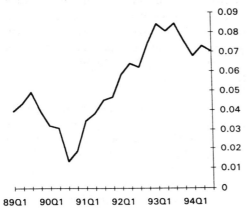

Figure 3
Average Deposit Insurance Liability

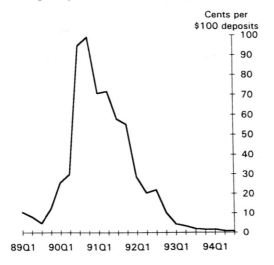

financial risk has worked to protect the deposit insurance system. With these changes at least partially offsetting one another, a summary measure of risk is indispensable.

DEPOSIT INSURANCE EXPOSURE

Figure 3 shows the average deposit insurance liability based on the estimates of bank asset-return volatility and capital. The estimate, expressed in cents per hundred dollars of deposits, reflects the economic cost of insuring bank deposits. As discussed above, it is not only a direct reflection of the risk of losses to the deposit insurance fund, but also a summary measure of bank risk that subsumes both operating risk and financial risk. The figures are sensitive to certain assumptions made in the modeling; as a result, the time pattern is more trustworthy than the precise dollar amounts, and it is the appropriate focus of attention.

Risk to the deposit insurance fund began to go up in the third quarter of 1989 as capital ratios began to fall, and soared markedly in mid-1990. Figure 2 showed that bank capital was at very low levels at that time. As operating risk began its sharp rise—perhaps partly as a result of the recession—the position of the deposit insurance fund became increasingly precarious. However, once the increase in asset volatility stabilized, the improving capital ratios brought the insurance liability down sharply through early 1993. Since then, the liability of the deposit insurance system has edged down further still, as modest declines in average capital ratios have been more than offset by falling operating risk. Consistent with this trend, bank failures in 1993 and 1994 were well below earlier FDIC projections. According to the estimates in Figure 3, the liability of the deposit insurance system was only a few cents per hundred dollars of deposits in September 1994, compared with over 90 cents in the early 1990s. This represents a substantial reduction in the risk exposure of the deposit insurance system.

CONCLUSION

Banks have been increasing the riskiness of their business since at least the beginning of the 1980s. Moreover, a jump in asset risk in mid-1990, combined with the depressed capital ratios prevailing at that time, caused a substantial increase in overall banking risk, as reflected in the potential for deposit insurance fund losses. However, a subsequent marked increase in the average capital ratio and small decline in operating risk has meant a substantial reduction in the liability of the deposit insurance system.

This recent decline in the risk faced by the deposit insurance system may help shape the debate in 1995, as the Congress considers removing legal barriers between banking and other activities. In particular, it should mitigate concerns over the deposit insurance system, and may help tip the balance of the legislative agenda toward the potential gains from removing barriers separating banking from other financial activities.

REFERENCES

Furlong, F. 1988. "Changes in Bank Risk-Taking." Federal Reserve Bank of San Francisco *Economic Review* (Spring) pp. 45-56.

Levonian, M. 1991. "Have Large Banks Become Riskier? Recent Evidence from Option Prices." Federal Reserve Bank of San Francisco *Economic Review* (Fall) pp. 3-17.

READING 18   Reduced Deposit Insurance Risk

QUESTIONS

1. How does deposit insurance remove a "natural check on risk-taking?" What two types of banking risk can stem from this?

2. A goal of bank regulatory reform has been to force banks and their liability holders to shoulder more risk. Evaluate the desirability of this goal and the reforms that have been implemented to achieve it.

3. What is Levonian and Furlong's evidence that risk to the deposit insurance fund has decreased in recent years? Does it support their conclusion regarding the removal of legal barriers separating banking from other financial activities?

READING 19

Making Sense of Mark to Market

Michelle A. Clark

U.S. bankers have been struggling lately to keep up with increased regulatory and congressional scrutiny of their activities. Now the accountants are getting in on the act. Within the last two years the Financial Accounting Standards Board, or FASB (pronounced FAZZBEE), the chief rule-making body for accountants, has approved several proposals that alter the way banks and other financial institutions make financial disclosures.

These new standards fall under the general category of market value accounting (MVA). MVA, also known as fair value accounting or marking to market, requires that an asset or liability be valued according to its market price, that is, the current price at which it could be sold. The call for MVA has gained momentum in recent years, in part because of the savings and loan (S&L) crisis, during which traditional bank accounting methods failed to reveal the huge unrealized losses imbedded in S&Ls' mortgage portfolios. Much of the S&L losses ultimately borne by taxpayers could have been averted, MVA proponents say, if bank accounting methods had reflected the current rather than historical value of assets and liabilities.

MARKET VALUE VS. HISTORICAL COST ACCOUNTING

Historical cost accounting (HCA) is the accounting method traditionally used by most financial institutions. With HCA, assets and liabilities are reported at their contractual values, which may or may not equal their market values.[1]

A simple example will illustrate the point. Suppose a banker purchases a one-year fixed-rate security (or makes a lump-sum, one-year loan) with an interest rate of 10 percent, the current market interest rate. Suppose midway through the year, market interest rates rise to 12 percent. This rise in interest rates would reduce the price (or market value) at which the bank could sell the loan or security at midyear.[2] The market value of the instrument would fall because a buyer would need to be compensated for the difference between the interest rate on that instrument (10 percent) and the going market interest rate (12 percent). In contrast, by HCA, this asset would be valued at $1,000. The possibility that changes in market rates will cause changes in earnings or the value of portfolios

Reprinted from Federal Reserve Bank of St. Louis *The Regional Economist*, January 1994, 10-11.

of assets and liabilities (and hence capital) is called interest rate risk.

Of course, the market value of that instrument would also decline if the borrower paid back only half the principal: The banker loses the opportunity to invest and earn interest on the remaining $500 outstanding in addition to the loss of principal. This type of risk is called credit or default risk.

Market values, then, are based on expected cash flows and foregone investment opportunities. For an asset that is actively traded, like a government bond, the market price is the best estimation of the asset's true economic value. Full market value accounting would require all assets and liabilities to be valued in a similar fashion.

IS HALF A LOAF BETTER THAN NO LOAF?

The use of MVA has been hotly debated for several decades. Proponents argue that MVA would reveal the closest approximation to the true economic value of a bank—its capital—and that it would help both shareholders and regulators better monitor a bank's financial condition. Opponents counter that MVA, while theoretically appealing, is impractical for financial institutions because the market values of most of their assets and liabilities are difficult, if not impossible, to measure accurately.

While the jury is still out on whether full MVA will ever be adopted, partial MVA is now a reality. The most recent FASB statement, FAS 115 (Accounting for Certain Investments in Debt and Equity Securities), went into effect January 1, [1994] and requires that all banks report certain portions of their investment portfolios at market value.[3] Under FAS 115, a bank's securities portfolio will be divided into three parts: held to maturity, available for sale and trading securities.

The "held to maturity" category will include only those instruments that the bank has the "positive intent and financial ability" to hold to maturity; these assets will continue to be reported at historical cost. The "trading account" will consist of securities that are frequently bought and sold to generate profits on short-term price movements; these assets will be marked to market with any unrealized gains and losses reported in the income statement, as they have been for a number of years. All other securities will fall into the category "available for sale"; these will also be marked to market, but their unrealized gains and losses will not be reflected in the income statement. Rather, they will form a separate component of shareholders' equity, and thus will affect the measured value of bank capital on the balance sheet.

According to proponents, one of FAS 115's major benefits is that bank capital will now reflect interest rate risk as well as credit risk. Credit risk is accounted for in a bank's allowance for loan losses, a contra item on the balance sheet. Until now, interest rate risk has not been reflected in banks' financial statements.[4] Interest rate risk can be significant for banks, especially for those banks with large securities holdings.

One of the primary economic factors affecting the value of investment securities, or any bond holding, is interest rates. As illustrated in the example above, the inverse relationship between interest rates and (fixed-rate) bond prices implies that an increase in interest rates will depress the market value of banks' outstanding investment securities. If a bank were forced to sell a security before its maturity in this environment, the bank would incur a loss (as the security's selling price drops below its purchase price). With MVA, these interest rate risk effects are accounted for in the capital account: Unrealized gains would supplement capital while unrealized losses would be deducted from capital. A bank with unrealized losses would be forced to hold more capital (or reduce assets) to meet regulatory standards, which would better protect depositors and the Bank Insurance Fund in the event of insolvency.

Moreover, marking a portion of the investment portfolio to market will eliminate the incentive for an accounting abuse known as "gains trading." Banks that gains trade tend to sell those securities with unrealized gains, bolstering income and perhaps book capital, while keeping securities with unrealized losses on the books at historical cost, keeping book capital artificially high. Because unrealized gains and losses will be reflected in capital under FAS 115, the incentive for gains trading will essentially be eliminated. Gains trading will also be discouraged by penalties for those banks that attempt to move securities from the "held to maturity" category into one of the other two categories to take advantage of market value gains.

MOST BANKERS WOULD RATHER GO WITHOUT

Most bankers oppose MVA, whether it is partial or full. While the objections are far-ranging, most have to do with feasibility and possible adverse effects on the banking industry. The principle objection to FAS 115 is that it ignores liabilities. Under partial MVA, measured capital is likely to be volatile as the value of assets fluctuates while the value of liabilities stays constant. Most banks hedge against interest rate risk by making adjustments on the liability side of the balance sheet—such as matching up fixed-rate assets with fixed-rate liabilities of equal duration—to offset fluctuations on the asset side. Under FAS 115, then, measured capital could be a misleading indicator of the actual amount of interest rate risk inherent in the banks' operations. Increased capital volatility could also raise the cost of capital for many banks.

The problem with full MVA is that most bank assets are difficult to measure at market value. Small commercial loans, for example, are not actively traded so an observable market price does not exist. A similar problem exists on the liability side, in that there is no agreed-upon method to determine the market value of nontraded liabilities like demand deposits. Methods of estimating market values for these nontraded assets and liabilities are likely to vary substantially across banks, making comparability a major problem. And because each market value estimate would have to be done on a case-by-case basis, banks are likely to incur significant costs.

Thus, while MVA accounting methods are theoretically appealing and could potentially give bank regulators and depositors a clear picture of banks' financial health, there are some significant real world costs associated with MVA that will not be easy to measure or mitigate. If MVA is to make further inroads into official bank accounting, its supporters should demonstrate that its real world benefits will exceed its real world costs.

ENDNOTES

1. Technically, most assets and all liabilities are currently reported at amortized cost, meaning that, for example, as borrowers make principal and interest payments, the amount outstanding of the loan or security is reduced. The value of liabilities reflects accrued interest due that has not been paid.

2. In this case, the market value of this asset can be calculated with the following formula: $MV = C_1/(1+r) + \ldots + C_n/(1+r)^n + P/(1+r)^n$, where C = interest payment, r = discount or interest rate, n = time to maturity, e.g., five years, and P = principal payment. Initially the present value of this asset is $1000: the bank could take this amount and invest it at 10 percent to earn the same return as the loan or security. If market interest rates rise to 12 percent immediately, the market value of this instrument falls to $982.14, since (C+P)/1.12) = $1100/1.12 = $982.14.

3. Technically, FAS 115 became effective with fiscal years beginning after December 15, 1993; because most banks' fiscal years coincide with the calendar year, January 1, 1994, was D-day for most.

4. In addition to accounting for interest rate risk with market value accounting of the investment portfolio, interest rate risk will soon be incorporated into banks' risk-based capital requirements.

REFERENCES

Hempel, George H., and Donald G. Simonson. "The Case for Comprehensive Market-Value Reporting," *Bank Accounting and Finance* (Spring 1992), pp. 23-29.

Morris, David M. "The Case Against Market-Value Accounting: A Pragmatic View," *Bank Accounting and Finance* (Spring 1992), pp. 30-36.

Morris, Charles S., and Gordon H. Sellon, Jr. "Market Value Accounting for Banks: Pros and Cons," Federal Reserve Bank of Kansas City *Economic Review* (March/April 1991), pp. 5-19.

Pickering, C.J., and Randy Wade. "Accounting for Investments: Understanding the Implications of FASB 115," *Independent Banker* (August 1993).

Shaffer, Sherrill. "Marking Banks to Market," Federal Reserve Bank of Philadelphia *Business Review* (July/August 1992), pp. 13-22.

PART III Financial Institutions

QUESTIONS

1. What change in bank accounting practice is called for by the Financial Accounting Standards Board's FAS 115? Why was this standard adopted?

2. What are the arguments for and against imposing market value accounting on banks?

READING 20

Glass-Steagall and the Regulatory Dialectic

João Cabral dos Santos

Congress, the Administration, and the bank regulatory agencies are considering various proposals to usher the U.S. banking system into the twenty-first century. The pace of financial innovation—spurred by advances in information technology, globalization of the economy, and competition from other financial institutions—has made this reform seem long overdue. However, any clear understanding of the causes and consequences of the reform movement must recognize that some of the financial innovations that have sprung up over the last three decades were specifically designed to avoid regulations that current reform efforts may repeal.

Like any other industry, banks are in business to earn profits by supplying the products that their customers demand. Similarly, the factors that motivate innovation in the nonfinancial industry—changes in technology and in the market environment—also motivate innovation in banking. But, because of their central place in creating money and credit, banks are considerably more regulated that are firms in the nonfinancial sector, and so have an extra incentive to innovate: Often, bankers aim to avoid regulations that prevent them from exploring profitable opportunities as they arise.

Although some financial innovations eventually become accepted practices, others are blocked by new regulations. These regulations motivate banks to develop other innovations, which in turn prompt further action by the regulators. This interaction sometimes resembles a cat-and-mouse game, or what Professor Edward Kane has termed the "regulatory dialectic."[1] That is, prohibiting banks from adopting a specific path to achieve one of their objectives creates an incentive for them to find an alternative route to the same goal.

Financial innovations are generally introduced by larger and more aggressive banks, and then are successively adopted by other banks until regulators eventually intervene. The nature and timing of this intervention are in turn influenced by interactions among the institutions that make up the bank regulatory system and that are ultimately responsible to Congress, which makes the laws.[2]

The last four decades have provided ample evidence of how banks attempt to circumvent regulations. In general, they either develop

Reprinted from Federal Reserve Bank of Cleveland *Economic Commentary*, February 15, 1996.

PART III Financial Institutions

new financial products or change their organization structure. Banks avoided deposit-rate ceilings by making implicit interest payments (for example, they offered gifts to depositors when market interest rates rose above the regulatory ceiling). They attempted to overcome the prohibition on interstate branching by creating bank holding companies (BHCs) with banks in multiple states. And they circumvented the Glass-Steagall Act by developing new financial products, like MID (market-indexed deposit) accounts.

The first half of this *Economic Commentary* presents a brief review of the interactions among banks and regulators as banks attempted to expand their activities across state lines. The second half discusses whether any lessons from those interactions can be applied to the ongoing debate over reforming the Glass-Steagall Act.

INTERSTATE BANKING AND THE REGULATORY DIALECTIC

Banks' efforts to circumvent the regulations that prohibit interstate banking—and regulators' subsequent reactions—are a classic example of the regulatory dialectic. Since the 1950s, banks have tried to exploit the loopholes in these regulations by changing their organizational structure or by altering their portfolio of activities. Regulators, on the other hand, have adjusted the regulations in reaction to each innovation.

Branching conditions for state banks (those chartered by states) have always been a matter of state discretion. Passage of the McFadden Act in 1927, and its amendment in 1933, gave national banks (chartered by the Comptroller of the Currency) branching capabilities identical to those of state banks. But because no states allowed interstate branching for state banks, the McFadden Act effectively imposed the same restriction on national banks.[3]

During the two decades following passage of the McFadden Act, banks seemed to lack the incentive (or the means) to profitably circumvent the prohibition on interstate branching. That changed in the 1950s, perhaps because of a perceived increase in economies of scale, additional competition from other U.S. financial institutions and foreign banks, and improvements in technology, all of which encouraged banks to find profitable ways around the branching prohibition.

Bankers first attempted to overcome the interstate branching restrictions by developing multibank holding companies with banks located in various states. Once lawmakers recognized bankers' intent, they responded with the Douglas Amendment to the Bank Holding Company Act, which prohibited BHCs from acquiring banks in other states without the home state's authorization. This provision, passed in 1956, effectively stopped the interstate banking movement, because no states permitted out-of-state acquisitions.

Banks' next step was to expand their activities across state lines by forming one-bank holding companies. These were parent corporations that owned a single bank plus other nonbank subsidiaries (such as mortgage companies and finance companies), which could be located in one or more states. This organizational structure allowed banks to circumvent the Bank Holding Company Act, which defined BHCs as corporations that controlled two or more banks. Again, Congress stepped in and closed this loophole in 1970 by revising the Act to cover one-bank holding companies.

The government's actions did not stop banks from further attempts to engage in interstate banking. The 1970 amendment to the Bank Holding Company Act defined a bank as any firm that accepted demand deposits *and* made commercial loans. The industry's answer was to develop "nonbank" banks—institutions that offered only one of these services. Some nonbanks chose to offer money market deposit accounts instead of transaction deposits. Others continued to offer transaction deposits, but restricted the extension of credit to the purchase of money market instruments, like commercial paper, or to consumer credit. Not surprisingly, Congress went into action again, closing this loophole in 1987 by redefining a bank as any institution that had deposit insurance or that offered demand or transaction deposits and engaged in commercial lending.

Banks' continuing attempts to expand their services across state lines finally met with some success in the early 1980s, when the regulatory barriers to interstate banking began to be dismantled. The first step in this movement was taken by a few states that began permitting out-of-state BHCs to acquire home-state banks. Since then, every state except Hawaii has passed legislation allowing either nationwide entry (with or without reciprocity) or regional entry (with reciprocity). However, interstate branching was still forbidden to most banks because states generally did not allow acquired banks to be converted into branches, and only a few states permitted entrance through a de novo branch.[4]

Another important development came in 1994, when Congress passed the Interstate Banking and Branching Efficiency Act. This legislation defined nationwide standards for BHCs' acquisition of a bank in any state, implying that state laws governing out-of-state acquisitions were no longer applicable. Furthermore, beginning on June 1, 1997, BHCs will be allowed to convert their bank subsidiaries into a single network of branches, provided that their home states have not enacted legislation opting out of the Act's branching provision.[5]

This latest regulatory change, though welcome among the nation's bankers, has left intact one potentially important barrier to the development of a full nationwide banking system: It does not provide for de novo branching across state lines. That is, in a state where a bank has no branches, it can set up a new branch only if the host state has passed legislation specifically allowing for de novo branching.

LESSONS FROM THE MOVEMENT TO INTERSTATE BANKING

The regulatory back and forth described here has been—and will continue to be—costly. Besides the resources involved in

PART III Financial Institutions

developing innovations and enacting legislation to prohibit them, further costs will be incurred once the regulatory barriers that inspired these innovations have been repealed. The reason is that some of these innovations will become inefficient.

For example, as a result of last year's regulatory change allowing interstate branching, most of the BHCs that were specifically created to undertake interstate banking will convert their organization structure into a network of branches. This setup avoids the need to maintain separate banks with separate boards of directors and reduces the cost of complying with other existing regulations, like capital requirements. The conversion will improve the efficiency of the financial system, but its costs would not have been incurred if such BHCs—a product of the regulatory dialectic—had not been developed in the first place.

As the history of the movement to interstate banking shows, the cost-benefit analysis of a regulation is incomplete unless it considers the cost of the regulatory cat-and-mouse game it might engender. This is a timely issue given the ongoing debate over reforming the Glass-Steagall Act. Its importance is further enhanced by the continuous increase in financial market competition and the constant progress in information technology, which together make innovation easier and more attractive.

REFORMING THE GLASS-STEAGALL ACT

Following the 1929 stock market crash, the U.S. economy went into recession and a large number of banks failed. In 1931, the Pecora Commission was established to study the causes of the crash. Its conclusions pointed to banks' securities activities as a major reason that many institutions had to close their doors—a view disputed by recent research.[6]

Partly because of the Commission's findings, in 1933 Congress passed the Glass-Steagall Act, which forced the separation of commercial banking (accepting deposits and making loans) from investment banking (underwriting, issuing, and distributing stocks, bonds, and other securities).

Between the enactment of Glass-Steagall and the beginning of the 1960s, both commercial banks and securities firms seemed to lack the incentive (or the ability) to explore some of the gray areas of that Act. Commercial banks, for example, limited themselves to the few securities activities left open to them, namely, trading and underwriting U.S. Treasury securities and municipal general obligation bonds, and participating in private placements of corporate securities.[7] Since then, however, commercial banks and securities firms have attempted to expand their activities into one another's historical strongholds. This movement has engendered many interactions among these institutions, their regulators, and the courts. For instance, the growing outflow of certain deposits from banks and the rapid increase in mutual fund investment gave commercial banks a strong incentive to enter this line of business. But there was a hitch: The Glass-Steagall Act had been interpreted as prohibiting commercial banks from underwriting and distributing mutual funds.

Bankers found a way around this restriction by entering into joint-venture-type agreements with investment companies in order to create mutual funds that were bought and sold by these companies, but managed and advertised by the banks. More recently, some banks have introduced MID accounts as another way of circumventing the restriction on their mutual-fund activities. MIDs are fixed-term deposits whose return is one part guaranteed and one part connected to the Standard & Poor's 500 stock index. Being treated as a deposit, the principal plus the guaranteed interest are insured up to $100,000 by the Federal Deposit Insurance Corporation. This resembles an indexed stock mutual fund with two exceptions: First, MIDs have a fixed maturity. Second, the price the investor pays for a minimum guaranteed return is that the account receives only a partial gain when the stock index rises.

Commercial banks' successive attempts to enter the securities business led to a certain amount of deregulation. Using a more flexible interpretation of the Glass-Steagall Act, regulators began allowing banks to undertake some additional investment banking activities, such as discount brokerage services and the underwriting of commercial paper, municipal revenue bonds, and, more recently, corporate bonds and equities. Some important conditions were attached to this permission, however. For instance, most of these activities had to be undertaken by an independent affiliate of the BHC, and their collective revenue could not exceed 10 percent of the affiliate's total revenue.

The proposal under discussion in the House of Representatives to reform the Glass-Steagall Act continues the deregulatory path initiated in the 1980s. If implemented in its current form, it would end some of the actual investment banking restrictions faced by commercial banks. However, some bankers have opined that the deregulation does not go far enough. At stake are the exclusion of certain businesses (such as insurance) from the set of activities that banks would be allowed to undertake, and, to a lesser extent, the degree of choice regarding the organizational structure that banks could adopt if they chose to enter the investment banking business.

Given the incentives already expressed by the nation's bankers, and the continuous technological progress that drives the development of financial innovations, it would seem sensible for Congress to evaluate whether the benefits from certain provisions of the proposed regulation are worth the costs of another round of the regulatory dialectic that might ensue.

CONCLUSION

Deposit-rate ceilings were implemented to restrict banks' competition for deposits, so banks turned to implicit interest payments. The prohibition on interstate banking was introduced to protect small local banks and to limit banks' growth, so banks changed their organization structure and adjusted the set of activities they undertook. Investment banking was closed to commercial banks because of potential conflicts of interest with their lending activity and its perceived risks, so banks entered into joint-venture-type agreements and developed new financial instruments.

Each of these cases demonstrates bankers' ability to innovate when regulations prevent them from exploring potentially profitable opportunities. However, these innovations are costly to develop, and they often become inefficient once the regulation that drove them is repealed.

A regulation that on its surface may contribute to the banking system's efficiency and stability can also harbor hidden costs and perverse outcomes if it fails to factor in banks' incentives and reactions. This issue is particularly timely because of the ongoing debate over reforming the Glass-Steagall Act. When the original legislation was enacted in 1933, it had a limited impact on commercial banks because investment banking was a relatively small business. The situation is now very different. Investment banking, as well as the competition, are far more important, and banks' ability to innovate has improved considerably.

Given the history of the regulations discussed here, it would seem prudent for lawmakers to consider banks' incentives when hammering out the final provisions of the reform bill. Otherwise, we should not be surprised to see banks challenging the new regulation with yet another round of cat and mouse.

ENDNOTES

1. See Edward J. Kane, "Accelerating Inflation, Technological Innovation, and the Decreasing Effectiveness of Banking Regulation," *Journal of Finance*, vol. 36, no. 2 (May 1981), pp. 355-67.
2. The bank regulatory system includes the Comptroller of the Currency, the Federal Reserve System, and the Federal Deposit Insurance Corporation, among others. This *Economic Commentary* refers to the regulatory system as a whole, and not to any particular institution.
3. The fundamental reasons why the interstate branching prohibitions were introduced remain unclear. Some believe that these restrictions were intended to protect small local banks from competition with out-of-state banks, while others point to the public's distrust of large banks.
4. See Donald T. Savage, "Interstate Banking: A Status Report," *Federal Reserve bulletin*, vol. 79, no. 2 (December 1993), pp. 1075-89.
5. As of December 1995, only Texas had opted out of the branching provision, while 25 other states had opted in. Of the latter group, only eight have opted into the de novo branching provision.
6. For a critique of the Pecora Commission's conclusions, see George J. Benston, *The Separation of Commercial and Investment Banking: The Glass-Steagall Act Revisited and Reconsidered*, New York: Oxford University Press, 1990.
7. See, for example, Larry r. Mote and George G. Kaufman, "Securities Activities of Commercial Banks: The Current Economic and Legal Environment," *Research in Financial Services*, vol. 1, Greenwich, Conn.: JAI Press, Inc. 1989, pp. 223-62.

READING 20   Glass-Steagall and the Regulatory Dialectic

QUESTIONS

1. What is the "regulatory dialectic"? How does interaction among banking regulations, technology, and bank incentives regarding interstate banking illustrate this dialectical process?

2. What are the provisions of the Glass-Steagall Act? When and why was it passed?

3. How and why have banks attempted to circumvent Glass-Steagall limits on their behavior?

4. Why is the regulatory dialectic costly to society?

PART FOUR

THE MONEY SUPPLY PROCESS

The complete money supply model developed in Part Four of the text helps students identify an assortment of factors which influence the money supply and cause it to change. One of those factors is currency in circulation. Reading 21, **"Where Is All the U.S. Currency Hiding?"** by John B. Carlson and Benjamin D. Keen, focuses on currency held outside the U.S., examining why foreigners hold U.S. dollars and how their holdings affect economic policy. This reading supplements Chapter 17's discussion of depositor behavior and the money supply model.

READING 21

Where Is All the U.S. Currency Hiding?

John B. Carlson and Benjamin D. Keen

The total amount of U.S. currency held by the nonbank public equals about $375 billion, or nearly $1,400 for every man, woman, and child in the country. Clearly, few individuals ever hold this much cash at any point in time. On the surface, the sheer volume of currency outstanding seems inconsistent with common sense. Even if one considers currency balances held by businesses involved largely in cash transactions—like retailers—and by participants in the underground economy—like drug dealers—it is hard to reconcile the difference between households' holdings and total currency outstanding. So where is this currency hiding?

Recent evidence suggests that a growing proportion of U.S. currency is held outside the country by individuals who are uncertain about their own currency's future value. To these people, the dollar is a refuge during times of political and economic uncertainty. Knowing precisely how much currency is held outside the United States, however, is no simple matter. Unlike checking accounts, currency flows do not leave a paper trail. However, informal reports to the Federal Reserve and the U.S. Customs Department regarding currency flows abroad do provide a rough indication of foreign demand.

Having some idea about the magnitude of overseas holdings is important for several reasons. First, if the demand for currency is becoming driven largely by foreign portfolio decisions, then fluctuations in the level of currency outstanding may have little to do with domestic economic activity. Second, movements in the narrow monetary aggregates—of which currency is a sizable component—will not provide the same information as they have historically. Third, to the extent that foreigners demand currency, which is non-interest-bearing debt, the U.S. Treasury's need to issue an interest-bearing alternative is reduced.

To address these issues, we will examine why individuals hold currency and why the U.S. dollar is so popular abroad. We will also discuss some recent research on the share of currency held abroad and look at the implications for policy.

WHY DO PEOPLE HOLD CURRENCY?

For most Americans, the answer to this question is simple: to make payments when

Reprinted from Federal Reserve Bank of Cleveland, *Economic Commentary*, April 15, 1996.

PART IV The Money Supply Process

neither checks nor credit cards are convenient or accepted. The U.S. dollar has the textbook qualities often used to define money. That is, it is both a unit of account and a medium of exchange. Although stories about currency stashed under the mattress occasionally come to light, most Americans choose to hold cash only for transaction purposes. Since it bears no interest, there is little incentive to hold currency when no transactions are anticipated.

Textbooks also identify "store of value" as a quality of money. This characteristic, however, applies to many nonmonetary assets as well. During inflationary periods, houses are often considered good stores of value. Gold, rare art, coins, and stamps can also serve this purpose.

The dollar, on the other hand, has some characteristics that make it preferable to other stores of value. First, it is both compact and portable. One can barely move a house across town, let alone abroad. Even carrying gold can be cumbersome. Second, currency affords anonymity not offered by, say, ownership of a Van Gogh. Third, the U.S. dollar is liquid in many parts of the world. That is, it is easily converted to spendable forms with no (or minimal) transactions costs and little risk of capital loss. And finally, unlike most real property, currency is divisible. If the denomination of a bill is larger than the price of an exchange, then change can be made.

WHY DO FOREIGNERS HOLD U.S. CURRENCY?

In contrast to domestic demand, foreign demand for the U.S. dollar owes more to the store-of-value quality of money. The dollar is preferred to many other currencies because it is a relatively stable source of purchasing power, widely accepted, and reasonably secure from counterfeiting. Another appealing feature is that unlike some other currencies, which may be recalled with little notice or limited opportunities for exchange, Federal Reserve Notes are ultimately exchangeable at full face value, regardless of when they were issued. Moreover, because shipments of less than $10,000 do not have to be reported, U.S. currency maintains a degree of anonymity for its holder.

These favorable features of the U.S. dollar ultimately reflect the political and economic stability we enjoy. For countries whose political situation is uncertain, the dollar offers a form of wealth that may be put in a suitcase and carried should a resident need to flee. Political instability is often associated with economic turmoil and a debasing of a country's currency. Despite the episodes of double-digit inflation in the 1970s and early 1980s, the United States has never experienced a hyperinflation.

TRENDS IN FOREIGN HOLDINGS OF U.S. CURRENCY

Foreign demand for the U.S. dollar is particularly strong in certain parts of the world. In Liberia and Panama, the dollar is the official currency. Large amounts of currency are known to be circulating in Central and South America, especially in Argentina, where it is often used to settle real estate and auto transactions. The dollar is also very popular in Eastern Europe, especially in the former Soviet Union, where inflation, declining exchange rates, and currency recalls have made the ruble a poor store of value. U.S. military personnel stationed overseas and many international travelers likewise rely on the dollar.

Measuring the *flow* of U.S. currency abroad is extremely difficult. Cash is often sent in the mail, and, as mentioned above, individual shipments of up to $10,000 do not have to be reported to the Customs Department. Customs does keep records of shipments above $10,000, however, and these provide some information on currency flows abroad. Another major source of data is found in the informal reports that commercial banks submit to the Federal Reserve regarding their overseas currency shipments. These reports suggest that sine 1988, about half of all U.S. currency sent overseas has gone to Europe (Russia is the most likely destination), 30 percent has gone to the Middle East and Far East, and around 20 percent has gone to Central and South America, with a fair amount of that ending up in Argentina.[1]

Determining the total *stock* of currency held abroad is even more difficult. In fact, the only available data are shipment numbers from informal reports to the Customs Department and the Federal Reserve. Currently, many analysts believe that a substantial portion of all U.S. currency is held overseas.

Researchers at the Federal Reserve Board have examined this issue in depth. A preliminary study conducted in 1993 estimated that more than 70 percent of all U.S. currency is held outside our borders, with most of the outflows occurring since 1970.[2] Recently, a broader examination set that figure at between 50 and 70 percent, with about 80 percent of all currency growth since 1980 tied to increased foreign demand.[3]

Figure 1 illustrates two estimates of the level of currency held abroad. Both are based on statistical approaches that exploit the similarity between seasonal fluctuations in the domestic demands for U.S. and Canadian currency.[4] Because the seasonal factor in currency for both countries is largely driven by similar season fluctuations in retail sales, one approach adjusts for differences in the seasonality of retail sales between the two countries.

SOME RECENT ISSUES

The strong international demand for the dollar inevitably makes it a target for would-be counterfeiters. Although the current design of U.S. currency is sufficient to prevent mass counterfeiting, photocopying technology may soon reach the point where nearly perfect copies can be easily produced. The Treasury anticipated this potential problem in 1983 and began working on a plan to redesign the currency. Even though Treasury officials believe that the amount of counterfeit currency in circulation is minimal, recent rumors of an

PART IV The Money Supply Process

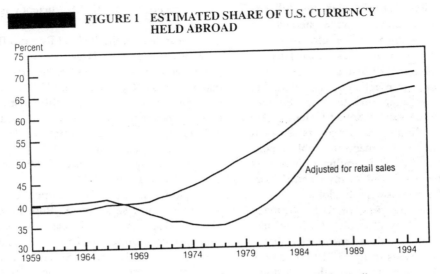

FIGURE 1 ESTIMATED SHARE OF U.S. CURRENCY HELD ABROAD

SOURCE: Richard D. Porter and Ruth A. Judson, "The Location of U.S. Currency" (footnote 1).

almost-perfect counterfeit produced in the Middle East—the so-called *supernote*—gave added incentive to the redesign effort.[5]

Because most foreigners prefer to hold $100 bills and most counterfeits are found overseas, the Treasury decided to redesign that note first and set a release date of March 1996. To avoid disturbing foreign economies and to protect the special anonymity feature of the dollar, officials announced that the old currency would not be recalled and would always be accepted at 100 percent of face value. To spread the word, the department is spending millions of dollars on advertising and on setting up toll-free hot lines around the world. Nevertheless, promises about cash are often viewed with deep suspicion by foreigners who have watched their own currencies become virtually worthless.

In early 1995, as news of the soon-to-be released $100 bill spread abroad, currency growth plummeted, from about 8.5 percent over the last two decades to about 3 percent in 1995. (see figure 2). Many analysts believe that this slowdown largely reflected foreign holders' concerns about the new currency. Moreover, now that the redesigned note has been released, currency growth is expected to accelerate to near previous levels. Preliminary data since the March introduction reveal no sharp rise in the currency numbers, but it must be stressed that this information is very limited (see figure 3). Only time will tell if the currency growth rate will return to a level more consistent with its previous trend.

READING 21 Where Is All the U.S. Currency Hiding?

FIGURE 2   U.S. CURRENCY GROWTH

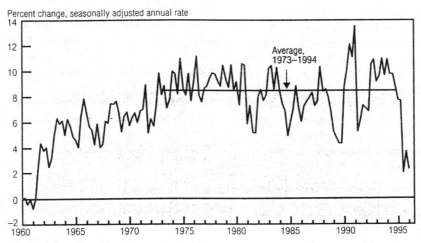

SOURCE: Board of Governors of the Federal Reserve System.

FIGURE 3   U.S. CURRENCY LEVELS

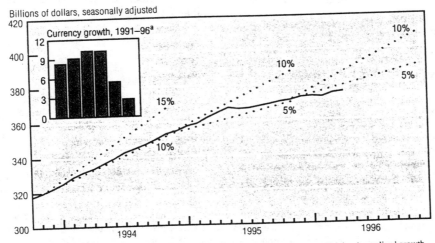

a. Growth rates are percentage rates calculated on a fourth-quarter over fourth-quarter basis. Annualized growth rate for 1996 is calculated on an April over 1995:IVQ basis.
NOTE: Dotted lines represent growth ranges and are for reference only.
SOURCE: Board of Governors of the Federal Reserve System.

PART IV The Money Supply Process

POLICY IMPLICATIONS

Large swings in overseas holdings of U.S. currency typically have little impact on the current level of domestic economic activity. Rather, such movements distort the historical relationship between currency and the economy, making currency a less reliable indicator. Although the level of currency has never received much attention in policy analysis, it is a substantial component of the monetary base (about seven-eights currency) and of M1 (about one-third currency), which are watched closely by some analysts.

Events such as the introduction of the new $100 bill can thus create misleading signals in the narrow money measures, making them less reliable for policy purposes. For example, the slowdown in currency growth in early 1995 accentuated the decline in both the monetary base and M1.[6] Because the currency slowdown most likely reflects reduced foreign demand, it seems doubtful that deceleration in the narrow money measures portends a weakening economy, as it might have in years past. Moreover, foreign demand tends to be induced by unpredictable events. To the extent that U.S. currency is becoming increasingly subject to the vagaries of foreign demand, the use of narrow money measures as guides for policy will prove problematic.

Another important implication concerns the federal budget, U.S. currency pays no interest, yet is ultimately a debt of the federal government. Essentially, it is an interest-free loan. The greater the level of currency outstanding, the less the level of interest-bearing debt outstanding and hence the smaller the interest bill of the U.S. Treasury. This implicit yield of currency—known as seigniorage—reduces the annual tax bill by between $15 and $20 billion. To the extent that foreign demand for the dollar increases, the tax burden of U.S. citizens is further lightened.

ENDNOTES

1. See Richard D. Porter and Ruth A. Judson, "The Location of U.S. Currency: How Much Is Abroad?" Board of Governors of the Federal Reserve System, manuscript, June 1995.
2. See Richard D. Porter, "Estimates of Foreign Holdings of Currency—An Approach Based on Relative Cross-Country Seasonal Variations," Board of Governors of the Federal Reserve System, manuscript, September 1993.
3. See Porter and Judson, "The Location of U.S. Currency" (footnote 1).
4. Essentially, both approaches assume that foreign demand for Canadian currency is negligible and that the foreign-held component of U.S. currency has no seasonal pattern. Hence, the difference between the seasonal factors in total demand for U.S. currency and Canadian currency largely reflects foreign demand for U.S. currency.
5. According to the U.S. General Accounting Office, "the total level of counterfeit-currency detections—$208.7 million in fiscal year 1994—represented less than one one-thousandth of U.S. currency in circulation." See *Counterfeit U.S. Currency Abroad: Issues and U.S. Deterrence Efforts*, Washington, D.C.: GAO, February 1996, p. 2.
6. The implementation of sweep accounts has also tended to dampen the growth of both of these aggregates relative to economic activity.

READING 21 Where Is All the U.S. Currency Hiding?

QUESTIONS

1. How does currency perform the classic textbook functions of money? What advantages does currency have over other assets in performing these functions?

2. Why do foreigners hold U.S. dollars rather than their own or other currencies?

3. How does an increase in the currency to checkable deposit ratio affect the U.S. money multiplier and money supply? Given this, how should foreign holdings of U.S. dollars affect the U.S. money supply?

PART FIVE

THE FEDERAL RESERVE SYSTEM AND THE CONDUCT OF MONETARY POLICY

As the nation's central bank, the Fed plays a major role in determining the money supply. The Fed conducts monetary policy in the midst of on-going public debate over how much independence it should have, what policy objectives it should pursue, and what economic indicators it should monitor. International considerations can also influence monetary policy. These issues are treated in the readings for Part Five.

Reading 22, **"Why Central Bank Independence Helps to Mitigate Inflationary Bias"** by Timothy Cogley, describes the effects of unexpected inflation on debtors and creditors. Cogley argues that unchecked factional politics leads to high inflation because of debtors' numerical superiority. An independent central bank publicly commits monetary authorities to a low-inflation policy. This reading is suggested for use with Chapter 18's discussion of Federal Reserve structure and independence; it could be used also with Chapter 30's treatment of policy credibility.

"The Natural Rate and Inflationary Pressures" by Stuart E. Weiner is Reading 23. Weiner presents a good introduction to the natural rate of unemployment and the implications the relationship between the natural rate and increases in inflation holds for policymakers. The reading will help students better understand the Fed's monetary policy stance over the past two years and can be used with Chapter 21 in discussing the Fed's policy framework or with Chapter 26 in covering the role of the natural rate and long-run equilibrium in the aggregate demand-aggregate supply model.

Reading 24, **"Primer on Monetary Policy I: Goals and Instruments,"** and Reading 25, **"Primer on Monetary Policy II: Targets and Indicators,"** are both by Carl E. Walsh. These readings give an overview of several important issues in the implementation of monetary policy, supplementing Chapter 21's discussion of these topics.

Reading 26 is **"U.S. Foreign Exchange Operations"** by Kristina Jacobson. Jacobson describes how the goals and methods of U.S. foreign exchange operations have evolved under the Bretton Woods fixed exchange rate system and, since 1973, under the floating exchange rate system. Her detailed look at foreign exchange operations can be used with Chapter 22's coverage of the evolution of the international financial system.

READING 22

Why Central Bank Independence Helps to Mitigate Inflationary Bias

Timothy Cogley

The President and Congress are directly responsible for fiscal policy, but Congress has chosen (through the Federal Reserve Act) to delegate authority for monetary policy to the Federal Reserve System. Furthermore, it has granted the Federal Reserve a substantial degree of independence. Decisions about monetary policy are made by the Federal Open Market Committee (FOMC), which consists of 7 Governors, who are appointed by the President and confirmed by Congress, and 12 regional bank Presidents, who are chosen jointly by the Federal Reserve Board and the boards of the regional banks. On a short-term basis, FOMC decisions are largely independent of direct input from the President or Congress. And since members of the FOMC serve long terms and do not stand for election, they are largely insulated from the political process.

Why did the founders of the Federal Reserve choose to insulate the central bank in this manner? One possibility is that they were concerned that there would be an inflationary bias if monetary policy were too strongly influenced by elected officials. The empirical evidence suggests that this concern is warranted: across countries, there appears to be an inverse relation between average inflation and the degree of central bank independence (for example, see Alesina 1988 and Grilli, Masciandaro, and Tabellini 1991). But what is it about the political process that tends to create an inflationary bias? A recent paper by Jon Faust (1996) provides an intriguing answer, and this *Weekly Letter* discusses his arguments.

AN ANALOGY WITH THE SUPREME COURT

In most circumstances, our system of government favors the rule of simple majorities as a way to decentralize political power, but this preference is far from universal. There are any number of examples in which governmental decisions are insulated to a greater or lesser extent from the rule of simple majorities. The best example is the U.S. Supreme Court. Like the Federal Reserve Board, Supreme Court Justices are nominated by the President and confirmed by Congress but do not stand for election. They

Reprinted from Federal Reserve Bank of San Francisco *Weekly Letter*, no. 96-08, February 23, 1996 serve life terms, and they can't be fired for rendering unpopular decisions. Hence, in the short run, the Supreme Court is largely insulated from the will of the electorate.

The rationale for having an independent Supreme Court is a belief that majority rule may sometimes produce undesirable outcomes. For example, in times of crisis, a majority of voters might be persuaded to temporarily suspend certain fundamental rights, such as that of free speech or assembly. While such an action might appear to be expedient, it might prove to be difficult to reverse once the crisis has passed. Once rights are suspended, they may be difficult to restore. There is also a moral hazard problem: some factions in society might provoke a crisis in order to undermine public support for basic rights. An independent Supreme Court limits the power of transient majorities to alter certain fundamental aspects of our political system and thus contributes to its long-term stability.

In the language of Alexis de Tocqueville (1969), an independent Supreme Court helps to protect against the "tyranny of the majority." Can the same be said for an independent central bank? Faust argues that it can.

UNEXPECTED INFLATION TRANSFERS WEALTH FROM CREDITORS TO DEBTORS

The first step in his argument concerns the effects of unexpected inflation on the distribution of wealth. In the United States, most debt contracts are written in nominal terms. A creditor agrees to lend a sum of money at a given nominal interest rate for a given period of time, and the borrower agrees to repay the principal plus interest at maturity. The interest payment consists of two components. First, borrowers must pay something in order to persuade lenders to part with their capital for the term of the loan. Second, inflation erodes the real value of the principal during the term of the loan, and borrowers must compensate lenders for this loss. Since the nominal interest rate is typically set at the beginning of the loan, the compensation for the erosion of purchasing power must reflect expected inflation, rather than actual inflation.

These two components are reflected in the Fisher equation, which states that the nominal interest rate is equal to the real interest rate (payment for use of capital) plus the expected inflation rate (compensation for the erosion of purchasing power).

If expectations turn out to be correct, then the inflation compensation that was agreed upon at the beginning of the loan exactly makes up for the erosion in purchasing power during the life of the contract. If actual inflation turns out to be higher than expected, the inflation compensation turns out too small. Since the creditor is only partially compensated for the erosion of purchasing power, the debtor gains at his expense. On the other hand, if actual inflation turns out to be lower than expected, the inflation compensation more than offsets the erosion of purchasing power, and the lender gains at the expense of the borrower. Thus, unexpected inflation transfers wealth between creditors and debtors. Debtors gain when inflation is unexpectedly high, and creditors gain when it is unexpectedly low.

SETTING MONETARY POLICY BY MAJORITY RULE

Now imagine what would happen if monetary policy were set by majority vote. Once loans are made, creditors would have a short-term incentive to vote for policies which would deliver an inflation rate that is lower than the one implicit in the debt contract, because this would redistribute wealth in their favor. Similarly, debtors would have a short-term incentive to vote for policies which would generate an inflation rate that is higher than the one implicit in the debt contract, because this would redistribute wealth in their favor. If monetary policy were set by majority vote, the more numerous faction would prevail.

This raises the question, "are debtors or creditors more numerous?" Direct evidence on this question is hard to come by, but two observations suggest that debtors may be more numerous. One follows from typical life-cycle spending patterns and the fact that the population grows over time. Early in life, people tend to borrow to invest in education, to smooth consumption between low income periods in their youth and higher income periods later in life, and to buy houses and other durable consumption goods. As people age, they pay off these debts and accumulate wealth for retirement. Thus, younger people are more likely to be debtors and older people more likely to be creditors. With population growth, there are more young people than old, and this suggests that debtors may be more numerous.

This life-cycle consideration is reinforced by the form in which many people finance their housing purchases. When people take out a mortgage, they acquire a real asset (land and a house) and a nominal debt (the mortgage). Like other fixed income securities, a fixed-rate mortgage incorporates a premium for expected inflation. Since this debt is nominal, its real value falls if inflation turns out to be higher than expected. Adjustable rate mortgages also tend to fall in real value when there is an unexpected increase in inflation, because they usually contain annual and lifetime caps on the nominal mortgage rate. These caps become especially important when there are big changes in inflation. On the other side of the balance sheet, households hold land and houses. Since these are real assets, their real (or inflation-adjusted) value is much less sensitive to unexpected changes in inflation. Thus, households who hold nominal debts and real assets would also benefit from monetary policies which generate surprisingly high inflation.

If debtors are more numerous than creditors, a majority of voters would have a short-term incentive to vote for policies which generate an unexpected increase in inflation. But over a long period of time, inflation cannot be higher than expected on average. Creditors are not fools. They would build this knowledge of voting patterns into their inflation forecasts and mark up the Fisher premium accordingly. Inflation would sometimes turn out to be higher than expected and sometimes lower, but on average the majority faction would not be able to use monetary policy to redistribute wealth. Systematic attempts to do so would just raise the average rate of inflation.

Moreover, although the majority would prefer low average inflation, they would not be able to achieve it. When seeking new loans, borrowers would like to promise to vote for low inflation, but once the contract is signed they would be free to vote as they please and would again have a short-term incentive to vote for high inflation. Creditors would see through this and give their promise little weight. They would insist upon a big Fisher premium to compensate for high expected inflation, and borrowers would support a high inflation policy in order to reduce the real value of the nominal interest rate, thus confirming creditors' expectations of high inflations. Setting monetary policy by majority vote generates an inflationary bias which makes everyone worse off. In particular, the majority is worse off because they suffer the costs of higher inflation without achieving any redistribution.

If everyone prefers low average inflation, why can't the electorate or the legislature solve the problem by giving the central bank explicit instructions in the form of official low-inflation targets? Creditors and debtors both have a long-term incentive to support low inflation, so both groups would presumably support such a plan. But how would these targets be enforced? Once debt contracts are signed, borrowers would have a short-term incentive to support an "exception" to the low inflation target in order to redistribute wealth in their favor. Hence the majority's support for low inflation would not be consistent over time. Their short-term interests for redistribution would undermine their long-term interests for low average inflation.

DELEGATING MONETARY POLICY TO AN INDEPENDENT COMMITTEE

The majority needs to find a way to commit to a low-inflation policy. One way to do so is to delegate authority to an independent committee and then let them make decisions about monetary policy. In effect, this makes it more difficult for the majority to change its mind. To achieve this independence, it may be important to insulate the central bank from the electorate and their representatives, so that they cannot easily punish central bankers for rendering decisions that are unpopular in the short run.

While central bank independence is important, it is not sufficient to solve this inflationary bias. The composition of the committee is also important. For example, if this committee were simply a microcosm of the general population, then majority voting within the committee would just replicate the inflationary bias in the general population. Thus, it may also be important to choose committee members so as to balance the forces for and against inflation. To achieve this balance, it may be necessary for the anti-inflation forces to be overly represented relative to their proportion in the general population.

READING 22 Why Central Bank Independence Helps to Mitigate Inflationary Bias

CONCLUSION

Unexpected inflation redistributes wealth from nominal creditors to nominal debtors. If debtors are more numerous than creditors, majorities may often favor monetary policy actions that generate unexpected inflation. But since monetary policy can't systematically generate surprisingly high rates of inflation, attempts to use it to redistribute wealth would just raise the average inflation rate without achieving the intended redistribution. In the end, policy by majority may lead to outcomes that are inferior even for the majority, and insulating monetary policy makers from the electorate may produce superior outcomes.

REFERENCES

Alesina, Alberto. 1988. "Macroeconomics and Politics." In *NBER Macroeconomics Annual*, Stanley Fischer, ed. Cambridge, MA: MIT Press.
Faust, Jon. 1996. "Whom Can We Trust to Run the Fed? Theoretical Support for the Founders' Views." *Journal of Monetary Economics* (forthcoming).
Grilli, Vittorio, Donato Masciandaro, and Guido Tabellini. 1991. "Political and Monetary Institutions and Public Financial Policies in the Industrial Countries." *Economic Policy* 13, pp. 341-392.
Tocqueville, Alexis de. 1969. *Democracy in America*. Garden City, NY: Doubleday.

QUESTIONS

1. Is the independence of the Supreme Court desirable? Why? Is an independent Federal Reserve equally desirable? Why?

2. What is the Fisher equation?

3. What arguments does Cogley make to support the view that debtors may outnumber creditors? Which of these groups prefers unexpectedly low inflation? Why?

4. According to Cogley, why does the U.S. have an independent central bank?

READING 23

The Natural Rate and Inflationary Pressures

Stuart E. Weiner

The natural rate of unemployment has become an important topic recently as the Federal Reserve has raised short-term interest rates in an attempt to keep the economy from overheating. The inflation outlook for the latter part of this year and next depends critically on how close the economy is to reaching capacity constraints. The natural rate of unemployment measures capacity constraints in labor markets.

BACKGROUND

The natural rate of unemployment is a key concept in monetary economics. It represents the lowest possible unemployment rate that is consistent with stable inflation. When the demand for workers is so strong that the actual unemployment rate falls below the natural rate, wage and price pressures intensify and inflation starts to rise.

The natural rate of unemployment cannot be observed but must be estimated. Chart 1 presents estimates of the natural rate for the years 1961 through 1994. To produce this series, a statistical technique was used that links inflation movements to unemployment movements. Also shown in the chart is the actual unemployment rate.

In looking at the chart, three features stand out. First, the actual unemployment rate has rarely equaled the natural unemployment rate. Second, the natural rate has remained at a relatively high level throughout the period. And third, after rising in the 1970s, the natural rate has drifted down a bit in the 1980s and 1990s.

The divergence of the actual and natural rates of unemployment is a reflection of the business cycle. In the chart, periods when the actual unemployment rate exceeds the natural unemployment rate are periods of recession or the early stages of recovery. Periods when the actual rate is below the natural rate are periods of a booming economy.

The relatively high level of the natural rate reflects imperfections in labor markets, imperfections that exist regardless of the overall state of the economy. Individuals unemployed at the natural rate may be unemployed for a variety of reasons. They may have the wrong skills, live in the wrong areas, or have little incentive to accept the jobs they are offered. Or, in an environment of expanding employer mandates, they may

Reprinted from Federal Reserve Bank of Kansas City *Economic Review*, Third Quarter 1994, 5-9.

READING 23 The Natural Rate and Inflationary Pressures

Chart 1
Unemployment

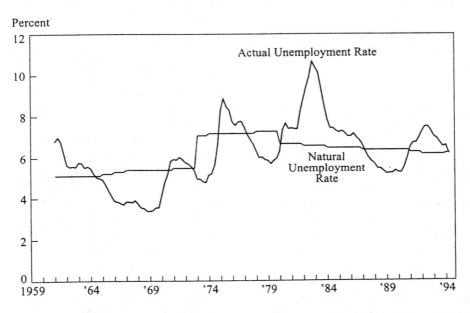

Sources: Actual unemployment rate: U.S. Department of Labor. Natural unemployment rate: Stuart E. Weiner, "New Estimates of the Natural Rate of Unemployment," Federal Reserve Bank of Kansas City *Economic Review,* 1993: Q4.

simply be too expensive for employers to hire. Whatever its many sources, unemployment at the natural rate is independent of cyclical factors and hence falls outside the domain of monetary policy.

The third feature that stands out in the chart, the change in the natural rate over time, reflects both demographic and structural forces. The natural rate rose in the 1970s in part because of the growing share of women and youths in the labor force. Because women and youths typically have higher unemployment rates than men, the overall unemployment rate consistent with stable inflation rose. Also contributing to the rise in the natural rate in the 1970s were the two oil shocks and the productivity decline, all of which increased the cost of labor to employers.

Since 1980, the natural rate has drifted down a bit on favorable demographic trends, the principal one being the sharp decline in the share of youths in the labor force. At the same time, however, structural forces have kept the natural rate high. These include the shift from manufacturing jobs to service jobs, the growing gap between high-tech job requirements and low-tech worker skills, and the downsizing and restructuring of firms throughout the economy. Thus, according to the estimates reported in the chart, the natural rate of unemployment is currently 6¼ percent. With the actual unemployment rate averaging 6.2 percent in the second quarter, this means that labor markets currently are operating at full capacity.

IMPLICATIONS

Historically, the gap between the actual unemployment rate and the natural unemployment rate has been a reliable indicator of future increases in inflation. This can be seen in Chart 2. The shaded areas represent periods of sustained rises in inflation, with beginning and ending inflation rates noted along the top edge. The "unemployment gap" is calculated from Chart 1 and equals the actual unemployment rate minus the natural unemployment rate. Thus, when the gap moves below the zero line, the actual unemployment rate is below the natural rate, and when the gap moves above the zero line, the actual unemployment rate is above the natural rate.

As shown by the shaded areas, the U.S. economy has experienced four periods of sustained increases in inflation over the past 35 years. In all four cases, the increases were accompanied by the actual unemployment rate. And at no time has there been a false signal; that is, at no time has the actual unemployment rate gone below the natural rate without the economy ultimately experiencing a rise in inflation.

The most recent inflationary episode began in 1987. In early 1987, the unemployment rate moved below the natural rate and stayed below the natural rate for four years. As a result, inflation began to edge upwards, from 3.8 percent to 5.5 percent, and it was not until early 1991 that it leveled off. A concern this year has been that the economy is facing a similar situation today. Or, to put it in terms of the chart, a concern has been that it might be necessary to draw in a fifth shaded area before too long.

In thinking about the policy implications of unemployment rate movements this year, several points need to be made.

The first involves the lead time between a move below the natural rate and the eventual increase in inflation. As can be seen in the chart, in three of the four inflationary episodes, the actual unemployment rate went below the natural rate in advance of the increase in inflation. Only in the most recent episode were the movements concurrent. Thus, there certainly is a precedent for the situation today, where the unemployment rate is at the natural rate but a general increase in inflationary pressures is not yet showing through. That is why relying on current inflation as an indicator of future inflation is dangerous, and why the Federal Reserve has taken timely policy action. Because of the inertia in the inflation process and the lags in the effect of policy, the Federal Reserve has needed to stay ahead of the curve if a rise in inflation is to be avoided.

A second point concerns the prospects for the natural rate itself. One could be less concerned about the inflation outlook if one believed the natural rate would be declining from its currently estimated 6¼ percent level. But there is little reason to think it is going to fall. On the demographics side, the share of

READING 23 The Natural Rate and Inflationary Pressures

Chart 2
Unemployment and Inflation

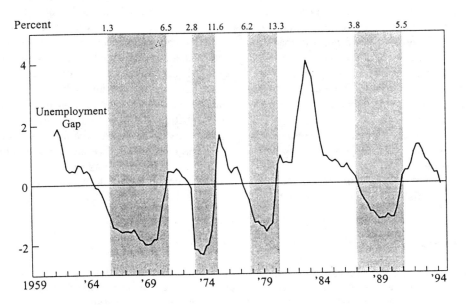

Notes: Shaded areas represent periods of rising inflation as measured by the consumer price index less food and energy; beginning and ending inflation rates are noted along the top edge. The unemployment gap is calculated by subtracting the natural rate of unemployment from the actual unemployment rate.

Sources: Actual unemployment rate and inflation: U.S. Department of Labor. Natural unemployment rate: Stuart E. Weiner, "New Estimates of the Natural Rate of Unemployment," Federal Reserve Bank of Kansas City *Economic Review*, 1993: Q4.

young workers is expected to stabilize and the share of minority workers is expected to rise. Both will keep the natural rate at a high level. Nor will structural forces be beneficial. Such factors as continued firm downsizing and continued skill mismatch will prevent the natural rate from declining. And in some instances structural forces will interact with demographic forces to exacerbate labor market problems. The U.S. Department of Labor, for example, has noted that while the fastest growing occupations in coming years will be those occupations that historically have required relatively higher levels of education, the composition of the labor force will be shifting toward groups that typically have attained lower levels of education.

Given the inherent difficulty of estimating the natural rate, it is possible that the natural rate is somewhat lower than 6¼ percent, and it is safer to think in terms of a range of estimates. However, a third point to make is that, even if the natural rate is as low as 6 percent, prior to the firming of policy earlier this year some private forecasters were looking for the actual unemployment rate to slip below this level by yearend. So a concern over potential inflationary pressures is not inextricably tied to any one specific estimate of the natural rate.

Finally, it should be emphasized that one need not be satisfied with an unemployment rate as high as 6¼ percent. On the contrary, unemployment this high represents a waste of resources, with substantial economic, social, and human costs. Rather, what the natural rate framework implies is that it is at this point that monetary policy can do no more. To further reduce unemployment, policymakers should be looking at potential labor market policies, such as improvements in education and job training programs and reductions in the cost of employer mandates.

The Federal Reserve has done about all it can to guide the economy to full employment. The challenge now is to ensure that inflation remains under control.

ENDNOTES

[1] A complicating factor this year has been the revisions to the Current Population Survey. With the January employment report, the U.S. Department of Labor started basing its unemployment rate calculations on a new questionnaire and new collection techniques. It was estimated that the new methodology would raise the measured unemployment rate by about one-half percentage point, and most analysts raised their estimates of the natural rate by an equal amount. To date, however, the differences between the new and old surveys have been less pronounced, and it now appears that a 0.5 adjustment factor may be too high. In this article, no adjustment factor is applied. Hence, the natural rate estimates used in this article are identical to those reported by the author in "New Estimates of the Natural Rate of Unemployment," Federal Reserve Bank of Kansas City, *Economic Review*, 1993:Q4.

READING 23 The Natural Rate and Inflationary Pressures

QUESTIONS

1. What is the natural rate of unemployment? What factors influenced its value during the 1970s and 1980s?

2. In early 1994 the Fed began raising short-term interest rates. What evidence does Weiner present that could be used to justify this policy?

3. Is the natural rate of unemployment likely to fall in the future? Why? Can monetary or other economic policies lower the natural rate? Explain.

READING 24

A Primer on Monetary Policy Part 1: Goals and Instruments

Carl E. Walsh

Recent interest rate increases have focused the public's attention on the conduct of monetary policy and the role of the Federal Reserve. In February, the Fed's policymaking body, the Federal Open Market Committee (FOMC), raised the federal funds rate a quarter of a percentage point, the first such increase since 1989. The FOMC voted again for two more 25 basis point increases in March and April, and at the May 17th meeting the federal funds rate was pushed up another half a percentage point.

These actions were designed to prevent inflation from rising above its current annual rate of under 3 percent. The interest rate hikes were consistent with the Fed's desire to move the economy gradually towards even lower rates of inflation in order to achieve price stability. Because these actions occurred before any actual increase in inflation, the FOMC's policy has generated wide debate among economists and in the popular press.

In order to grasp the issues at the heart of the recent debates, it is helpful to understand some of the elements involved in setting monetary policy. This *Weekly Letter* provides the first of a two-part primer designed to give an overview of issues in how monetary policy is conducted. Part one reviews the goals of monetary policy and the basic instruments the Fed can use to conduct policy. The next *Weekly Letter* will discuss the role of intermediate targets, indicators, rules and forecasts in the implementation of monetary policy.

THE GOALS OF MONETARY POLICY

In the lobby of the Federal Reserve Bank of San Francisco, visitors are exposed to the difficulties of implementing monetary policy through an electronic video game. The object is to time the release of a dart from a moving arm in order to hit the bulls-eye of a moving target. The moving bulls-eye reflects, in a graphic manner, the uncertainty that exists over the appropriate goals of monetary policy and the changing values of these goals as a result of developments both in the economy and in our understanding of the economy.

The "official" goals of monetary policy, enshrined in the Federal Reserve Act (Section 2A(1)), are to "promote . . . maximum employment, stable prices, and moderate long-

Reprinted from Federal Reserve Bank of San Francisco *Weekly Letter*, August 5, 1994.

READING 24 Monetary Policy: Goals and Instruments

term interest rates." If maximum employment is interpreted as that level of employment consistent with the numerical goals of 4 percent unemployment established by the Humphrey-Hawkins "Full Employment and Balanced Growth Act of 1978," then few economists believe it is possible to achieve all these goals at once in the U.S. economy.

The belief that 4 percent unemployment and stable prices are inconsistent is shaped by the widely accepted "natural rate hypothesis." It argues that the economy's average equilibrium unemployment rate, often called the natural rate of unemployment, is independent of monetary policy. Most current estimates of the natural rate place it in the range of 6 to 6½ percent. Taken together, these imply that the unemployment rate will tend to average around the 6 to 6½ percent range in the long run, regardless of the conduct of monetary policy.

What if the Federal Reserve tried to achieve 4 percent unemployment in the long run? *Consistent* attempts to expand the economy beyond its potential for production will result in higher inflation while ultimately failing to produce lower average unemployment. In fact, extreme rates of inflation (or deflation) may so disrupt the role of the price system in directing resources in a market economy that the result could be slower average growth *and* higher average unemployment. Although economists continue to debate whether reducing inflation from moderate to low rates would significantly improve the long-run performance of the economy, most believe that there are no long-term gains from consistently pursuing expansionary policies.

While the Fed has little effect on the natural rate of unemployment, the Fed can determine the economy's average rate of inflation. Thus, many recent commentators have emphasized the need to define the goals of monetary policy in terms of low or zero inflation, which *is* achievable. In 1989, Representative Neal (D, NC) actually introduced a bill in Congress that would have amended the Federal Reserve Act to make price stability the sole goal of U.S. monetary policy. The idea that central banks should have goals defined only in terms of price stability or low inflation is not new. John Maynard Keynes wrote in 1924 that ". . . they (Treasury and Bank of England) should adopt the stability of sterling prices as their primary objective" (p.202).

In practice, the Fed, like most central banks, cares about both inflation and measures of the short-run cyclical performance of the economy. However, pursuing multiple goals can create conflicts for policy; for example, the desire to mitigate short-run downturns raises the issue of whether this goal should take precedence over a low-inflation goal at any particular point in time. Thus, it is important to avoid allowing short-run, temporary successes in preventing employment losses during recessions from leading to longer-run failures in maintaining low inflation. Proponents of more activist policy argue, however, that monetary policy can help to stabilize the economy and should act to offset temporary downturns in economic activity. They argue that responding to temporary, cyclical fluctuations need not be inconsistent with maintaining a firm commitment to low average inflation.

One effect of having multiple, conflicting goals is that it leads to political pressures on the Fed, varying in strength and intensity over time, for lower interest rates, for faster growth, or for lower inflation. Political pressure on monetary policy is usually criticized for its tendency to emphasize short-run considerations over longer-run objectives. For example, politicians who may have time horizons that extend only to the next election will be tempted to push for more expansionary policy, which may produce lower unemployment and faster real growth in the short run, even though in the long run it can only lead to higher inflation. Unless the central bank has sufficient independence from political institutions to resist such pressures, the result is likely to be higher average inflation with no appreciable effect on average unemployment or real growth. Alesina and Summers (1993) find that greater central bank independence is associated with lower average inflation, but they find no association with average real growth among the industrialized economies.

In sum, monetary policy is continually faced with a conflict between what it can temporarily achieve in the short run and what it can permanently achieve in the longer run. That is why even those economists who believe monetary policy has an important role to play in helping to stabilize short-run business cycle fluctuations also have, in recent years, increasingly emphasized the importance of maintaining a commitment to low average rates of inflation.

THE INSTRUMENTS OF MONETARY POLICY

The Fed does not control inflation or unemployment directly; instead, the Fed must decide on the settings for the tools, or instruments, of policy that it does control directly as it attempts to achieve its objectives of low inflation and stable economic growth. It is predominantly through *open market operations*—purchases and sales of government securities—that the Fed attempts to influence the economy and achieve its policy goals. Open market operations influence the level of bank reserves in the economy, which in turn influences the level of interest rates, the provision of money and credit, investment spending, and the pace of economic activity.

Banks are legally required to hold a fraction of certain types of deposit accounts that they issue as reserves. They keep these reserves in the form of vault cash or deposits with the Fed. When banks need additional reserves on a short-term basis, they can borrow them from other banks who happen to have more reserves than they need. The interest rate on the overnight borrowing of reserves is called the federal funds rate. The funds rate adjusts to balance the supply and demand for reserves.

Open market operations affect the supply of reserves in the banking system. If the Fed buys government securities, it pays for them by adding reserves to the banking system; this increases the supply of reserves, which lowers the cost of borrowing reserves—the federal funds rate falls. When the Fed sells

READING 24 Monetary Policy: Goals and Instruments

government securities, the reverse happens: the supply of reserves falls, and the federal funds rate rises.

If the demand for reserves were perfectly predictable, the Fed could predict exactly the relationship between the quantity of reserves and the funds rate. In this case, it could use either reserves or the funds rate as its policy instrument equally well. But, because reserve demand can fluctuate unpredictably, the choice between the use of a quantity and the use of an interest rate as the chief instrument of policy does make a difference. To see why, suppose the economy grows faster than predicted, putting upward pressure on interest rates as credit demand increases. If the Fed tries to control the quantity of reserves, it will not accommodate the greater demand for credit, and the funds rate will rise. This will tend to push up other interest rates and act as an automatic brake on the economy. If the Fed is using the funds rate as its instrument, this pressure for higher interest rates will automatically produce a rise in the supply of reserves as the Fed acts to prevent the funds rate from rising. In this example, policy that focuses on the quantity of reserves would be less likely to let inflation rise.

If, in contrast, pressures for higher interest rates came from a financial market development, such as tighter regulatory supervision of bank lending practices, a policy that acted to keep the quantity of reserves constant would lead some key lending rates to rise, which would tend to have a contractionary effect on the economy. If policy acted to keep the funds rate constant, then the supply of reserves would automatically increase to offset the contractionary effect of the financial disturbance. During most of the post-war era, the interest rate approach to implementing policy—setting the level of the funds rate—provides a more accurate description of Fed operating procedures.

The link between open market activities and the federal funds rate is fairly straightforward. The other linkages between policy actions and the behavior of the economy are subject to more controversy. The roles played by intermediate targets, forecasts and policy rules in linking policy actions with the behavior of the economy will be discussed in the second part of this primer.

REFERENCES

Alesina, A., and L. Summers. 1993. "Central Bank Independence and Macroeconomic Performance." *Journal of Money, Credit and Banking* 25 (May) pp. 151-162.

Keynes, J.M. 1924. *Monetary Reform.* New York: Harcourt Brace and Company.

PART V The Federal Reserve System and the Conduct of Monetary Policy

QUESTIONS

1. What is the natural rate hypothesis?

2. The Fed has multiple, conflicting goals. Which one should have top priority? Why?

3. The Fed can control the federal funds rate by using open market operations to adjust the supply of reserves to the banking system. If the demand for reserves is unpredictable, does it matter whether the Fed uses the funds rate or the level or reserves as its policy instrument? Explain.

READING 25

A Primer on Monetary Policy Part II: Targets and Indicators

Carl E. Walsh

The last issue of the *Weekly Letter* (Walsh 1994) discussed the goals of monetary policy and the main instruments actually controlled by the Federal Reserve. It noted that most economists believe monetary policy can have important effects on output and employment only in the short-run; in the longer run, the Fed can affect inflation but not employment. This *Letter* focuses on issues related to the actual implementation of monetary policy.

CHANNELS OF MONETARY POLICY

Economists disagree about the exact linkages among monetary policy actions, inflation, and economic activity. Most agree that banks play a critical role in the transmission process, although evidence is inconclusive about whether it is through the liability side of banks' balance sheets (deposits and other components of the money supply) or through the asset side (bank loans). In either case, the general view is that monetary policy works by affecting interest rates. Increases in interest rates raise the cost of borrowing and lead to reductions in business investment spending and household purchases of durable goods such as autos and new homes. These declines in spending reduce the aggregate demand for the economy's output, leading firms to cut back on production and employment. Conversely, interest rate declines stimulate aggregate spending and lead to increases in production and employment.

Since the Fed can control the federal funds rate, it would appear to be a simple matter to link policy actions—changes in the funds rate—to real economic activity. Unfortunately, four critical problems arise in implementing monetary policy. First, while the Fed can affect market interest rates, spending decisions and economic activity depend on *real* interest rates, that is, market rates corrected for expected rates of inflation. Second, economic activity is likely to be related to both short-term and long-term real interest rates, while the Fed most directly controls very short-term market rates. Third, the Fed is interested ultimately in measures of economic performance like inflation, real economic growth and employment, yet data on these variables that might be used to guide policy are not available every day or every week or even every month. And fourth,

Reprinted from Federal Reserve Bank of San Francisco *Weekly Letter*, August 19, 1994.

policy actions taken today will affect the economy only with a significant lag so that policy changes must be made in anticipation of future developments in the economy. Because the first two of these issues have been recently discussed by Trehan (1993) and Cogley (1993), they are touched upon only briefly here.

REAL INTEREST RATES

Aggregate spending is related not to market interest rates but to the expected real rate of interest. Since it is difficult to measure expected inflation, it is hard to know the current level of real interest rates. And variations in expected inflation can make a big difference. In 1978, the funds rate averaged 7.93 percent, but the rate of inflation was 9.1 percent; if the inflation was fully anticipated, that 7.93 funds rate was equivalent to an expected real rate of negative 1.17 percent. Today the funds rate is 4.25. If the market expects a continuation of the current 3 percent inflation rate, then today's funds rate translates into a positive 1.25 percent expected real rate. So a funds rate of 4.25 percent today may be more restrictive than the 7.93 funds rate was in 1978. With inflation expectations difficult to measure, economists can disagree about the current level of real rates and therefore the stance of monetary policy.

In addition, the Fed can only influence the level of real interest rates in the short-run; it cannot permanently prevent the real rate from returning to its equilibrium level without risking accelerating inflation or deflation.

Persistent attempts to keep real rates too low will initially generate an economic expansion that will lead to more rapid inflation. As individuals come to expect higher inflation, real rates will tend to adjust back to their equilibrium level. Further expansionary policy would be needed to keep the real rate down, leading to further increases in inflation.

Most estimates of expected inflation imply that real short-term interest rates earlier this year were very low, too low to be consistent with steady real growth at a sustainable rate. However, the real rate of interest consistent with sustained growth varies over time in ways that are difficult to measure or predict. Thus, the benchmark against which any estimate of the current real rate should be compared is itself not directly measured. So economists can disagree about whether current real rates are too high or too low.

LONG-TERM INTEREST RATES

Aggregate spending is related both to long-term real interest rates and to the short-term rates the Fed can affect directly. Long-term rates will be equal to the average of the expected future short-term rates plus a risk factor that reflects the premium necessary to induce risk-averse investors to hold long-term bonds. An increase in short-term rates that is viewed to be temporary will have a much smaller impact on long rates than would an increase expected to be relatively persistent.

Long-term interest rates can be expressed as the sum of an expected real return and an adjustment for expected inflation. Long rates have the potential, therefore, to provide information about the market's expectations about inflation. Long rates will tend to rise (fall) if higher (lower) inflation is expected. After the Fed's most recent increase in the funds rate on May 17th, long-term interest rates actually declined. This was interpreted as evidence that financial market participants were confident the Fed had tightened sufficiently to ensure inflation would not increase. Unfortunately, long-term interest rates also vary because of variations in the expected rate of return. Because of the difficulties in predicting these variations, it is not always possible to interpret changes in long-term interest rates as providing information about inflation expectations.

INTERMEDIATE TARGETS

Ideally, the Fed would like to be able to monitor continuously its ultimate goals, like the rate of inflation, in order to adjust its policy instruments. Unfortunately, new data on inflation are available only monthly, while data on GDP growth are available only quarterly. Consequently, the Fed must rely on data available more frequently, such as interest rates, which it can observe continuously, or monetary aggregates, which are available weekly, as *intermediate targets* to help guide policy. An intermediate target is a variable that, while not directly under the control of the Fed (that is, it is not an instrument like the federal funds rate), responds fairly quickly to policy actions, is observable frequently, and bears a predictable relationship to the ultimate goals of policy.

To use an intermediate target, the Fed must first determine the value for the intermediate target consistent with the desired goals. The Fed then adjusts its instruments in order to ensure the intermediate target variable takes on the chosen value. That is, policy is conducted as if the intermediate target value were the goal of policy. If new information suggests the intermediate target variable is diverging from the targeted value, policy instruments are adjusted to return it to target.

During the early 1980s, several different measures of the money supply served as intermediate targets; for example, when M2 was growing above its target range, this signaled a need to tighten policy by contracting the growth of bank reserves. Slow M2 growth was a signal to expand reserve growth. However, the relationship between the monetary aggregates and the ultimate goals of monetary policy became increasingly unpredictable, reducing the value of the aggregates as intermediate targets (see Judd-Trehan 1992).

POLICY INDICATORS

Currently, the Fed has no single reliable intermediate target that could be used to guide policy; consequently, the Fed must rely on many variables for information to guide policy. These variables are indicators of the current state of the economy or of future developments in the economy.

Indicators of future developments are needed because it takes time for a monetary policy action to affect the economy. Policy actions taken in early 1994 are likely to have their greatest effect on the economy in late 1994 and early 1995. This makes it imperative that policy actions be taken not on the basis of current economic conditions, but on the basis of forecasts of future economic conditions. To wait to shift the Fed's policy stance until inflation actually increases, for example, would mean that inflationary momentum will have already developed, making the task of reducing inflation that much harder and more costly in terms of job losses. In the past, the Fed has been criticized for waiting too long before adjusting its policies.

Basing policy on forecasts creates its own difficulties. Because economic developments are difficult to predict, forecasts often turn out to be wrong. And because forecasters often disagree, there will be corresponding differences over the appropriate stance of policy. The current situation is a case in point. The Fed has tightened policy, not in response to any current rise in inflation, but on the basis of its forecast of rising inflation in the future if it maintained its previous policy stance. Critics have claimed that future inflation increases are unlikely. Because the debate is over forecasts of what inflation would have done under the Fed's previous policy, they are difficult to resolve.

In the absence of an agreed upon intermediate target to guide policy, the Fed must evaluate a number of variables that may serve to indicate future economic developments in order to determine if policy changes are appropriate. Among the indicators that have been proposed are nominal income growth, real interest rates, commodity prices, exchange rates and the price of gold. For example, the Fed could use nominal income growth as an indicator by comparing the most recent data on nominal growth to the growth rate consistent with sustained real growth and low inflation. Since most estimates of the economy's long-run sustainable growth rate of real income are in the 2 to 2½ percent range, if the inflation target were 1 percent, nominal income growth should be in the 3 to 3½ percent range.

Because no single indicator variable consistently provides accurate information on the future of the economy or the stance of monetary policy, the Fed must rely on a number of indicators; it "looks at everything." In principle, this is just what the Fed should do. Exchange rates, nominal income growth, real interest rates, money supply growth, commodity prices, and so on all provide some information that is useful for conducting policy.

Unfortunately, each indicator also can provide misleading signals about the economy and often the signals they give are contradictory. During the last two years, for example, while real interest rates were low indicating expansionary monetary policy, the M2 definition of the money supply was growing very slowly, indicating a more contractionary stance of policy.

As an alternative to using forecasts or relying on a number of indicator variables, many economists have proposed simple rules to guide Fed behavior. The most famous was Milton Friedman's rule of maintaining a constant growth rate of the money supply. More recently, rules for the monetary base (currency plus bank reserves), M2, nominal GDP, and the funds rate have been studied (for example, see Judd and Motley 1991). In general, these alternatives are "feedback rules": The Fed's policy instrument is adjusted on the basis of recent movements in measures of economic activity such as nominal income growth, the unemployment rate, or actual inflation. Such rules can help to reduce the uncertainty associated with monetary policy actions by making policy more predictable.

CONCLUSIONS

The conduct of monetary policy often consists of balancing inconsistent goals using sometimes unreliable indicators to manipulate tools whose effects on the economy are uncertain. Despite these uncertainties, the general conduct of monetary policy in recent years has received surprisingly wide approval. The current controversy over interest rate increases is not about the fundamental need to prevent a resurgence of inflation, but instead has centered on the difficulty of forecasting the future course of inflation.

REFERENCES

Cogley, Timothy. 1993. "Monetary Policy and the Long-Term Real Interest Rate." Federal Reserve Bank of San Francisco *Weekly Letter* (December 3).

Judd, John P., and Brian Motley. 1993. "Nominal Feedback Rules for Monetary Policy." Federal Reserve Bank of San Francisco *Economic Review* (3) pp. 3-17.

Judd, John P., and Bharat Trehan. 1992. "Money, Credit, and M2." Federal Reserve Bank of San Francisco *Weekly Letter* (September 4).

Trehan, Bharat. 1993. "Real Interest Rates." Federal Reserve Bank of San Francisco *Weekly Letter* (November 5).

Walsh, Carl E. 1994. "A Primer on Monetary Policy Part 1: Goals and Instruments." Federal Reserve Bank of San Francisco *Weekly Letter* (August 5).

PART V The Federal Reserve System and the Conduct of Monetary Policy

> **QUESTIONS**
>
> 1. Why doesn't the Fed's control over the federal funds rate give it a similar degree of control over real economic activity?
>
> 2. What are intermediate targets? Why does the Fed use them in implementing monetary policy?
>
> 3. Why were the Fed's interest rate increases in early 1994 controversial?
>
> 4. What are Walsh's arguments in support of rules to guide Fed policy?

READING 26

U.S. Foreign Exchange Operations

Kristina Jacobson

The volume of U.S. official foreign exchange operations has grown substantially in recent years. In 1989, the total volume of U.S. transactions in the exchange market was over $20 billion, the highest ever. At the same time, because recent U.S. operations have usually involved the purchase of foreign currency, U.S. foreign currency balances have grown to record levels, reaching nearly $45 billion in December 1989.[1]

Such changes in U.S. foreign exchange operations reflect the evolving nature of U.S. exchange rate policy over the postwar period. During the Bretton Woods system of fixed exchange rates, which lasted from 1947 to 1973, the primary goal of U.S. operations was to maintain the dollar price of gold, chiefly through official transactions with foreign authorities. With the shift to floating exchange rates in the early 1970s, the focus of U.S. operations has been to counter disorderly conditions, primarily through direct intervention in the market.

This article describes how the goals and methods of U.S. foreign exchange operations have changed over time. The first section reviews the institutional framework for U.S. foreign exchange operations. The second section discusses the role of the United States in the Bretton Woods system of fixed exchange rates and U.S. exchange rate policy goals and methods during that time. The third section discusses the goals and methods of U.S. operations during the floating-rate regime.

I. FRAMEWORK FOR OPERATIONS

The U.S. Treasury and the Federal Reserve System cooperate in formulating and implementing U.S. exchange rate policy. In a broad sense, because foreign economic policy falls under the Treasury's domain, the Treasury is ultimately responsible for exchange rate policy. However, the Fed consults with the Treasury on deciding exchange rate policy and directly implements that policy.

The foreign exchange desk at the Federal Reserve Bank of New York conducts all U.S. foreign exchange operations, using Treasury and Federal Reserve funds. Since 1978, the Fed and the Treasury have generally shared equally in financing operations. The Treasury

Reprinted from Federal Reserve Bank of Kansas City *Economic Review*, September/October 1990, 37-50.

pays for its portion of operations with its Exchange Stabilization Fund (ESF).[2] The Federal Reserve System pays for its operations with an account owned by all 12 Federal Reserve banks. The Federal Open Market Committee (FOMC), the Fed's principle policymaking body, regulates operations for the Fed's foreign exchange account.[3]

The Treasury reports the U.S. foreign exchange policy goal in general terms to the International Monetary Fund (IMF). The IMF is an international organization designed to promote cooperation in international monetary and payment issues. Currently, the goal of U.S. foreign exchange operations as reported to the IMF is to counter disorderly market conditions or to act when "otherwise deemed appropriate" (International Monetary Fund 1986). The Federal Reserve recognizes the Treasury's goal and ensures that operations for the System foreign exchange account will follow the Treasury's commitment to the IMF.

The FOMC manages the System account through three formal documents: the Foreign Currency Directive, the Authorization for Foreign Currency Operations, and the Procedural Instructions. These documents require that Fed operations be "conducted in close and continuous consultation and cooperation with the United States Treasury" (Board of Governors 1989). The documents also provide guidelines on financing arrangements between the Fed and foreign authorities or the U.S. Treasury. The FOMC also formally and informally monitors the size of System foreign currency balances. For any operations not falling within the guidelines, the foreign desk must seek approval from the entire FOMC or a delegated subcommittee of the members.

Each day, the foreign desk must decide whether and how to intervene within the guidelines agreed upon with the Treasury. To provide the desk with up-to-the-minute information, staff members at the New York Fed continuously watch the 24-hour, worldwide foreign exchange market and convey significant developments to the Treasury and the Fed's Board of Governors in Washington, D.C. Treasury and Board staffs also study the market, but the New York Fed follows developments most closely. Each morning, New York staff members call various commercial banks to obtain the latest exchange rate quotes and to get a "feel" for the market. New York staff members may also call foreign central banks to coordinate foreign exchange operations. If the desk plans to conduct operations, the manager of the foreign desk determines exactly when and how to act. In making intervention decisions, the manager consults officials at the Treasury and the Board.

The rest of this article reviews the goals and methods of U.S. foreign exchange operations, first during the fixed-rate regime and then during the floating-rate regime.

II. FIXED-RATE REGIME: GOALS AND METHODS

The Bretton Woods system of fixed exchange rates lasted from 1947 to March 1973. The U.S. dollar was the center of the system and the value to which other countries pegged their currencies. The role of foreign authorities was to intervene in the foreign exchange market to maintain the value of their currency relative to the dollar. For example, if it was deemed necessary to cause the pound to rise against the dollar, British authorities bought pounds, increasing the demand for the pound and pushing up its price. Alternatively, to cause the pound to fall against the dollar, British authorities sold pounds, increasing the supply of pounds and pushing down the pound's price.

In contrast to the role of foreign authorities, the role of the United States was to maintain the dollar price of gold at $35 an ounce. The United States stood ready to sell gold to foreign authorities who wished to convert dollars acquired through foreign exchange operations. The annual U.S. notification of its exchange rate goal to the IMF stated this commitment.[4]

The allowable limits of exchange rate fluctuation were small during the fixed-rate regime, except for occasional currency devaluations or revaluations.[5] For example, in the mid-1960s, the pound was frequently under downward pressure in part because of a large British trade deficit. The downward pressure continued despite efforts of global monetary authorities to maintain the currency's value. Consequently, in 1967, British authorities devalued the pound (Chart 1).

Although exchange rate fluctuations were generally small during the fixed-rate period, exchange rate pressures surfaced in other ways. Because authorities used their reserves to intervene in the market to maintain fixed exchange rates, pressure on exchange rates was evident through changes in the size of official reserves, such as dollar holdings of foreign officials and the U.S. gold stock. For example, the U.S. gold stock dropped substantially during the 1960s, as the United States upheld its obligation to sell gold for dollars obtained by foreign authorities through their foreign exchange operations (Chart 2). In addition, as a result of exchange rate pressures, governments sometimes changed monetary and fiscal policy.[6]

Operations to Protect the U.S. Gold Stock

The convertibility of dollars into gold was the foundation of the Bretton Woods regime. Foreign authorities were willing to hold dollars because the United States assured their convertibility into gold at a fixed price. During the 1960s, however, the fixed-rate system showed signs of strain. The dollar was under downward pressure, largely because of the U.S. current account deficit. To counter downward pressure on the dollar, foreign authorities bought dollars in the market and consequently built up large dollar reserves. As foreign authorities exchanged their excess dollar balances for gold and the U.S. gold stock fell, concern grew about whether the United States could continue to convert dollars into gold. Early in the decade, with downward pressure on the dollar intensifying, the United States began to act to protect its gold stock and the global monetary system. Four basic methods were used in this effort.

First, the United States borrowed foreign currency through a swap network. The swap

PART V The Federal Reserve System and the Conduct of Monetary Policy

Chart 1
The Bretton Woods Period: Foreign Exchange Value of the Dollar
(Foreign currency units per dollar)

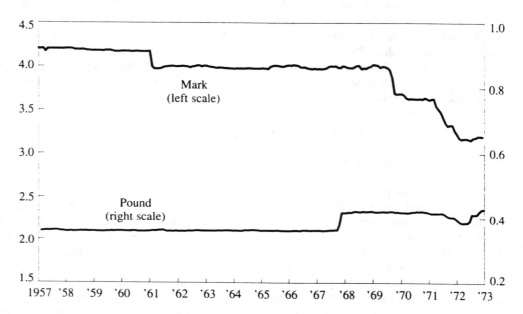

Source: *Federal Reserve Bulletin*, various issues.

network is a mechanism through which U.S. and foreign authorities may temporarily exchange domestic and foreign currency. The swap network consists of a series of reciprocal credit agreements between U.S. and foreign authorities.[7] In effect, each country agrees to exchange its currency for foreign currency on demand, up to an agreed-amount. The country initiating the exchange is the borrower; the other country is the creditor. The borrower purchases foreign currency from the creditor and agrees to sell the currency back at the same exchange rate on a specified date, usually in three months. The borrower may extend the swap if both parties agree.[8]

During the fixed-rate regime, the United States borrowed through the swap network primarily to relieve exchange rate risk on dollars held by foreign authorities. Because the dollar was frequently under downward pressure, foreign authorities holding large amounts of their reserves in dollars were at risk that the dollar would be devalued, causing their reserves to lose value. Through the swap network, the United States borrowed

READING 26 U.S. Foreign Exchange Operations

Chart 2
The Bretton Woods Period: U.S. Gold Stock

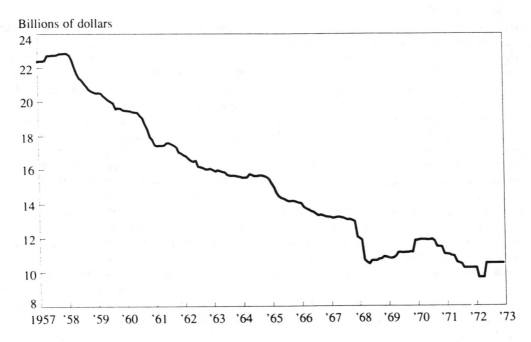

Source: Data Resources, Inc.

foreign currency to purchase a portion of the dollars held by foreign authorities, decreasing the dollar holdings of the foreign authorities. In this way, U.S. authorities hoped to limit the amount of dollars foreign authorities converted into gold. By absorbing some of the dollars foreign authorities did not want, the Unites States hoped to buy time for exchange market conditions to stabilize.

The United States also loaned dollars to foreign authorities through the swap network. For example, with the pound under downward pressure in the mid-1960s, the United States loaned dollars to the Bank of England so it could intervene to maintain the pound's value.

A second method U.S. authorities used during the fixed-rate regime was to sell foreign-currency-denominated bonds, called "Roosa bonds," to foreign authorities.[9] These bonds served as a source of foreign currency to purchase the dollar reserves of foreign authorities and to repay swap debt. For example, in May 1963, the United States sold $30 million equivalent of Belgian-franc-

PART V The Federal Reserve System and the Conduct of Monetary Policy

denominated bonds to the Belgian authorities and used the proceeds to buy surplus dollars held by the Belgian authorities. Also, in August 1963, the United States sold a $50 million two-year mark bond to the West German authorities and used the proceeds to repay earlier U.S. borrowing of marks through the swap network. In this way, the United States limited how long a swap remained outstanding (Coombs 1963).

The third method used to protect the gold stock involved drawing on the U.S. reserve position in the IMF. The United States and other IMF members pay quotas, or membership fees, to the IMF. These quotas provide most of the resources the IMF lends to member countries in pursuit of its goals. The United States drew down from its reserve position at various times during the Bretton Woods period. For example, in 1965, the United States drew foreign currency to buy excess dollars from foreign authorities and to pay off swap borrowing. Paying off swap borrowing by drawing from the IMF provided another way to limit how long a swap was outstanding.

Finally, as a fourth method to protect the U.S. gold stock, U.S. and foreign authorities cooperated to keep the market price of gold from rising above the official $35 rate. The United States was concerned that a high market price for gold would induce foreign authorities to exchange their dollar reserves at the U.S. gold window. To keep the market price of gold from rising above the official price, the United States and other nations formed an organization called the gold pool, which sold gold in the London market from 1961 to 1968. However, this effort met with limited success.

Operations in the Foreign Exchange Market

Although the chief role of the United States during the fixed-rate period was to maintain the fixed price of gold, U.S. authorities also on rare instances intervened directly in the foreign exchange market. At times, the intervention was undertaken to reduce pressure on foreign authorities to buy dollars—by limiting the number of dollars bought and held by foreign authorities, the United States hoped to decrease the amount of gold it would have to sell. At other times, the intervention was undertaken to calm financial markets. For example, after the assassination of President Kennedy in 1963, U.S. authorities entered the exchange market to counter speculative pressures and provide assurance that U.S. international financial policy had not changed. Two other notable episodes of U.S. intervention came in 1965 and in 1967, both in response to downward pressure on the British pound. In these episodes, the United States purchased pounds to help British authorities maintain the value of the pound. Although U.S. intervention was infrequent during the fixed-rate period, U.S. authorities did undertake various types of intervention. In conducting its direct intervention, the desk had several choices on how to approach the market, depending on exchange market conditions and the goal of the intervention. For example, the desk at times dealt directly with a commercial bank. The commercial bank in turn was free to inform other market participants as it saw fit. The market may have interpreted such operations as a signal about how U.S. officials viewed exchange rates.

At other times, the desk preferred to approach the market indirectly by asking a commercial bank to act on its behalf. The commercial bank would act just as it would act for any other customer and would be precluded from revealing on whose behalf it was acting. Also, the desk on occasion chose to act passively, responding to an offer privately placed in the market rather than initiating an operation at a certain rate. The desk might have used this approach when trading was thin in order to restrain the impact that an aggressively pursued transaction might have had on the market.

Intervention by the foreign desk, no matter what the approach, has had implications for the operations of the domestic desk at the Federal Reserve Bank of New York. The domestic desk automatically offsets, or sterilizes, the effect of any U.S. exchange market intervention on the U.S. money supply. It does so by buying or selling U.S. Treasury securities as part of its "open market operations."[10] For example, when the foreign desk sells dollars for foreign currency to counter upward pressure on the dollar, the U.S. money supply increases as the dollars enter the U.S. banking system. To offset this intervention, the domestic desk sells Treasury securities to drain the dollars created by the intervention.

Because the United States sterilizes all of its intervention, the end result of a U.S. exchange market intervention is a change in the relative supplies of U.S. and foreign bonds held by the public. In the above example, the domestic desk's sale of Treasury securities adds to the supply of Treasury securities held by the public; hence, the relative supply of U.S. Treasury securities increases as a result of the sterilized intervention.

Sterilized intervention is generally thought to affect exchange rates less than nonsterilized intervention does. Nonsterilized intervention changes the size of the U.S. money supply because no offsetting purchase or sale of Treasury securities occurs. A change in the U.S. money supply directly affects the exchange rate because the supply of dollars relative to foreign currency changes. Also, a change in the U.S. money supply may influence U.S. interest rates and U.S. economic activity, which in turn may affect the exchange rate. Sterilized intervention, on the other hand, does not change the size of the U.S. money supply. However, to the extent investors regard foreign and domestic bonds as imperfect substitutes, the change in relative bond supplies may cause some exchange rate adjustment. In addition, sterilized intervention may influence the exchange rate by signaling a change in U.S. economic policy.[11] Nevertheless, most research suggests that sterilized intervention—in the absence of a fundamental change in U.S. economic policy—probably does not have a lasting effect on the foreign exchange value of the dollar.[12]

III. FLOATING-RATE REGIME: GOALS AND METHODS

Despite efforts by U.S. and foreign authorities, the Bretton Woods system remained under pressure in the 1960s and early 1970s. This pressure resulted mainly from imbalances in international payments positions of several countries. Concern about U.S. ability to maintain convertibility of the dollar also persisted. In 1971, the U.S. Treasury suspended converting dollars into gold and foreign currency. Although efforts to maintain the Bretton Woods regime continued over the next two years, the fixed-rate system collapsed by March 1973. Fixed exchange rates between the dollar and most major currencies no longer were in effect, and exchange rates moved in response to market forces.[13]

During the floating-rate regime, from March 1973 to the present, the United States has conducted foreign exchange operations primarily to counter disorderly markets. The U.S. report to the IMF has reflected this goal.[14] At times, U.S. authorities have interpreted the objective narrowly, focusing market operations on efforts to counter short-term market disorder. At other times, U.S. authorities have interpreted the objective more broadly, acting to adjust exchange rates considered out of line with economic fundamentals. In 1985, the United States officially broadened its foreign exchange market goal to include both countering disorderly markets and entering the market when "otherwise deemed appropriate" (International Monetary Fund 1986). During the floating-rate regime, the focus of U.S. operations has been direct intervention in the foreign exchange market in response to movements in exchange rates. The dollar's value has varied substantially over the period (Chart 3). This section reviews the changes in U.S. foreign exchange market goals and methods during the floating-rate regime.

Narrow Interpretation: 1973 to 1977

In the years immediately after the Bretton Woods system broke down, the United States directed most of its foreign exchange market intervention toward countering disorderly markets in the narrow sense. Narrowly defined, characteristics of a disorderly market include sharp exchange rate movements, thin trading, and wide spreads between the rates at which market participants are willing to buy (bid rates) and the rates at which they are willing to sell (ask rates). The volume of U.S. intervention from 1973 to 1977 was relatively small. The dollar rose and fell during these years in response to changing market perceptions of economic fundamentals. When the dollar fell sharply, U.S. authorities frequently bought dollars to stabilize market conditions. The United States paid for these purchase by using its foreign currency reserves and by borrowing through the swap network. To accommodate this borrowing, U.S. authorities expanded swap lines with several countries. During periods when the dollar rose, U.S. authorities took the opportunity to purchase foreign currency to repay debts.

READING 26 U.S. Foreign Exchange Operations

Chart 3
The Floating-Rate Period: Trade-Weighted Value of the Dollar

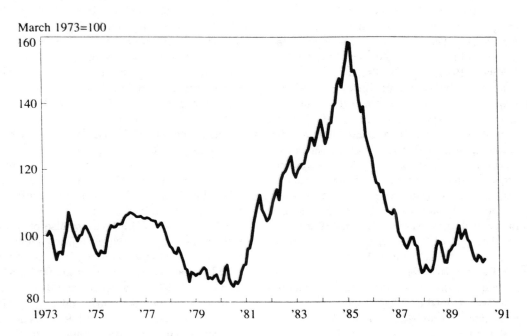

Source: Board of Governors of the Federal Reserve System.

An example of U.S. operations during this period was the purchase of dollars in July 1973 to "assist the market in finding solid footing" (Coombs 1973). At the time, the dollar was under downward pressure, in part because of rising interest rates in Europe and market concern about inflationary pressures in the United States. The foreign exchange market showed signs of disorder, including wide bid-ask spreads and thin trading. Trading became so disorderly at times that some New York banks withdrew from the market.

Another notable episode of U.S. intervention was in February 1975, when the United States, Germany, and Switzerland purchased dollars in the first major concerted intervention during the floating-rate period. The dollar was falling because of a severe U.S. recession, a decline in U.S. interest rates relative to foreign rates, and rising inflation in the United States relative to several other countries. These developments had a strong impact because the market doubted whether U.S. economic policy could contain inflationary pressures.

PART V The Federal Reserve System and the Conduct of Monetary Policy

Broad Interpretation: 1978 to 1980

In the late 1970s, the dollar declined sharply, prompting authorities to act more forcefully. The trade-weighted value of the dollar declined 20 percent from June 1976 to October 1978, largely because of market concern about economic imbalances among major industrial nations (Chart 3). The U.S. economy was experiencing rising inflation and a worsening current account deficit. In contrast, other countries, such as Japan and Germany, were experiencing weak economic growth and substantial current account surpluses. Initially, U.S. authorities purchased dollars "to deal...with the disorder in the exchange market" (Holmes 1978).

The United States began a series of steps to stop the dollar's fall in 1978. In January, the Federal Reserve and Treasury began to participate equally in financing intervention. This was a notable change in tactics because most intervention had previously been for the Fed account. In addition, the Treasury and the Bundesbank agreed to set up a swap arrangement, augmenting U.S. resources for foreign exchange intervention. Over the following months, the Treasury borrowed under this agreement, obtaining marks to use for dollar purchases in the market. During 1978, the Federal Reserve also tightened domestic monetary policy, which increased U.S. interest rates and helped strengthen the dollar.

On November 1, 1978, U.S. authorities announced a major plan to halt the dollar's decline. This plan included, among other efforts, the purchase of dollars in the exchange market. The United States had decided the dollar's decline "had gone beyond what could be justified by underlying economic conditions" (Holmes 1979, p.67). The plan was the first major departure from a narrow interpretation of the U.S. exchange rate objective. Increases in Federal Reserve swap agreements with various central banks helped finance the intervention, and tighter monetary policy bolstered the move. The United States also used several financing arrangements to increase the Treasury's resources for intervention.

The Treasury drew on the resources available from the IMF. For example, in 1978, the Treasury drew from its position at the IMF to obtain foreign currency to purchase dollars. The Treasury also obtained foreign currency by selling Special Drawing Rights (SDRs) to foreign authorities. An SDR is an international reserve asset the IMF began creating in 1970 to supplement other world reserve assets like the dollar and gold. IMF member nations receive SDR allocations according to the size of their quotas. In 1978, the Treasury sold SDRs for marks, yen, and Swiss francs.

The Treasury also issued foreign-currency-denominated securities, or "Carter bonds." In contrast to the Roosa bonds sold to foreign authorities during the fixed-rate regime, the Carter bonds were sold to the public. The Treasury issued nearly $2.8 billion equivalent of Carter bonds by January 1979 and ultimately issued over $6 billion equivalent before it began redeeming the bonds in 1981 (Holmes 1979, p.203, and Cross 1981). In addition, the Treasury increased gold sales to obtain foreign currency.

The Treasury also made use of financing arrangements with the Federal Reserve. Warehousing, for example, is a method of exchanging dollars in return for foreign currency not needed at the time. The Fed buys foreign currency from the Treasury and simultaneously agrees to sell the currency back at the same exchange rate as in the purchase at some specified date in the future. The FOMC regulates System warehousing of foreign currency for the Treasury and in 1978 the FOMC broadened its warehousing authorization, allowing the System to warehouse foreign currency for the general Treasury account as well as for the ESF.[15] In this way, the System could warehouse the foreign currency proceeds of the Carter bonds until the Treasury used them.[16]

Narrow Interpretation: 1981 to 1984

With the arrival of the Reagan Administration in 1981 and a more hands-off approach to government, U.S. authorities once again interpreted the goal of countering disorderly markets narrowly. From 1981 to 1984, the United States rarely intervened in the foreign exchange market. This policy stance reflected the view of the Treasury during the first Reagan term that the market should determine exchange rates. The new policy limited intervention to extreme circumstances, such as after the shooting of President Reagan in March 1981. Furthermore, the administration questioned whether intervention could have much effect on the exchange rate.[17]

The dollar rose dramatically during the early 1980s (Chart 3). This rise has been attributed to the strong U.S. economy, large budget deficit, tight U.S. monetary policy, and high real interest rates relative to the rest of the world. From July 1980 to its peak in February 1985, the dollar's value increased over 85 percent. As the dollar rose, the domestic business community began to complain that the dollar's strength limited the competitiveness of U.S. products against foreign competitors.

Broad Interpretation: 1985 to Present

In 1985, against the backdrop of a very strong dollar, the Treasury during the second Reagan term returned the United States to a broad interpretation of its exchange rate policy goal. Since then, the United States has intervened both to calm disorderly markets and to correct apparent inconsistencies between exchange rate levels and economic fundamentals. In pursuit of its goals, the United States has intensified cooperation with foreign authorities on international economic policy. Also, in contrast to operations during most of the postwar period—which had largely consisted of dollar purchases—recent U.S. intervention has consisted mostly of dollar sales, resulting in record U.S. holdings of foreign currency.

During 1985, the United States intervened more heavily than it had for several years. From January to March 1985, U.S. authorities sold over $650 million in the foreign exchange market. These actions were taken to prevent a further rise in the dollar's value, thus reflecting a broader interpretation of U.S. intervention goals. During 1985, official intervention goals as reported to the IMF were broadened to include intervening "to counter disorderly conditions in the exchange markets or when otherwise deemed appropriate" (International Monetary Fund 1986). The major episode of U.S. intervention in 1985 occurred after the meeting of the five industrialized G-5 nations at the Plaza Hotel in September.[18] At this meeting, G-5 officials agreed that appreciation of foreign currencies was desirable because exchange rates did not reflect economic fundamentals. Officials were also concerned about the threat of rising protectionism in the United St .. In the weeks after the Plaza Accord, the United Sates sold dollars in the largest U.S. intervention since the late 1970s. Foreign authorities also sold substantial amounts of dollars. The volume of U.S. intervention from September to October exceeded $3 billion, nearly five times the volume of the U.S. intervention earlier in the year. As the dollar continued to fall throughout the rest of 1985 and 1986, further U.S. intervention became unnecessary.

By early 1987, the dollar had fallen to its lowest level in seven years. The weak dollar reflected a growing U.S. trade deficit and signs of a weakening U.S. economy. At a meeting in February at the Louvre in Paris, G-7 officials decided that exchange rates reflected economic fundamentals.[19] As a result, these officials decided to "cooperate closely to foster stability of exchange rates around current levels" (Bank for International Settlements 1987). This agreement, the Louvre Accord, has guided international cooperation in exchange rate policy to the present. The Louvre Accord also signaled a shift in U.S. policy from encouraging the appreciation of foreign currencies to fostering exchange rate stability.

During the rest of 1987, the dollar generally fell and U.S. intervention consisted primarily of dollar purchases. The dollar's continued decline reflected in part large U.S. trade deficits. The October stock market crash and the associated easing of monetary policy by the Federal Reserve also placed downward pressure on the dollar. In 1987, the United States conducted an even higher volume of intervention than in 1985. This intervention largely consisted of dollar purchases to stop the dollar's slide. Foreign officials cooperated with the U.S. effort and in December 1987, G-7 officials restated their Louvre commitment to cooperate in the foreign exchange market. In an effort to calm the market, these officials also announced that "either excessive fluctuation of exchange rates, a further decline of the dollar, or a rise in the dollar to an extent that becomes destabilizing to the adjustment process, could be counterproductive by damaging growth prospects in the world economy" (U.S. Department of the Treasury 1987).

The next major increase in the volume of U.S. intervention came in 1989. This intervention again was consistent with the G-7 commitment to exchange rate stability. The bulk of U.S. intervention in 1989 was during the first half of the year. For example, the dollar came under upward pressure at times during the spring and summer because of political uncertainty abroad and interest-rate differentials favorable to the dollar. In

READING 26 U.S. Foreign Exchange Operations

response, U.S. authorities sold dollars.[20] Also, after their September 23 meeting, G-7 officials issued a communique stating that the dollar's rise was inconsistent with longer run economic fundamentals (Bank for International Settlements 1989). During the last months of the year, upward pressure on the dollar subsided and the dollar fell.

Recent U.S. intervention has resulted in the largest U.S. holdings of foreign currency ever. Total holdings of the Federal Reserve and the Treasury combined have risen from $8 million in 1973 to nearly $45 billion in December 1989.[21] The growth of these balances reflects the fact that recent intervention has usually involved dollar sales.

IV. SUMMARY

The goals and methods of foreign exchange operations have changed over time. Under the Bretton Woods regime, the role of the United States was to convert officially held dollars into gold. In the 1960s, concern for the U.S. gold stock grew, as foreign monetary authorities accumulated large amounts of dollars. To protect the gold stock, the United States borrowed foreign currency to buy dollars from foreign authorities. The United States also on rare occasions intervened directly in the foreign exchange market.

The primary objective of U.S. exchange rate policy during the floating exchange rate period has been to counter disorderly market conditions. Over time, U.S. authorities have interpreted this objective both narrowly and broadly. Major episodes of U.S. intervention occurred in the late 1970s, in 1985, and from 1987 to the present. In the late 1970s, U.S. authorities intervened to support the weak dollar and, in 1985, to counter the strong dollar. From 1987 to the present, U.S. operations have been mixed, with the underlying goal to maintain exchange rate stability. Direct intervention was particularly heavy in 1989, totaling over $20 billion, the highest volume ever.

ENDNOTES

1. Data on the size of U.S. foreign currency holdings in 1989 were obtained from Board of Governors of the Federal Reserve System 1990a. Data on the volume of U.S. transactions in the foreign exchange market were taken from various issues of the Federal Reserve Bank of New York's *Quarterly Review*.
2. The ESF fund was established by the Gold Reserve Act of 1934 to be operated by the Treasury to stabilize the exchange value of the dollar. The Treasury maintains its ESF and its general accounts at the Federal Reserve, which acts as the government's banker.
3. The FOMC is made up of seven members of the Board of Governors and five of the 12 district Federal Reserve Bank presidents.
4. During the fixed-rate regime, the United States was committed to buying gold at $35 an ounce "for settlement of international balances and other legitimate monetary purposes" (International Monetary Fund 1967).
5. During the fixed-rate regime, the foreign exchange value of a country's currency was officially set by that country's government. Countries occasionally revalued (officially raised) or devalued (officially lowered) their currencies against the dollar. For more information, see Federal Reserve Bank of New York 1983.

PART V The Federal Reserve System and the Conduct of Monetary Policy

6. For example, in the early 1960s, the United States undertook "Operation Twist," which was designed both to limit outflows of short-term capital by keeping short-term interest rates high and to foster economic growth by keeping long-term interest rates low (Salvatore 1983).
7. The Bank for International Settlements (BIS) also may participate in swaps.
8. The Federal Reserve conducts most swaps for the United States. The Treasury has conducted swaps infrequently for relatively small amounts. The FOMC monitors Federal Reserve swap arrangements and in 1963 decided the Fed should not extend its borrowing through the swap network for more than one year.
9. These bonds were named after Robert Roosa, Undersecretary for Monetary Affairs, U.S. Treasury, 1961-64.
10. For a discussion of open market techniques, see Roth 1986.
11. These two ways that sterilized intervention may affect the exchange rate are more formally called the portfolio balance channel and the signaling channel. The portfolio balance channel operates if interest rates and the exchange rate adjust to reestablish equilibrium in the bond market because foreign and domestic bonds are not perfect substitutes. In the example in the text, for instance, market participants initially may not want to hold the additional U.S. Treasury securities added to the market by the sterilization. But, if the dollar's value falls, market participants may become willing to purchase the new "cheaper" dollar-denominated securities. If domestic and foreign bonds are perfect substitutes, however, sterilized intervention (operating through the portfolio balance channel) is ineffective. The signaling channel operates if the intervention signals the market about a change in macroeconomic policy, which obviously would affect the exchange rate. For further discussion, see Edison 1990.
12. A 1983 G-7 study, for example, found that from 1973 to 1981, sterilized intervention "did not generally have a lasting effect, but that intervention in conjunction with domestic policy changes did have a more durable impact" (Jurgensen 1983). For a discussion of other studies, also see Edison 1990, and Frenkel 1990.
13. During a floating-rate regime, currencies either appreciate or depreciate in response to market forces. The terms revalue and devalue apply only in fixed-rate systems. For more information, see Federal Reserve Bank of New York 1983.
14. During the floating-rate regime, the goal of U.S. policy has generally been "to counter disorderly conditions in the exchange markets" (International Monetary Fund 1988).
15. For information about the effect of warehousing on the money supply and for information about other aspects of U.S. foreign exchange operation, see Meulendyke 1989.
16. Another type of financing arrangement between the Fed and the Treasury is for the Fed to monetize SDRs and gold. If the ESF wishes to supplement its dollar balances, it may ask the Fed to monetize SDRs. The Fed does this by purchasing SDRs from the ESF for dollars. More precisely, the Fed purchases SDR certificates, which represent the Fed's claim on a specified amount of SDRs. If the ESF wishes to use monetized SDRs, it must first repurchase them from the Fed. Monetizing gold is similar to monetizing SDRs except, instead of SDR certificates, the Fed purchases gold certificates, representing the Fed's claim on a specified amount of the Treasury's gold.
17. Beryl Sprinkel, then Chairman of the President's Council of Economic Advisers, expressed this view in his 1981 Congressional testimony, saying that he was "not at all certain that intervention in a market as massive as our dollar exchange market can have much effect, certainly not in the longer run" (International Economic Policy 1981).
18. The G-5 includes the United States, Japan, West Germany, France, and the United Kingdom.
19. The G-7 includes members of the G-5 plus Canada and Italy.
20. Over time, the ESF has increased the amount of SDRs it has asked the Federal Reserve to monetize. In 1989, the ESF increased the amount of SDRs monetized by the Federal Reserve to $8.5 billion, a 70 percent increase over the year before, to supplement its resources for foreign currency operation. These figures were taken from various issues of the *Federal Reserve Bulletin*.
21. Over time, the FOMC has increased the limit on the amount of foreign currency the Federal Reserve may hold. The current maximum, is $25 billion. The Federal Reserve also continues to warehouse foreign currency for the Treasury to supplement the Treasury's resources for foreign currency operations. At its March 1990 meeting, the FOMC increased the amount of foreign currency the Fed may warehouse for the Treasury to $15 billion. The previous increase in the limit

was from $5 billion to $10 billion in September 1989. Such increases reflect the Treasury's need of dollars for foreign currency purchases rather than foreign currency for dollar purchases (Board of Governors 1990b).

REFERENCES

Abrams, Richard K. 1979. "Federal Reserve Intervention Policy," *Economic Review*, Federal Reserve Bank of Kansas City, March.
Balbach, Anatol B. 1978. "The Mechanics of Intervention in Exchange Markets," *Economic Review*, Federal Reserve Bank of St. Louis, February.
Batten, D.S., and Mack Ott. 1984. "What Can Central Banks Do about the Value of the Dollar?" *Economic Review*, Federal Reserve Bank of St. Louis, May.
Bank for International Settlements. 1987. "Chronology of Economic Policy Developments: February and March 1987," April 15, p.8.
___. 1989. "Chronology of Economic Policy Developments: September and October 1989," November 15, p.11.
Board of Governors of the Federal Reserve System. 1962. *Federal Reserve Bulletin*, September.
___. 1963. *Federal Reserve Bulletin*, September.
___. 1970. *Federal Reserve Bulletin*, March.
___. 1988. *75th Annual Report 1988*, BOG.
___. 1989. *76th Annual Report 1989*, BOG, p.75.
___. 1990a. *Federal Reserve Bulletin*, May, Table 3.12.
___. 1990b. "Record of Policy Actions of the Federal Open Market Committee, Meeting Held on March 27, 1990," press release, May 18.
Coombs, Charles A. 1962. "Treasury and Federal Reserve Foreign Exchange Operations," *Federal Reserve Bulletin*, Board of Governors of the Federal Reserve System, September.
___. 1963. "Treasury and Federal Reserve Foreign Exchange Operations," *Federal Reserve Bulletin*, Board of Governors of the Federal Reserve System, September.
___. 1970. "Treasury and Federal Reserve Foreign Exchange Operations," *Federal Reserve Bulletin*, Board of Governors of the Federal Reserve System, March, p.227.
___. 1973. "Treasury and Federal Reserve Foreign Exchange Operations," *Federal Reserve Bulletin*, Board of Governors of the Federal Reserve System, September, p.216-17.
Cross, Sam Y. 1981. "Treasury and Federal Reserve Foreign Exchange Operations," *Federal Reserve Bulletin*, Board of Governors of the Federal Reserve System, September.
Destler, J.M., and C.R. Henning. 1989. *Dollar Politics: Exchange Rate Policymaking in the United States*. Washington: Institute for International Economics.
Edison, Hali J. 1990. "Foreign Currency Operations: An Annotated Bibliography," *International Finance Discussion Papers*, May.
Federal Reserve Bank of New York, 1983. "Fedpoints 38, Currency Devaluation and Revaluation."
___. 1981. *Statfacts, Understanding Federal Reserve Statistical Reports*, November.
Frenkel, Jacob A., Morris Goldstein, and Paul R. Masson. 1990. "International Dimensions of Monetary Policy: Coordination Versus Autonomy," *Monetary Policy Issues in the 1990s*, Federal Reserve Bank of Kansas City, pp.201-02.
Holmes, Alan R., and Scott E. Pardee. 1975. "Treasury and Federal Reserve Foreign Exchange Operations, February-July 1975," *Monthly Review*, Federal Reserve Bank of New York, September.

PART V The Federal Reserve System and the Conduct of Monetary Policy

___. 1978. "Treasury and Federal Reserve Foreign Exchange Operations," *Quarterly Review*, Federal Reserve Bank of New York, Spring, p.56.
___. 1979. "Treasury and Federal Reserve Foreign Exchange Operations," Quarterly Review, Federal Reserve Bank of New York, Spring.
International Economic Policy. 1981. Hearing before the Joint Economic Committee, U.S. Congress, 1 Sess. Washington: Government Printing Office, p.19.
International Monetary Fund. 1967. *Eighteenth Annual Report, Exchange Restrictions*, Washington, p.667.
___. 1986. *Exchange Arrangements and Exchange Restrictions, Annual Report*, Washington, p.523.
___. 1988. *Exchange Arrangements and Exchange Restrictions, Annual Report*. Washington, p.500.
Jurgensen, P. 1983. *Report of the Working Group on Exchange Market Intervention*, March, p.17.
Meulendyke, Ann-Marie. 1989. *U.S. Monetary Policy and Financial Markets*, Federal Reserve Bank of New York, pp.144-47, 222-24.
Roth, Howard L. 1986. "Federal Reserve Open Market Techniques," *Economic Review*, Federal Reserve Bank of Kansas City, March.
Salvatore, Dominick. 1983. *International Economics*. New York: Macmillan Publishing Co., Inc., p.517.
U.S. Department of the Treasury. 1987. Press release. Washington, December 22.

QUESTIONS

1. What options were available to the U.S. to protect its gold stock under the Bretton Woods system of fixed exchange rates? Explain how each worked to reduce pressure on the dollar.

2. How is U.S. intervention in foreign exchange markets "sterilized"? What does this mean regarding the effects of such intervention?

3. Why did the dollar rise in the early 1980s and then fall in the latter half of the 1980s? What foreign exchange operations did the U.S. undertake during this period, and why were these operations performed?

PART SIX

MONETARY THEORY

Monetary theory considers how the money supply and the Fed's monetary policy affect aggregate spending on goods and services, aggregate output and employment, and the price level and inflation rate. The readings for Part Six discuss some of the central topics and controversies of monetary theory: the demand for money; the nature and stability of the relationship between money and output; the transmission of monetary policy; the causes of inflation; rational expectations and efficient markets; and the activist/nonactivist policy debate.

Reading 27, **"M2 Growth in 1995: A Return to Normalcy?"** by John B. Carlson and Benjamin D. Keen, describe the slowdown in M2 growth relative to output in the early 1990s and identify factors responsible for M2's weakness. Carlson and Keen also discuss research efforts to alter economic measures and models in response to the apparent shift in the relationship between M2 and economic activity. This reading augments Chapter 23's discussion of velocity and the demand for money.

W. Michael Cox, in Reading 28, **"Is There an Output-Inflation Trade-Off,"** analyzes the historical relationship between output and inflation. He argues that the long-term costs of higher inflation outweigh its short-term benefits. This reading goes with Chapter 26's discussion of the Phillips Curve.

Reading 29, **"Bank Lending and the Transmission of Monetary Policy"** by Bharat Trehan, compares the "conventional" view and the "lending view" of the effects of monetary policy. The conventional view stresses monetary policy's effect on bank liabilities (transactions deposits), and the lending view emphasizes its effect on bank loans and their special importance to credit constrained borrowers. Trehan argues that the existence and strength of a lending channel is important to policymakers even though evidence supporting the lending hypothesis is inconclusive. This reading can be used with Chapter 27's discussion of money and economic activity or Chapter 21's treatment of the conduct of monetary policy.

"What Causes Inflation?" by Laurence Ball, Reading 30, supplements Chapter 28's discussion of inflation. Ball summarizes modern inflation theory: long-run inflation trends are determined by the extent to which the rate of money supply growth exceeds the growth rate of output, and short-run fluctuations in the inflation rate are influenced by demand and supply shocks. He mentions the roles of price inertia, budget deficits, inflationary expectations, and accommodating monetary policy in the inflation process and explains why price increases for specific items do not *cause* inflation.

Reading 31 is **"Challenges to Stock Market Efficiency: Evidence from Mean Reversion Studies"** by Charles Engel and Charles S. Morris. Engel and Morris discuss the expected behavior of stock prices in an efficient market. They then explain mean reversion of stock prices in an inefficient market and review the evidence from a number of studies of stock prices and returns. They conclude that, despite some evidence that stock prices are mean reverting, more evidence is needed before concluding the stock market is inefficient. This reading supplements the discussion of efficient markets theory in Chapter 29.

Reading 32 is **"Activist Monetary Policy for Good or Evil? The New Keynesians vs. the New Classicals"** by Tom Stark and Herb Taylor. This reading delineates the essential elements of these two schools and explains why their positions on activist policy differ. It ties in with Chapter 30's discussion of New Classical and nonclassical rational expectations models. Alternatively, instructors may wish to use this reading with the coverage of the activist/nonactivist policy debate in Chapter 28.

READING 27

M2 Growth in 1995: A Return to Normalcy?

John B. Carlson and Benjamin D. Keen

In years past, the growth rates of money measures such as M2 received considerable attention because evidence showed that there was a simple and stable long-run relationship between M2, nominal income, and inflation. Many analysts believed that abrupt changes in money growth induced swings in output, while changes in the trend rate of money growth led to changes in the underlying rate of inflation. Indeed, the view that M2 is an important monetary policy guide is reflected in the fact that the Federal Reserve is required by law to specify growth ranges for the monetary and credit aggregates.[1]

In recent years, however, the reliability of money measures as indicators of monetary policy has been called into question. Since 1990, the relationship between M2 and the variables mentioned above seems to have been permanently disturbed. As a result, policymakers' focus on money measures has diminished significantly. In July 1993, Federal Reserve Chairman Alan Greenspan reported that "...at least for the time being, M2 has been downgraded as a reliable indicator of financial conditions in the economy, and no single variable has yet been identified to take its place."[2]

The latest data, however, suggest that M2 may have begun to regain its value as a policy indicator. After decelerating for five successive years, the growth rate of the aggregate has turned up substantially in 1995. Year to date, M2 has advanced at a 4.3 percent annual pace, approaching the upper end of its Humphrey-Hawkins specified growth range (see figure 1). This recent strength raises a number of questions. Can we infer that the relationship of M2, output, and inflation has stabilized again? Will M2 regain its lost status? This *Economic Commentary* discusses the breakdown and diminished role of M2, then looks at evidence suggesting that the relationship among these variables has indeed been restored.

THE DEMAND FOR M2

The link between money and economic activity has long been succinctly represented in the quantity theory of money. In his influential restatement of this idea, Milton Friedman argues that "the quantity theory is in the first instance a theory of money demand."[3] Simply put, the notion is that over the long

---

Reprinted from Federal Reserve Bank of Cleveland *Economic Commentary*, December 1995.

PART VI Monetary Theory

FIGURE 1 THE M2 AGGREGATE

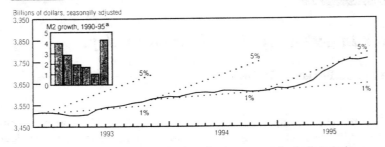

a. Growth rates are percentage rates calculated on a fourth-quarter over fourth-quarter basis. Annualized growth rate for 1995 is calculated on a November over 1994:IVQ basis.
NOTE: Last plot is for November 1995. Dotted lines represent M2 growth ranges and are for reference only.
SOURCE: Board of Governors of the Federal Reserve System.

FIGURE 2 M2 VELOCITY AND OPPORTUNITY COST

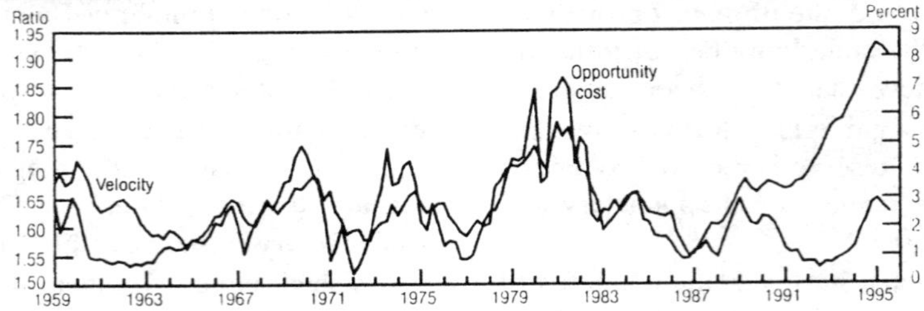

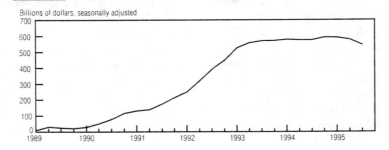

SOURCES: Board of Governors of the Federal Reserve System; and U.S. Department of Commerce, Bureau of Economic Analysis.

FIGURE 3 THE M2 FORECAST ERROR

SOURCE: Federal Reserve Bank of Cleveland.

run, money-balance holders tend to demand a level of balances proportionate to their income. Providing a steady supply of money equal to that demanded should thereby foster noninflationary economic growth. It was largely on the belief that money demand is one of the most stable and reliable relationships in economics that money measures earned their status in the monetary policy process.

From the mid-1980s to the early 1990s, the demand for M2 was perceived to be reasonably stable and the most reliable of the alternative money measures. M2 and nominal GDP had grown at approximately the same rate over the previous 30 years, suggesting a simple and enduring relationship that provided policymakers with a reliable and uncomplicated framework for setting monetary targets. This relationship is summarized by the trendless long-run average of M2 velocity, defined as the ratio of GDP to M2.

Although M2 velocity had been trendless in the long run, it exhibited considerable variation in the short run. Most of this variation, however, was associated with changes in the opportunity cost of holding M2 deposits, defined as the difference between short-term market interest rates and the rate of return on M2 deposits (see figure 2). Specifically, an increase in the opportunity cost of M2 encourages balance holders to shed M2 deposits in favor of higher-yielding alternatives. Hence, M2 deposits are pared down and velocity increases. Before the 1990s, Federal Reserve Board estimates of the response of M2 demand to interest-rate changes were fairly good predictors of the observed variability of M2 velocity.

THE DEMISE OF M2

Beginning in 1990, however, M2 growth began to slow despite a considerable reduction in its opportunity cost. At the same time, M2 velocity remained unexpectedly high. Although part of the M2 slowdown reflected a weakened economy, the magnitude of the downturn could not be reconciled with the aggregate's demand framework or with the historical experience of its velocity. For the next three years, velocity began to drift upward, even though M2 opportunity cost fell. As this anomaly persisted, it became apparent that the estimated relationship linking M2, its opportunity cost, and nominal GDP had broken down. Most standard M2 demand models began to substantially overpredict M2 (see figure 3).

A fundamental factor underlying the aggregate's weakness relates to the credit-market restructuring that occurred in the late 1980s and early 1990s. Specifically, the troubles faced by many financial intermediaries—most notably savings and loans—placed them in a position where they could not assume any additional risk. Consequently, such depositories were forced to tighten their lending standards. Investors seeking financing for marginal business opportunities had to look elsewhere for funds or else abandon their projects. With limited loan expansion, depositories found little need for funds and hence did not price deposits attractively.

Another relevant factor was the steepening in the maturity structure of interest rates. A weakened economy and higher lending standards in the early 1990s ultimately led short-term interest rates to fall to levels not seen in years. This dramatic downturn was not accompanied by a one-to-one decline in long-term interest rates. As a result, long-term instruments were paying significantly more than short-term instruments.

The wide divergence between long- and short-term yields acted as a catalyst for financial innovation. Chief among these innovations were instruments that reduced the transaction costs of bond mutual funds and increased their accessibility to households. This allowed individuals to buy into a diversified portfolio of long-term bonds with check-writing privileges that made the funds quite liquid.

Bond mutual funds are subject to capital losses in the short run, but in the long run, they yield relatively higher rates than do deposit instruments. When short-term interest rates were falling in the early 1990s, marketing strategies encouraged households to learn about bond mutual funds, which were yielding significantly higher returns. As a result, many Americans chose, for the first time, to move some of their wealth from M2 deposits to bond funds. It now appears that for many of these people, bond funds have become a permanent and significant part of their portfolios, supplanting bank CDs (previously the only major form of financial wealth for most households).

EFFORTS TO SALVAGE M2

The breakdown of the relationship between M2, nominal income, and opportunity cost provoked substantial research. One Federal Reserve board study sought to correct the problem by improving the opportunity-cost measure.[4] Specifically, this approach accounted for a broader menu of alternative rates—including some longer-term interest rates—in an M2 demand model. Although the extended opportunity-cost model improved out-of-sample prediction performance, it started to overpredict money demand in mid-1993, when long-term interest rates fell dramatically.

Other researchers tried to redefine the M2 aggregate to include additional instruments such as bond mutual funds.[5] Models using these broader measures were able to explain some of the M2 shortfall by internalizing part of the substitution between M2 balances and these funds. However, adding bond funds to M2 did not fully restore its relationship with nominal income and opportunity cost.[6]

Finally, with the abrupt turnaround in interest rates in 1994 and the flattening of the maturity structure, some analysts predicted that households might abandon bond funds as a form of wealth holding, especially as capital losses sharply reduced reported yields. Although the changing interest-rate structure stanched the flow of money into bond funds, there is no evidence of any significant net outflow. Hence, a large component of the shift in household funds from CDs to bond funds appears to be permanent. The question remains, however, whether household portfolio management has stabilized, and, if so, what that implies for the future relationship between M2, inflation, and output.

HAS M2 STABILIZED?

Preliminary evidence suggests that the relationship between M2, inflation, and output may have stabilized. The prediction errors of the M2 demand model have essentially remained unchanged since 1992. This is consistent with a permanent one-time shift in the level of M2 relative to income. Such an outcome would be the case if the forces underlying the deceleration of M2—restructuring of the nation's credit markets and financial innovation—had worked themselves out, resulting in a one-time effect on M2 demand.

When the M2 model is reestimated to allow for such a change, we find that the historical relationship is largely restored.[7] One implication of this result is that M2 velocity has stabilized at a new level, and that its short-run relationship with M2 opportunity cost is essentially unchanged.[8] Based on our estimates, mean M2 velocity increased from around 1.64 before 1990 to near 1.89 after 1992 (see figure 4). Deviations of M2 velocity from its estimated mean are closely linked to changes in its opportunity cost (see figure 5).

We stress, however, that these estimates are based on a limited amount of data covering only part of a business cycle; hence, skepticism about their durability and precision is warranted. A convincing case might require the new estimates to hold up over a wide range of interest-rate environments, especially one similar to that which existed around 1990, when long rates greatly exceeded short rates. Nevertheless, it seems prudent to begin monitoring this relationship now.

CONCLUSION

Even if M2 continues on a trajectory consistent with the new, higher level of velocity, it seems unlikely that it will soon regain its lost status. One of the most attractive features of the M2 aggregate—the long-run stability of its velocity around a fixed value—has been spoiled. More than 30 years of experience supported the view that M2 velocity would ultimately return to its mean value of around 1.64. The recent evidence that its velocity is higher is based, at most, on five years of experience. Clearly, it will take more time (perhaps another business cycle) to gain confidence that the new average level approximates a long-run equilibrium value.

Nevertheless, if the recent evidence continues to hold, then M2 will probably grow at about the same rate as nominal income, assuming that interest rates remain relatively unchanged. Thus, M2 velocity would remain around its current level. On the other hand, a sharp decline in interest rates, and hence in the opportunity cost of M2, could induce a substantial rise in M2 demand. The consequent reduction in the aggregate's velocity would be interest-rate induced and hence would be consistent with the new stabilized relationship. It seems highly doubtful, however, that M2 velocity will return to anywhere near its previous level.

PART VI   Monetary Theory

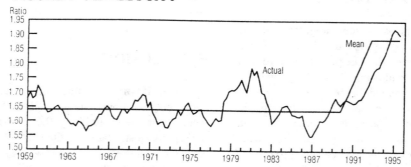

FIGURE 4   M2 VELOCITY

SOURCES: Board of Governors of the Federal Reserve System; U.S. Department of Commerce, Bureau of Economic Analysis; and the Federal Reserve Bank of Cleveland.

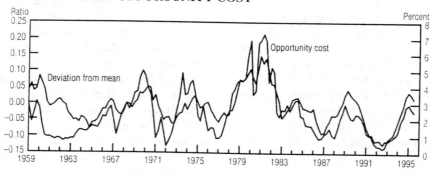

FIGURE 5   M2 VELOCITY'S DEVIATION FROM ITS MEAN AND OPPORTUNITY COST

SOURCES: Board of Governors of the Federal Reserve System; U.S. Department of Commerce, Bureau of Economic Analysis; and the Federal Reserve Bank of Cleveland.

ENDNOTES

1. In February and July of each year, the Federal Open Market Committee (the main policymaking arm of the Federal Reserve Board) sets annual growth ranges for the monetary and credit aggregates. The Federal Reserve Board chairman presents these ranges in testimony before Congress pursuant to the Humphrey-Hawkins Act of 1978.
2. See *1993 Monetary Policy Objectives: Summary Report of the Federal Reserve Board*, July 20, 1993, p. 8.
3. See Milton Friedman, "The Quantity theory of Money—A Restatement," in Milton Friedman, ed., *Studies in the Quantity of Theory of Money*. Chicago: University of Chicago Press, 1956, pp. 3-21.

READING 27 M2 Growth in 1995: A Return to Normalcy?

4. See Joshua N. Feinman and Richard D. Porter, "The Continuing Weakness in M2," Board of Governors of the Federal Reserve System, Finance and Economics Discussion Series, No. 209, September 1992.

5. See Sean Collins and Cheryl L. Edwards, "An Alternative Monetary Aggregate: M2 Plus Household Holdings of Bond and Equity Mutual Funds," Federal Reserve Bank of St. Louis, *Review*, November/December 1994, pp. 7-29.

6. See John V. Duca, "Should Bond Funds Be Added to M2?" *Journal of Banking and Finance*, vol. 19, no. 1 (April 1995), pp. 131-52. See also Athanasios Orphanides, Brian Reid, and David H. Small, "The Empirical Properties of a Monetary Aggregate That Adds Bond and Stock Funds to M2," Federal Reserve Bank of St. Louis, *Review*, November/December 1994, pp. 31-51.

7. We estimate a one-time level shift in M2 demand of approximately $500 billion, occurring smoothly over the 1990:IQ to 1992:IVQ period.

8. Indeed, the goodness-of-fit over the whole sample is superior to that in the sample period leading up to the level shift.

QUESTIONS

1. What determines the opportunity cost of M2? How are the size and velocity of the M2 aggregate expected to change as this opportunity cost rises and falls? Why?

2. What specific reasons do Carlson and Keen give for the slowdown of M2 growth in the early 1990s? How and why did economists attempt to modify models of the relationship between M2, income, and interest rates following this slowdown?

3. What evidence supports the claim that the relationship between M2, income, and interest rates has stabilized? What implications does stability of this relationship have for policymakers?

READING 28

Is There an Output-Inflation Trade-Off?

Evan F. Koenig and Mark A. Wynne

Critics of recent monetary policy have suggested that the Federal Reserve ought to run the economy a little hotter, meaning that the Fed should risk higher inflation down the road in exchange for greater output and lower unemployment today. Is there a connection between inflation and the level of output? Is an attempt to buy the economy more output by risking inflation a good bet? Not according to our analysis of the historical relationship between output and inflation. We compare the output gains from a more stimulatory monetary policy with its inflationary costs and show that the costs of permanently higher inflation substantially outweigh any potential short-term benefits.

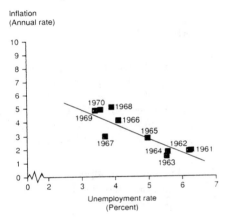

Chart 1
The Unemployment–Inflation Relationship, 1961–70

THE OUTPUT-INFLATION RELATIONSHIP: 1961-70

The negative relationship between unemployment and inflation shown in Chart 1 is called the Phillips curve, after New Zealand economist Alban W. Phillips, who showed that a similar curve could be fit to almost 100 years of British data. During the 1960s, many economists believed that policymakers could choose any point along the Phillips curve and hold the economy there indefinitely. In the opinion of two of the more illustrious advocates of this view, the Phillips curve presented policymakers with a menu of policy choices.[1] By accepting higher inflation, according to this view, it was possible to obtain a permanently lower rate of unemployment. Conversely, lower inflation

Reprinted from Federal Reserve Bank of Dallas *The Southwest Economy*, September 1994, 1-4.

READING 28 Is There an Output-Inflation Trade-Off

could only be attained at the cost of higher unemployment.

Because of shifts in the composition of the labor force and changes in minimum-wage legislation and unemployment insurance benefits, 5-percent unemployment has substantially different economic implications today than it did during the 1960s. To facilitate comparisons across time periods, we focus on a slightly different version of the Phillips curve. Each point in Chart 2 represents a combination of output and inflation rather than unemployment and inflation. Output is measured relative to a long-term growth trend that takes into account the demographic and other changes that complicate interpretation of the traditional Phillips curve. Note that the *negative* unemployment-inflation relationship of the traditional Phillips curve translates into a *positive* output-inflation relationship in Chart 2. This difference simply reflects the fact that when output is high, unemployment tends to be low, and vice versa. Chart 2 shows that in 1961, for example, the level of output was about 5.5 percent below trend, and prices rose just under 2 percent. By 1970, output was 2.5 percent *above* trend, and inflation was running at just under a 5-percent annual rate.

Looking at this chart, it's easy to understand why many people thought that an increase in the inflation rate would permanently increase the level of output.

Chart 2
The Output–Inflation Relationship, 1961–70

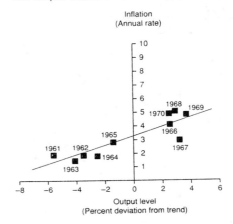

THE PHILLIPS CURVE BREAKS DOWN

During the 1970s, however, inflation rose past 5 percent to rates above 9 percent, yet output did not expand by nearly the expected amount. The output-inflation experience of the late 1970s and early 1980s effectively destroyed economists' belief in a stable Phillips curve.

If we fit a line through the output-inflation combinations observed during the late 1970s and early 1980s, as in Chart 3, we can see that the Phillips curve of this period was about 5 percentage points higher than the Phillips curve of the 1960s. Thus, a level of output equal to trend, which had been associated with 3-percent inflation, was now associated with 7-percent inflation.

PART VI   Monetary Theory

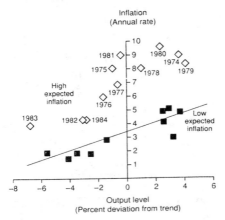

Chart 3
The Effect of Inflation Expectations on the Phillips Curve

What explains the shift in the Phillips curve? It's useful to think of stimulatory monetary policy as a drug for which the economy can build up a tolerance, so that larger and larger doses are required to achieve a given effect. If the Fed unexpectedly increases the rate of growth of the money stock, the economy will initially experience an increase in the level of output accompanied by a relatively small rise in inflation.

Such was the U.S. experience during the 1960s. If rapid money growth continues, however, the economy begins to adapt to it. The inflation rate catches up with the faster rate of growth of the money stock. Workers find that they have increased bargaining leverage and are successful in raising wages. They come to expect that rapid wage increases will continue. Similarly, firms find that they can pass on higher costs to their customers and expect continued rapid price increases. As wages and prices catch up to the money supply, the stimulus to output fades away. The higher inflation continues.

Milton friedman emphasized this point in a 1967 address to the American Economic Association, in which he correctly predicted—many years before the event—the breakdown of the Phillips curve:

> [T]he monetary authority controls nominal quantities—directly [only] the quantity of its own liabilities. In principle, it can use this control to peg a nominal quantity—an exchange rate, the price level, the nominal level of national income, the quantity of money by one or another definition. ...It cannot use its control over nominal quantities to peg a real quantity...[2]

In other words, the Fed's control of the money stock gives it no more than an ephemeral influence on real variables such as the level of output or unemployment.

The hard truth is that there is no lasting output-inflation trade-off in the U.S. economy. Chart 5 shows that, despite an average annual inflation rate of 7 percent, output in the late 1970s and early 1980s was on average no higher relative to trend than it was during the 1960s, when inflation averaged 3 percent a year. Graphically, the Phillips curve is vertical in the long run: over any extended period of time, output is no greater with a high inflation rate than with a low inflation rate. In fact, a case can be made that when properly measured, output may in fact be

READING 28 Is There an Output-Inflation Trade-Off

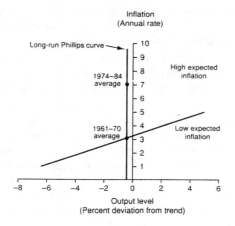

Chart 4
The Long-Run Phillips Curve

lower when inflation is high.

RECENT OUTPUT-INFLATION EXPERIENCE

The problem with easy money is that the economy will not just adapt to rapid money growth and inflation but actually come to depend on it—just as the human body can become dependent on a narcotic. To reduce inflation may then require a painful process of withdrawal, during which output is temporarily depressed. In the early 1980s, the U.S. economy went through just such a withdrawal process. Judging by the output-inflation realizations displayed in Chart 5, that process succeeded in lowering inflation expectations back to 1960s levels. Still, expectations remain at levels nearly twice those consistent with price stability. That is, if we define price stability as inflation in the zero- to 2-percent range, recent output-inflation performance lies on a Phillips curve consistent with expected inflation nearly twice this rate.

If the Fed followed its critics' advice, it would now abandon the pursuit of price stability. Far from trying to overcome the addiction to easy money, the Fed would seek yet another easy-money high. Would a little more inflation really be so bad? Inflation distorts the economy in many ways; here we consider only the most fundamental of these distortions.[3]

At the most basic level, inflation is a tax on the use of money. If inflation is running at, say, 5 percent a year, $100 today will be worth only $95 in a year's time. Inflation

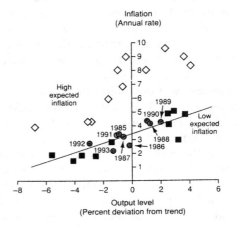

Chart 5
Recent Output–Inflation:
A Return to the Pattern of the 1960s

225

erodes the purchasing power of money in much the same way as the purchasing power of an individual's income is eroded by having to pay income taxes or sales taxes.

Just as individuals try to come up with ways to avoid paying, or at least minimizing their liability for, regular taxes, so, too, will they try to find ways of minimizing the inflation tax they pay. The more rapidly prices increase, the less people hold money. Each dollar changes hands more frequently. In economists' jargon, the velocity of money rises.

This increased attention to financial management consumes real resources. In any one year, the cost is small—on the order of 0.1 percent of gross domestic product (GDP) for each percentage point of inflation. But the cost is incurred year after year after year and grows over time in proportion to the volume of transactions.

Unfortunately, the costs of inflation are not captured fully in the national income accounts, which are the data statisticians compile each year and use to calculate GDP. To the contrary, some of the spending on financial services that is caused by inflation but contributes nothing to people's well-being is counted as real output in the GDP statistics. In much the same way, the additional military spending that accompanied the cold war boosted real GDP, although the threat of nuclear annihilation was hardly welfare-enhancing.

If the benefits of inflation exceeded the costs, Argentina would be an economic powerhouse. Formal analysis confirms the verdict of common sense. Estimates of the total amount of output to be gained from a permanent 1-percentage-point increase in U.S. inflation range from 2.5 percent to 5 percent of GDP.[4] The gains are short-lived, dissipating entirely within a few years.

In contrast, the cash-management costs that accompany higher inflation are small in any single year but grow along with the economy and continue indefinitely. Estimates that take the recurrent nature of these costs into account place their size between 6.5 percent and 10 percent of GDP.[5] Thus, the costs of higher inflation are roughly twice the benefits. The governors of the Federal Reserve System were given 14-year terms precisely so that they would be farsighted in their policy deliberations and not ignore the costs that inflation imposes on society in future years.

CONCLUSION

In short, although higher inflation may be associated with increased output in the short run, there is no lasting output-inflation trade-off. Furthermore, inflation distorts the composition of output, encouraging excessive spending on cash management. The welfare cost of this distortion is small in any single year. Over time, however, the cumulative costs of inflation far outweigh its short-term benefits. If inflation also lowers the economy's growth rate, as some suspect, this would tilt the results of the cost-benefit calculus even more against inflation.[6]

The lesson to be learned from the breakdown of the Phillips curve is that monetary policy cannot have more than a fleeting effect on real variables, such as output and employment. Therefore, the proper focus of the Federal Reserve is not on these variables, but, rather, on the variables over which it *does* exert lasting influence—*nominal* variables such as prices and spending.

ENDNOTES

1. Paul A. Samuelson and Robert M. Solow, "Analytical Aspects of Anti-Inflation Policy," *American Economic Review: Papers and Proceedings* 50 (May 1960): 177-94.
2. Milton Friedman, "The Role of Monetary Policy," *American Economic Review* 58 (March 1968): 1-17.
3. For a comprehensive discussion of the costs of inflation, see Stanley Fischer and Franco Modigliani, "Toward an Understanding of the Real Effects and Costs of Inflation," in Stanley Fischer, ed., *Indexing, Inflation and Economic Policy* (Cambridge, Mass.: MIT Press), 7-33.
4. These figures are based on calculations in Dean Croushore, "What Are the Costs of Disinflation?" Federal Reserve Bank of Philadelphia *Business Review*, May/June 1992, 3-16; Laurence Ball, "How Costly Is Disinflation? The Historical Evidence," Federal Reserve Bank of Philadelphia *Business Review*, November/December 1993, 17-28; and Charles Carlstrom and William Gavin, "Zero Inflation: Transition Costs and Shoe Leather Benefits," *Contemporary Policy Issues* 11 (January 1993): 9-17.
5. These figures are based on estimates presented in Charles Carlstrom and William Gavin, "Zero Inflation: Transition Costs and Shoe Leather Benefits," *Contemporary Policy Issues* 11 (January 1993): 9-17, and Robert E. Lucas, "On the Welfare Cost of Inflation," mimeo, February 1994.
6. Some of the evidence on the relationship between inflation and economic growth is reviewed in Glenn D. Rudebusch and David W. Wilcox, "Productivity and Inflation: Evidence and Interpretation," mimeo, Board of Governors of the Federal Reserve System, May 1994, and Mark A. Wynne, "Price Stability and Economic Growth," *Southwest Economy*, May/June 1993.

QUESTIONS

1. Why should economic policies which increase output relative to its long-run trend also cause higher inflation?

2. Use short-run and long-run Phillips curves to explain U.S. inflation and output patterns from the 1960s to the 1990s.

3. What are the implications of the long-run Phillips curve for monetary policy?

READING 29

Bank Lending and the Transmission of Monetary Policy

Bharat Trehan

How does monetary policy affect the economy? According to the conventional view, a change in monetary policy affects the economy by causing individuals to alter their holdings of short-term bank liabilities (money). However, other channels have been suggested as well, either in addition to or in place of the conventional channel. Some recent work has returned to an earlier theme, emphasizing the role played by bank lending in this process. If this view is correct, it suggests that close attention should be paid to bank lending. For example, it suggests that variables that alter the ability of banks to make loans--such as capital requirements or the health of the banking sector--may alter the efficacy of monetary policy. This *Weekly Letter* compares the conventional view with the so-called lending view and discusses the empirical evidence.

THE "CONVENTIONAL" VIEW

According to the conventional view, monetary policy works as follows. To tighten policy, for example, the Fed sells securities to the public in exchange for reserves. Because banks must hold reserves against transactions deposits, a reduction in available reserves generally means a reduction in these deposits. To make firms and households willing to hold more bonds and fewer transactions balances, the yield on bonds must rise. Higher interest rates, in turn, serve to restrain spending on goods and services throughout the economy. (In the long run lower spending will lead to a fall in the price level such that inflation-adjusted money balances rise, and interest rates fall, to where they were prior to the tightening.)

According to this view, then, monetary policy works because there are no perfect substitutes available for transactions deposits. Individuals are unwilling to change the quantity of transactions balances they hold unless the cost of holding these balances changes. (In this case the cost is the interest that could have been earned if the individual held bonds instead of money.) In terms of bank balance sheets, this view stresses the liability side, and assumes that there is nothing special about the asset side. When monetary policy is tightened (for example), the reduction in bank assets required to balance the reduction in deposits is assumed to be

---

Reprinted from Federal Reserve Bank of San Francisco *Weekly Letter*, September 3, 1993.

costless, essentially because bank loans are assumed to be no different from other kinds of loans in the economy.

THE LENDING VIEW

Suppose, instead, that there were something special about bank loans. In that case the reduction in loans required to rebalance bank balance sheets would have effects in addition to those caused by higher interest rates. This is the view put forward by the proponents of the "lending view." (In the past the lending channel has been suggested as an alternative to the conventional channel; most recent discussion suggests that it is something that works in addition to the conventional channel.) As Bernanke (1993) points out, the conventional view is overly restrictive since it assumes that "...currency and bank deposits [are] the *only* assets for which there are not perfect or nearly perfect substitutes." By contrast, all other assets are grouped under the general heading of "bonds." This grouping is clearly problematic; for instance, it is difficult to argue that commercial paper issued by General Motors and the loan carried on a credit card are perfect substitutes.

What would make bank loans special? One prominent explanation is that banks have information about borrowers that is not easily available to other lenders. The bank might acquire such information, for instance, in the course of repeated dealings with a particular customer. Since other lenders would not have the same information, they would be unwilling to step in to compensate for a (monetary policy induced) reduction in lending by banks. Credit constrained borrowers would then be forced to cut spending. Firms, for example, might have to reduce employment or shut down plants.

POTENTIAL PROBLEMS

While this view of the transmission mechanism is intuitively plausible, a number of objections have been raised against it. Some economists have argued that there is no particular reason for bank loans to be special. They argue that while there may be borrowers about whom it is difficult to acquire information, there is no particular reason that deposit-taking institutions should be making loans to these borrowers. Finance companies, for example, can easily acquire the same information and make the same loans. The existence of alternative institutions willing to make the same loans means that bank lending is not special, since companies that are denied loans by banks can easily turn elsewhere.

Proponents of the lending view have countered by saying that because banks can easily monitor the transactions activities of borrowers they are likely to have an informational advantage over other lenders. Such an advantage would mean that banks could provide loans at a lower cost than other lenders, and bank loans would be special. While banks could have some sort of informational advantage over nonbank lenders, the strength of any such advantage is still an open question.

Some have also questioned the Fed's ability to control bank lending through

PART VI   Monetary Theory

variations in reserves. Romer and Romer (1990) point out that, in addition to issuing transactions deposits, banks can also raise funds by issuing CDs. Since banks are no longer required to hold reserves against CDs, they can respond to a tightening of monetary policy by issuing fewer transactions deposits (against which reserves must be held) and more CDs, while keeping loans constant. If this were indeed the case, Fed induced variations in reserves would have little effect on banks' ability to make loans.

However, this argument assumes that banks could issue as many CDs as they wanted at prevailing interest rates. In fact, it is unlikely that firms and households would be willing to increase CD holdings without being offered some kind of inducement to do so; specifically, banks would have to raise the interest rates they offered on CDs. The cost of making loans would go up as a consequence, and banks would end up making fewer loans than they were making before the Fed tightening. Thus, while CDs with zero reserve requirements make loan volume less sensitive to variations in reserves, loan volume is not totally immune.

EMPIRICAL EVIDENCE

A look at the data reveals that the quantity of bank lending tends to move together with economy-wide aggregates such as output, employment and firm inventories. However, this evidence by itself is not conclusive; such a pattern could be caused either because changes in the supply of loans lead to changes in the level of economic activity or because firms react to changes in economic activity by changing their demand for loans.

One response to such arguments is to try to determine whether changes in bank lending predict changes in economic activity. If changes in bank lending provide a channel through which changes in monetary policy affect the economy, then changes in bank lending should be observed to precede changes in economic activity. While detecting such patterns can be a subtle matter, empirical studies generally have found little evidence to support this hypothesis; instead, bank lending tends to change at about the same time as economic activity. This would suggest that bank lending is not a significant channel for the transmission of monetary policy to the economy.

However, proponents of the lending view have pointed out that such studies are inappropriate because the volume of bank loans is difficult to adjust immediately after a change in policy, and that banks are likely to react first by reducing the securities they hold and only later by changing the amount of loans. While the available evidence is consistent with this hypothesis, the fact that the quantity of outstanding loans falls at the same time as economic activity also means that we cannot rule out the possibility that loan demand is falling because of lower levels of activity.

It has also been suggested that some of the observed sluggishness in loan behavior may be the result of the fact that banks often precommit to making loans. Here the evidence is somewhat more favorable to the lending hypothesis; indeed, it has been shown that while loans made under commitment react relatively slowly, loans made without commitment fall relatively quickly in response to positive interest rate shocks.

Another way to test this hypothesis is to isolate the set of borrowers that is likely to be more dependent upon bank credit and compare the behavior of these borrowers to others who are not as dependent upon banks. Under the lending view a tightening of monetary policy would cause banks to cut down lending to all borrowers; however, small firms would find it difficult to obtain credit from other sources, while large firms would find it easier to go and borrow elsewhere. Consistent with this hypothesis, Gertler and Gilchrist (1991) find that the sales of small firms are more sensitive to changes in interest rates and to certain constructed measures of monetary policy.

More problematic for the lending hypothesis is their finding that bank lending to large firms actually tends to increase in response to positive interest rate shocks, while lending to small firms falls. Since small borrowers are unable to borrow elsewhere while large firms find it easier to move, one would expect that monetary policy tightening would lead to relatively more bank lending to small firms. The contradictory finding suggests that the decline in lending has more to do with the special characteristics of small firms (small firms may be more likely to fail in a recession, for example) than with the way in which monetary policy affects the economy.

A TENTATIVE ASSESSMENT

As our selective review of recent research indicates, the available evidence offers only mixed support to the lending hypothesis. Yet this does not mean that we should dismiss this hypothesis out of hand. On an a priori basis, the hypothesis appears plausible. While the financial system is evolving, at least at this point in time there seem to be a substantial number of borrowers who find it difficult to go elsewhere when denied lending by banks. It also is difficult to believe that banks can isolate lending completely from changes in the stance of monetary policy. Empirically, the issue seems to be whether the lending channel is important enough to matter once the effects of the conventional channel are allowed for.

Determining the strength of this channel is important. Kashyap and Stein (1993) point out that the existence of a lending channel implies that factors affecting bank lending are likely to have an influence on the effectiveness of monetary policy. The example they present has to do with the capital requirements that banks are subject to when making loans. Suppose, for example, that banks do not have enough capital to make new loans. In such a situation they will be unable to make new loans even after the Fed eases policy. Consequently, the easing of policy will have a smaller effect than it would if banks were not constrained by capital requirements. Kashyap and Stein suggest that this may help explain why many people considered monetary policy to be relatively ineffectual during the 1990-1991 recession; in other words, it might explain why the economy has not grown robustly even after policy eased. While this is not much more than conjecture at this point, it does illustrate why the existence and strength of such a channel may be of concern to policymakers.

PART VI   Monetary Theory

REFERENCES

Bernanke, Ben S. 1993. "Credit in the Macroeconomy." Federal Reserve Bank of New York *Quarterly Review* (Spring).
Gertler, Mark, and Simon Gilchrist. 1991. "Monetary Policy, Business Cycles and the Behavior of Small Manufacturing Firms." *NBER Working Paper* No. 3892.
Kashyap, Anil K., and Jeremy C. Stein. 1993. "Monetary Policy and Bank Lending." *NBER Working Paper* No. 4317.
Romer, Christina D., and David H. Romer. 1990. "New Evidence on the Monetary Transmission Mechanism." *Brookings Papers on Economic Activity* vol. 1.

QUESTIONS

1. Compare and contrast the conventional view and the lending view of how monetary policy affects the economy.

2. What evidence supports the lending hypothesis? What evidence contradicts it?

3. If the lending channel operates along side the conventional channel, how does this modify the effects of monetary policy on the economy?

READING 30

What Causes Inflation?

Laurence Ball

Inflation is universally unpopular; everyone from ordinary consumers to top government officials bemoans the perpetual process of rising prices. Frequently, discussions of inflation have an air of resignation. Inflation is like bad weather: we can complain about it, but it seems to be a fact of life. For most people, the causes of inflation are murky. Popular writers lay the blame on a variety of scapegoats: governments that spend too much money, the OPEC cartel, skyrocketing costs of medical care. What causes inflation, and is there any way to eliminate it?

Economists have both good news and bad news about inflation. The good news is that we know a lot about its causes and how it could be ended. The bad news—and the reason that inflation has not been ended—is that doing so could be costly. This article describes what economists understand about inflation and what issues remain mysterious. There is a clear consensus about the long-run causes of inflation—the determinants of average inflation over a decade or more. The short-run behavior of inflation—the ups and downs from year to year—is only partly understood.

INFLATION IN THE LONG RUN

The year-to-year movements in inflation that make newspaper headlines are small compared with the differences in inflation across different eras or different countries. In the United States, inflation as measured by the gross-national-product deflator averaged 7.4 percent per year from 1970 through 1979, but only 2.4 percent from 1950 through 1959.[1] From 1930 through 1939, inflation averaged -1.7 percent per year—the price level was lower at the end of the decade than at the beginning. And these differences across periods in the United States, while substantial, are dwarfed by differences across countries. From the 1950s to the mid-1980s, inflation averaged 4.2 percent per year in the United States, only 2.7 percent in Switzerland, but 8.0 percent in Italy, 21.2 percent in Israel, and 54.4 percent in Argentina (see Ball, Mankiw, and Romer, 1988).[2] What causes these differences in inflation over long periods?

The Culprit: Too Rapid Money Growth. While economists disagree about many issues, there is near unanimity about this one: continuing inflation occurs when the

Reprinted from Federal Reserve Bank of Philadelphia *Business Review*, March/April 1993, 3-12.

PART VI   Monetary Theory

rate of growth of the money supply consistently exceeds the growth rate of output. In the long run, as Milton Friedman puts it, "inflation is always and everywhere a monetary phenomenon." When the money supply grows much more quickly than output of goods and services, inflation is high; when it grows only slightly faster than output, inflation is low; and when it consistently decreases relative to output there is deflation: the price level falls. (The most recent example of deflation in the United States is the early 1930s).

Why does too rapid growth in the money supply cause inflation? To see the answer, consider how the economy responds when the money supply rises. According to mainstream economics, firms do not immediately adjust their prices in response to an increase in the money supply. Because prices do not respond immediately, there is an increase in the real money supply—the money supply relative to the price level. The increase in the real supply of money pushes down the price of money—that is, the interest rate. Over time, lower interest rates stimulate borrowing and spending by firms and consumers, and the economy expands. The story ends when firms react to the booming economy and their strained capacity by raising prices. Prices rise until they match the increase in the money supply, pushing the real money supply back to its original level and choking off the boom. That is, the long-run effect of a 10 percent increase in the money supply relative to output is a 10 percent increase in the price level and no change in the ratio of money to prices. It follows that if the money supply increases 10 percent faster than output every year, prices must eventually rise 10 percent per year. The gap between the average rate of money growth and the average growth rate of output determines average inflation.[3]

In principal, differences in inflation across countries or time periods could be explained by differences in either money growth or output growth, since the gap between the two determines inflation. In practice, however, the most important factor is money growth, which varies widely, with levels near zero in some countries and over 100 percent per year in others. Variation in output growth is smaller and thus is a secondary factor in explaining differences in the gap between money growth and output growth. As a first approximation, then, differences in inflation across time periods or countries can be explained by differences in money growth.

To provide evidence for this point, Figure 1 plots average inflation and money growth in the United States for various decades. Figure 2 presents average inflation and money growth from 1986-89 for a number of countries.[4] In Figure 1, the decades with the highest inflation, such as the 1910s and the 1970s, are those with the highest money growth. Similarly, Figure 2 shows a close relationship between inflation and money growth across countries. Countries such as Switzerland and France produce low inflation through low money growth; countries such as Turkey and Mexico produce high inflation through high money growth. Along with the theoretical arguments discussed above, this evidence has convinced economists that trend or average inflation is determined by money growth.

Why Is Money Growth Excessive? The question of what causes inflation has, at one

READING 30 What Causes Inflation?

FIGURE 1
Money Growth and Inflation (U.S.)
(1870 - 1980)

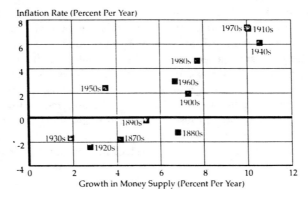

Recreated from: Milton Friedman and Anna J. Schwartz, *Monetary Trends in the United States and the United Kingdom.* Chicago: University of Chicago Press, 1982, with permission.

FIGURE 2
Money Growth and Inflation Across Countries
(1986 - 1989)

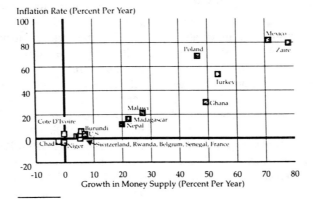

Recreated from: Andrew B. Abel and Ben S. Bernanke, *Macroeconomics.* Reading, MA: Addison-Wesley, 1992, p. 141, with permission.

PART VI   Monetary Theory

level, an easy answer: money growth. This answer, however, raises another, deeper question: why do policymakers allow the money supply to grow quickly? The Federal Reserve and corresponding monetary authorities in other countries possess effective techniques for controlling the average growth rate of the money supply.[5] Policymakers could slow average money growth enough to keep the average inflation rate at zero (although shocks to the economy would cause temporary movements above and below zero). Since both the public and the Federal Reserve dislike inflation, why isn't it eliminated?

The answer to this question is different in different types of economies. In some countries, the answer is simple: the government prints money at a rapid rate to finance budget deficits. This explains most episodes of very high inflation—the annual inflation of several hundred percent or more that has affected South American countries and Israel within the past decade. These countries have had high levels of government spending and have been unable politically to match this spending with tax revenues; thus they have financed their spending by creating new money. Predictably, rapid money creation has produced high inflation. Inflation has been brought under control only when the underlying budget deficit was reduced. (In Israel, for example, such a stabilization occurred in 1985.)

Budget deficits are not, however, the basic source of inflation in the United States or in most European economies. The U.S. government has, of course, run large deficits over the past decade. But these deficits have been financed primarily by borrowing, not by printing money. That is, the government covers its deficit mostly by issuing bonds. The Federal Reserve contributes to government revenue by creating new money, but this "seignorage" is small: less than 1 percent of total revenue. In countries like the United States, policymakers would gladly eliminate inflation through lower money growth if the only cost were a small revenue loss. The deterrent to lowering inflation must arise from a different source.

The reason U.S. policymakers are reluctant to push inflation to zero is that doing so is likely to cause a recession, or at least slower economic growth. This fear is supported by both macroeconomic theory and historical experience. Slower money growth reduces inflation in the long run, but there is a lag, as discussed earlier. When money growth falls, firms initially continue to raise prices at the rate to which they are accustomed. With money growing more slowly than prices, the real money supply falls, causing a recession. Only the experience of the recession causes inflation to fall.

This theoretical story fits much of the U.S. experience. One cause of the recession that began in 1990 was, arguably, the Fed's efforts to reduce inflation in the late 1980s. More clearly, disinflation was a major cause of the recession of 1981-82—the worst recession since the 1930s. Paul Volcker, the chairman of the Federal Reserve from 1979 to 1986, moved decisively to eliminate the double-digit inflation of the late 1970s. He succeeded, but at a price: inflation fell from 10.1 percent in 1980 to 4.0 percent in 1983, but unemployment rose from 5.8 percent in

1979 to 9.5 percent in both 1982 and 1983. Research by economic historians has shown that this experience is part of a regular pattern: when the Fed slows money growth substantially to reduce inflation, a recession occurs almost invariably.[6]

While some policymakers are willing to pay this price to reduce inflation, others are not. And the Fed's eagerness to fight inflation appears to depend on the severity of the inflation problem. Volcker was sufficiently concerned about double-digit inflation to implement the monetary tightening needed to reduce inflation. But inflation of around four percent, the level through much of the 1980s, did not create enough distress to prompt a further tightening. Thus inflation continued. (For more on this subject, the reader is referred to "What Are the Costs of Disinflation?" by Dean Croushore, in the May/June 1992 issue of the Federal Reserve Bank of Philadelphia *Business Review*.)

SHORT-RUN FLUCTUATIONS IN INFLATION

Although money growth determines average inflation in the long run, the short-run behavior of inflation is more complicated. Inflation fluctuates around its long-term trend from year to year; for example, annual inflation rates in the second half of the 1980s varied around their average of 3.6 percent, with annual rates from 1985 to 1989 of 3.6, 2.5, 3.3, 4.3, and 4.2 percent. Short-term fluctuations in inflation were larger in the 1970s: the annual rates from 1970 to 1974 were 4.7, 5.6, 5.0, 7.6, and 9.6 percent. One source of these inflation movements is temporary fluctuations in the growth of the money supply. In contrast to the long run, however, too rapid money growth is not the only, or even the primary, determination of inflation. Figure 3 plots inflation against money growth for each year during the 1970s and 1980s. Clearly, annual inflation can differ considerably from money growth. What causes this short-run divergence?

Demand Shocks. One source of short-run changes in inflation is shifts in aggregate demand—in desired spending by government, businesses, and consumers. Suppose that the government spends more to finance a war or businesses become more confident about the future and invest in factories and machines. As the demand for military hardware or for factories rises, the economy expands: firms increase production and hire more workers, cutting unemployment. But again, high output and low unemployment eventually spur faster increases in wages and prices: inflation rises. Similarly, a fall in aggregate demand causes a recession, leading firms to raise prices more slowly. The economy's short-run movements between booms and recessions produce fluctuations in inflation as well.

A good example of inflation arising from a shift in aggregate demand—a shift that was not initiated by monetary policy—is the increase in inflation in the late 1960s. Annual inflation varied from 0.8 percent to 2.3 percent over the period of 1960-64, but rose to 5.3 percent in 1969. The consensus explanation for this experience is increased government spending. As the Vietnam War escalated, the Johnson administration raised

PART VI Monetary Theory

FIGURE 3
Money Growth and Inflation During the 1970s (U.S.)

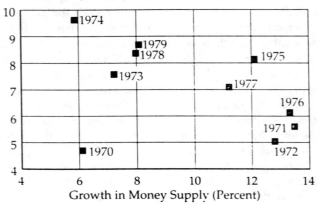

Money Growth and Inflation During the 1980s (U.S.)

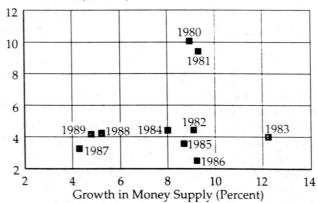

military spending while also continuing the social programs of the "Great Society." As a result, the federal budget deficit grew from $1.4 billion in fiscal year 1965 to $25.2 billion in 1968, and the economy overheated: unemployment fell, but inflation rose.

Price Shocks. Until the 1970s, most economists believed that shifts in aggregate demand were the dominant source of short-run movements in inflation. This view had to be modified, however, after the experience of the 1970s, when price shocks—a.k.a. "supply shocks"—caused large increases in inflation. These shocks were sharp increases in the prices of particular goods, namely food and energy products, arising ultimately from poor weather and the emergence of the OPEC cartel. These shocks created "stagflation": inflation rose while unemployment rose and real output fell (in contrast to the experience of demand shocks, which push inflation and unemployment in opposite directions). From 1972 to 1974, annual inflation rose from 5.0 percent to 9.6 percent as a result of a rise in food prices and the first OPEC price increase. OPECII raised inflation from 7.1 percent in 1977 to 10.1 percent in 1980. These increases dwarfed the fluctuations in inflation arising from the demand shocks of the previous 20 years. More recently, the spike in oil prices during the gulf crisis raised inflation in the second half of 1990.

Why do rises in food and energy prices create inflation? The reader will be forgiven for thinking that the answer is obvious: food and energy are a significant fraction of the economy, and rises in prices are the *definition* of inflation. Economists, however, believe that the issue is not so simple because of the distinction between the overall price level and *relative* prices.

In classical economic theory, the price level is determined by the money supply, as described above. Changes in supply and demand for various products arising from weather conditions, cartel decisions, and so on affect not the price level but relative prices: OPEC makes oil more expensive *relative* to other goods. Theoretically, this is accomplished partly by an increase in the absolute price of oil and partly by *decreases* in all other prices. With these price adjustments, oil can become relatively more expensive while the price level remains unchanged at the equilibrium level determined by the money supply. In practice, this is not what happens: OPEC in fact raised the average price level. But it is not obvious why this is so.[7]

This issue is the subject of recent research by me and Gregory Mankiw of Harvard University (Ball and Mankiw, 1992). Our explanation for the inflationary effects of price shocks rests on two ideas. First, there is some inertia in prices. Firms do not instantly adjust prices to every change in circumstances; instead, they adjust only if their desired price change is large enough to justify the costs of adjustment. For example, a mail-order company will print a new catalog to announce a 50 percent sale, but it is not worth the effort to announce a one-cent price change arising from a tiny change in costs; instead, the firm will simply keep its prices fixed. This behavior implies that large shocks have disproportionately large effects on prices: firms adjust to them quickly, while they make smaller adjustments more slowly.

The second key idea is that "price shocks" are episodes in which certain relative prices rise or fall by unusually large amounts. In the OPEC episodes, for example, some relative prices—those for oil-related products—rose 50 percent or more in response to the trebling of oil prices. By definition, other relative prices went down to balance these increases: if some prices are relatively higher, others must be relatively lower. It was not the case, however, that equilibrium prices of some nonoil products needed to fall by more than 50 percent. Instead, the relative price decreases were spread over all nonoil goods: a fraction of relative prices rose a large amount, balanced by smaller relative decreases in the majority of prices.

Combining this idea with the previous one—that large shocks have disproportionate effects—explains why OPEC was inflationary. The large relative shocks to oil-related prices triggered quick upward adjustments. For example, given the large increase in oil prices, gas stations would have suffered huge losses had they not quickly raised prices at the pump. In contrast, while prices of many other goods came under downward pressure, the required price decreases were small and hence occurred more slowly.

When consumers spend more money on oil, they had less available for toothbrushes, soft drinks, and all other nonoil goods, creating an incentive for the sellers of these products to reduce prices. But the desired decreases were only a few percentage points because OPEC did not cut heavily into toothbrush or soft drink demand. Thus firms were slow to adjust prices downward. In the short run, oil-related prices rose, and the offsetting decreases did not fully occur. Thus prices rose on average: there was inflation.

This theoretical story explains a large number of rises and falls in inflation in the United States. The oil and food price episodes in the 1970s are examples. Another example is the large *decrease* in oil prices in 1985-86. Our theory predicts that inflation should fall in this episode because the decreases in oil prices occur more quickly than the smaller increases in other prices. And, indeed, inflation fell from 4.4 percent in 1984 to 2.5 percent in 1986.

Our theory also explains episodes before the famous supply shocks of the 1970s. For example, inflation rose above 10 percent in 1951, largely due to a demand shock: the Korean War. Inflation then plummeted to near zero in 1952, and the cause appears to be a price shock. Specifically, the prices of meat, rubber, vegetable oil, and several other products fell steeply. More generally, my research with Mankiw suggests that a combination of demand and price shocks explains most of the year-to-year fluctuations in U.S. inflation since 1950.

Although some relative price increases are inflationary according to our theory, others are not. One example is the steady increase in the cost of medical care. These price increases probably have little to do with inflation, despite frequent claims to the contrary in popular discussions. A relative price increase affects inflation only if there is an unusually large shock during a particular year, so that the upward price adjustment occurs more quickly than the offsetting downward adjustments. Medical costs have risen faster than the overall price level for several decades, but the rise has been steady; there are no cases of 50 percent or 100 percent increases within a year, as in the case of oil. This smooth adjustment of relative prices could occur without inflation. If the Federal Reserve pursued noninflationary monetary policy, the average price level would remain steady, with rises in the price of medical care offset by price decreases in other industries.

FROM THE SHORT RUN TO THE LONG RUN

According to the analysis so far, the average rate of inflation over a long period is determined by the amount that average growth of the money supply exceeds average output growth. Inflation fluctuates around its trend from year to year in response to various demand and price shocks. We have seen that these ideas explain much of the U.S. inflation experience, but they do not capture one aspect: the link between the short run and the long run.

Suppose that inflation is proceeding at the level determined by trend money and output growth and that oil prices rise sharply. The theories reviewed so far suggest that this price shock should raise inflation in the short run but that inflation should then return to its long-run trend if trend money growth is unchanged. In fact, shifts in inflation arising from demand or price shocks appear quite persistent. When government spending raised inflation in the late 1960s, and when OPEC raised inflation in the 1970s, there was little sign that inflation would naturally return to its previous level. Instead, inflation continued until the Federal Reserve became sufficiently concerned to tighten policy, producing a recession. (Such policy tightenings occurred in 1970 in response to the high inflation of the late 1960s and in 1974 and 1978-79 after the OPEC shocks. See Romer and Romer, 1989.) Absent a policy tightening and recession, inflation arising from price or demand shocks seems to continue indefinitely: short-run shifts in inflation have long-run effects on trend inflation. How can this evidence by squared with our earlier theories?

Recall the crucial fact that trend inflation is ultimately caused by faster growth in the money supply than in output. Logically, if shocks such as OPEC shift trend inflation, they must induce the Federal Reserve to raise trend money growth (until the point when policymakers decide that inflation is too high and accept the cost of disinflation). Why does a short-run spurt in inflation lead the Fed to raise the average level of money growth?

The usual answer to this question focuses on the behavior of inflationary expectations. In past experience, individuals have seen that increases or decreases in inflation usually persist for a substantial period. Thus, when they see a new rise in inflation (because of an OPEC shock, for example), they expect inflation to stay high. Crucially, this expectation is self-fulfilling: the expectation that inflation will stay high causes it to stay high. The reason expectations affect actual inflation is that they affect decisions about wage- and price-setting. If everyone expects a 10 percent rate of inflation to continue, workers will demand 10 percent wage

PART VI   Monetary Theory

increases to keep up. Firms will raise prices 10 percent to match the higher wages they pay and also the 10 percent increases they expect from their competitors. Thus inflation will continue at 10 percent, fulfilling expectations.

The Federal Reserve is not helpless in the face of this self-fulfilling inflationary spiral. The spiral can continue only as long as it is "accommodated" by the Fed—as long as the Fed raises money growth as much as inflation has risen. However, a price shock such as that caused by OPEC is not only inflationary for the U.S., it also is contractionary. Because the higher price of imported oil leaves Americans with less of their incomes to spend on domestic goods and services, it causes output and employment to fall, at least temporarily. The Federal Reserve could bring inflation back down by slowing money growth. The result will be to reduce output further, causing a recession that eventually forces inflation down. Over substantial periods, however, such as the 1970s, the Fed has been unwilling to impose this cost on the economy. Thus, once a shock such as OPEC raises inflation, it can stay high for a long period before a Paul Volcker takes charge and disinflates. The price shock creates a vicious circle in which persistence in inflation creates the expectation of persistence, which in turn creates persistence.

While this story is widely accepted, it is not airtight. At an empirical level, it appears true that changes in inflation are expected to persist. Surveys of the expectations of forecasters and of ordinary citizens show that a rise in current inflation leads to higher forecasts of future inflation. At a deeper level, however, it is not clear *why* expectations behave that way. Since the expectation of persistence is self-fulfilling, it proves itself correct. But there are other expectations that would also be self-fulfilling. Suppose that a price shock raised inflation in one year, but everyone expected that inflation would return to its original level in the next year. With the expectation of moderate inflation, workers would moderate their wage demands, and firms would moderate their price increases. Thus the expectation of low inflation would also prove itself correct. Since expectations of either persistent or nonpersistent inflation are self-fulfilling, it appears that either expectation would be rational. The U.S. economy has settled into a situation in which people expect inflation to persist, perhaps only because it has in the past.

CONCLUSIONS

The behavior of inflation is one of the better-understood areas of macroeconomics. There is a wide consensus about the long-run determinants of inflation and, arguably, a consensus about much of its short-run behavior. The average inflation rate over long periods is determined by the extent to which the average rate of money growth (which, in the United States, is chosen by the Federal Reserve) exceeds the average growth rate of real output. Short-run inflation fluctuates around its long-run average because of demand shocks, such as large increases in government spending, and supply shocks, such as sharp rises in the prices of food and energy.

Some countries have persistently high inflation because they continuously create new money to finance large, ongoing budget deficits. Such countries are unable to reduce money growth enough to halt inflation because their governments have been unable to eliminate budget deficits and because they do not have effective alternatives for financing those deficits. In the United States, however, the government budget deficit is financed almost entirely with Treasury debt, not money creation. The United States had low average inflation in the 1980s because money growth, on average, only slightly exceeded output growth.

Finally, the distinction between short-run and long-run determinants of inflation is blurred by the fact that short-run changes often influence the long-run trend. When a demand or price shock raises short-run inflation in the United States, expectations of future inflation rise. Historically, the Fed often accommodated these expectations by allowing money growth to rise, so expectations were fulfilled. Not allowing money growth to rise would have slowed output growth and perhaps caused a recession.

These conclusions—a summary of the thinking of mainstream economists—partly fit ideas that are popular among journalists and the public and partly contradict such ideas. It is common, for example, to blame inflation on excessive deficit spending by the government. This view is on target for the case of Argentina, but not for the United States. Little of the U.S. deficit is financed by printing money. Thus it was possible for U.S. inflation to fall between the 1970s and the 1980s even though the U.S. budget deficit rose substantially. On the other hand, the view that government spending fuels U.S. inflation has a grain of truth. There are periods, notably the Vietnam era, when too much spending overheats the economy, producing inflation that persists as long as monetary policy is accommodative.

Perhaps the most common scapegoats for inflation are the particular prices that the public observes to rise most rapidly. In some eras, these are oil or food prices; a current favorite is medical care. When journalists and citizens blame individual prices for inflation, they confuse average and relative prices. Particular prices could rise just as much in relative terms even if the overall price level were constant. Again, however, there is a grain of truth in conventional thinking. Particularly sharp increases in prices, such as OPEC shocks, are inflationary.

ENDNOTES

1. Unless otherwise noted, all inflation figures refer to the percentage change in the GNP deflator. This variable is a broad index of the level of all prices in the economy. The more famous Consumer Price Index covers only prices paid by consumers, not those paid by governments or businesses.
2. Citations to all papers mentioned in the text are included in the "References" section at the end of this article.

PART VI   Monetary Theory

3. To be complete, inflation depends on the growth rate of the "velocity" of money—the frequency with which money is turned over—as well as on the gap between the average growth rates of money and output. For the United States, the average growth rate of velocity (for the M2 measure of money) has been zero over the past 40 years. In practice, then, money growth of 2 or 3 percent per year is consistent with stable prices. This rate of money growth matches the natural growth of output and spending.

4. The data for Figures 1 and 2 are taken from Friedman and Schwartz (1982) and Abel and Bernanke (1992), respectively.

5. Specifically, the Fed manipulates the supply of money through "open market operations"—purchases and sales of government bonds. Buying bonds with money adds to the economy's money stock, and selling bonds drains money out of the economy.

6. Romer and Romer (1989) identify six episodes since World War II in which the Fed sharply tightened policy to reduce inflation. In each case, a recession occurred within two or three years.

7. Writing in 1975, Milton Friedman puts the point this way: "It is essential to distinguish changes in *relative* prices from changes in *absolute* prices. The special conditions that drove up the prices of oil and food required purchasers to spend more on them, leaving them less to spend on other items. Did that not force other prices to go down or to rise less rapidly than otherwise? Why should the *average* level of prices be affected significantly by changes in the price of some things relative to others?"

REFERENCES

Abel, Andrew, and Ben Bernanke. *Macroeconomics*. Addison-Wesley, 1992.

Ball, Laurence, and N. Gregory Mankiw. "Relative-Price Changes as Aggregate Supply Shocks," mimeo, Princeton University (April, 1992).

Ball, Laurence, N. Gregory Mankiw, and David Romer. "The New Keynesian Economics and the Output-Inflation Trade-off," *Brookings Papers on Economic Activity* (1988:1).

Croushore, Dean. "What Are the Costs of Disinflation?" Federal Reserve Bank of Philadelphia *Business Review* (May/June, 1992).

Friedman, Milton. "Perspectives on Inflation," *Newsweek* (June 24, 1975).

Friedman, Milton, and Anna J. Schwartz. *Monetary Trends in the United States and the United Kingdom*. University of Chicago Press, 1982.

Romer, Christina, and David Romer. "Does Monetary Policy Matter? A New Test in the Spirit of Friedman and Schwartz," *NBER Macroeconomics Annual*, 1989.

READING 30 What Causes Inflation?

QUESTIONS

1. Why does excessive monetary growth cause inflation? What evidence does Ball present to support this argument?

2. Do increases in the prices of particular goods or services necessarily cause inflation? Under what circumstances may they be the cause of inflation?

3. What causes short-run fluctuations of inflation rates around the long-run trend?

4. Suppose the inflation rate increases above its long-run trend. Is the inflation rate likely to persist at this higher level or return to its long-run trend? Why?

READING 31

Challenges to Stock Market Efficiency: Evidence from Mean Reversion Studies

Charles Engel and Charles S. Morris

Analysts have traditionally regarded the stock market as an efficient market because they believe stock prices reflect the market value of future dividends. Dividends, in turn, depend on a company's profits. As a result, stock prices should change only in response to new information about future profits. For example, a company's stock price will rise if it patents a new way to harness solar power because future profits will rise. Conversely, its stock price will fall if its chief competitor discovers the new way first.

In recent years, however, many analysts have begun to question the efficiency of the stock market. What information, they ask, could have possibly caused the profitability of the companies in the Dow Jones Industrial Average to fall 23 percent on October 19, 1987? These analysts claim the stock market is inefficient because many traders pay attention to information unrelated to future profits. For example, some traders may jump on the bandwagon and buy stocks only because past returns were high. While prices will ultimately reflect true values, such behavior causes prices to overshoot true values in the short run. The tendency for prices to overshoot but eventually revert to true values is called *mean reversion*.

Is the stock market efficient? This article surveys the mean reversion evidence. The article finds that stock prices might be mean reverting, but the evidence is not strong enough to rule out market efficiency. The first section of the article discusses the features of an efficient stock market. The second section shows why prices may be mean reverting in an inefficient stock market. The third section shows that the evidence on mean reversion is mixed. Thus, more evidence is needed before declaring the stock market inefficient.

EFFICIENT MARKETS

The efficient market theory describes how prices are determined in a securities market. In an efficient stock market, a stock's price reflects the current market value of its expected future income stream. If a stock's price is less than the value of its expected income stream, investors will quickly buy the stock. As they do, the price will rise until it

Reprinted from Federal Reserve Bank of Kansas City *Economic Review*, September/October 1991, 21-35.

equals the current value of the income. Conversely, if a stock's price is above the current value of expected income, selling pressure will quickly drive down the price to its current value.[1]

The income from a stock can be divided into two parts. One part is the dividends that are paid over the investment horizon. The second part is the price for which investors can sell the stock at the end of the investment horizon.

The market value of the expected income from a stock depends on the size of the income stream relative to the return on other investments that are equally risky. The return on equally risky investments can be represented by the inflation-adjusted, or real, interest rate on such investments. The real interest rate on a risky investment is the sum of the real interest rate on a riskless investment, such as Treasury bills, and a risk adjustment factor that rises with the riskiness of an investment. Thus, the current price of a stock, P_0, is

$$P_0 = \frac{ED_1 + EP_1}{1+r}$$

where, ED_1 is the dividends that investors expect to be paid at the end of the investment period, EP_1 is the expected end-of-period price, and r is the real interest rate.[2] Thus, a stock will have a high price if it is expected to pay high dividend (high ED_1), if it is expected to appreciate rapidly (high EP_1), or if it is not very risky (low r).[3]

One feature of an efficient stock market is that highly profitable companies will have higher stock prices than unprofitable companies. In an efficient market, stock prices reflect the market value of future dividends, which ultimately depend on profits. Thus, stock prices reflect the market value of a company's future profits—that is, the company's *fundamental* value.

The economy benefits when stock prices reflect fundamental values because investment funds flow to their most valuable uses. Companies with profitable investment opportunities have high fundamental values, while companies without such opportunities have low fundamental values. As a result, companies with profitable investment opportunities can sell their stock for a higher price, and therefore get more investment funds, than companies without such opportunities.

A second feature of an efficient stock market is that expected real returns on stocks should be constant and equal to the real interest rate (Figure 1). Like most stock price indexes, such as the Dow Jones Industrial Average, the price in the figure includes the returns from dividends so that the percentage change in price is the total return.[4] If the real interest rate is constant over time, prices will grow along a straight line with a slope equal to the interest rate. The slope of the line is just the percentage change in price.[5] Thus, because the percentage change in price is the total return, the expected return on the stock is constant and equal to the real interest rate.

A third feature is that only new information about future profits causes real stock returns to deviate from the real interest rate. Because stock prices already reflect everything that investors expect about future

PART VI Monetary Theory

Figure 1
Stock Prices in an Efficient Market

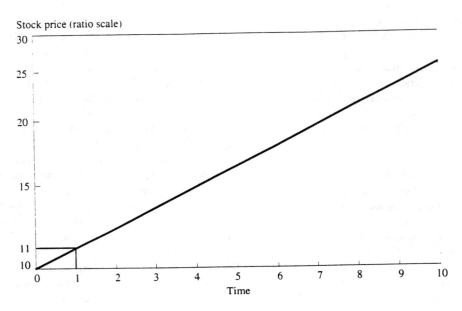

profits, prices should rise more or less than expected only if investors get new information about future profits. For example, suppose the interest rate is 10 percent and the stock price is $10 (Figure 2). At the end of period one, the stock price can be expected to rise to $11. But if the company announces it will pay higher dividends with the profits from a new discovery, the stock is a bargain at $11. As investors buy more of the stock, the price might rise to $13. Thus, while the expected return on the stock was only 10 percent, the unexpected news led to a 30 percent return.

A final feature of efficient markets is that when actual returns differ from what was expected, investors should still expect future returns to be constant and equal to the real interest rate. In other words, if prices rise more than expected, investors should not expect prices to continue to grow faster just because they did so in the past. Furthermore, investors should not expect prices to grow slower to offset the unexpected increase. For example, in Figure 2, the stock price rose 20 percent more than expected over the first period. The unexpected increase reflected the *entire* value of the increase in future dividends. As a result, the stock price should resume growing at the old rate. This is shown in Figure 2 by the high-dividend path having the same slope as the low-dividend path.

READING 31 Challenges to Stock Market Efficiency

Figure 2
Stock Prices in an Efficient Market: Change in Dividends

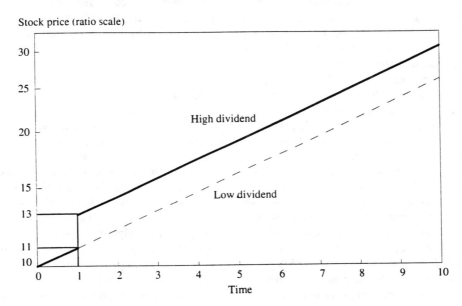

INEFFICIENT MARKETS

Many analysts claim the stock market is inefficient because they believe prices often overreact to new information and overshoot fundamental values in the short run. If stock prices do not always reflect fundamental values, the stock market will not direct investment funds to where they are most valuable. Moreover, expected returns will vary over time because prices will be mean reverting. Finally, stock prices that overreact to new information are excessively.

Why Might the Stock Market Be Inefficient?

In an efficient market, stock prices reflect the current value of the future income that stocks generate because prices depend on *future* dividends, prices, and interest rates. If other factors, such as *past* prices and dividends, affect the value investors place on stocks, stock prices will deviate from fundamental values. When prices deviate from fundamental values, the market is inefficient.

One theory of why stock prices deviate from fundamental values is that many traders pay attention to recent trends in returns

PART VI Monetary Theory

(Cutler, Poterba, and Summers). These "feedback traders" believe that if a stock's returns have been high in the recent past, they are likely to be high in the future. As feedback traders buy the stock to capture the excess returns, the price will rise above the stock's fundamental value. Likewise, if returns have been low in the recent past, feedback traders will sell the stock, driving the price below its fundamental value. Thus, in the short run, increases in stock prices are followed by further increases and decreases are followed by decreases.

According to the theory, however, stock prices will ultimately return to fundamental values. Arbitragers and traders who pay attention to fundamental values will discover which stocks are overvalued and which are undervalued. As they sell the overvalued stocks and buy the undervalued stocks, prices eventually reach their fundamental values.

An example may clarify how stock prices in an inefficient stock market differ from prices in an efficient stock market (Figure 3). Suppose a company's stock price jumps when it announces it will pay higher dividends with the profits from a new discovery. Because the return over the first period is 30 percent instead of 10 percent, feedback traders buy the stock. The upward pressure on the price drives the price above its fundamental value (shown by the dashed line segment). Traders who pay attention to fundamentals will then begin selling the overvalued stock, putting downward pressure on its price and causing the average return to fall over the next few periods. With lower past returns, fewer feedback traders buy the stock. Indeed, some may start selling the stock, producing even greater downward pressure on the price. Eventually, the price returns to its fundamental value. Prices that follow such a pattern of rising above their fundamental trend and then returning are said to be *mean reverting*.

Implications

In contrast to an efficient stock market, an inefficient stock market does not direct investment funds to their best use because prices do not necessarily reflect fundamental values. For example, feedback traders may irrationally drive the stock prices of companies with low fundamental values too high. Conversely, stock prices of companies with high fundamental values may be too low. As a result, companies with low fundamental values may be able to raise a lot of capital, while companies with high fundamental values may find it difficult to raise capital.

A second implication of an inefficient stock market is that mean reverting prices cause expected returns to vary. For example, although the average return in Figure 3 from the end of period one to the end of period five is 10 percent, the return is far from constant. As the price rises above the fundamental value, the return is 30 percent. But as the price reverts to the fundamental value, the average return is just 4 percent. Thus, greater than average returns are followed by less than average returns, while less than average returns are followed by greater than average returns.

A third implication is that prices are excessively volatile in the short run. Stock

Figure 3
Stock Prices in an Inefficient Market

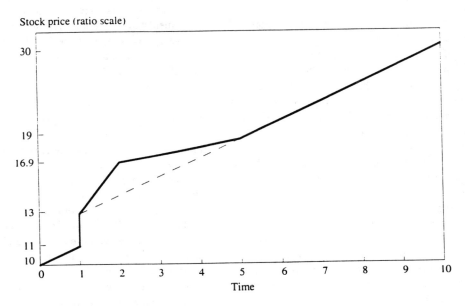

prices are volatile in an efficient market because new information causes unexpected changes in prices. However, prices are even more volatile in an inefficient market because prices will change by more than the value of the new information. In the long run, though, prices are not excessively volatile because they eventually revert to their fundamental trend. In other words, as shown in Figure 3, the long-run change in stock prices in an inefficient market is the same as in an efficient market.

IS THE STOCK MARKET EFFICIENT?

The evidence is mixed on whether the stock market is efficient. Some recent studies have found that stock prices are mean reverting, leading some analysts to conclude that the stock market is inefficient. Other studies cast doubt on this conclusion.

PART VI Monetary Theory

Evidence That Stock Prices Are Mean Reverting

After years of testing the efficient market hypothesis, financial economists have generally agreed that the stock market is efficient. In recent years, however, new research strategies have shown that stock prices are mean reverting over long investment horizons. The strategies rely on new statistical techniques that are potentially better able to detect regularities in stock prices. In addition, some researchers have begun to pay more attention to the long-run behavior of stock prices.

Variance-ratio tests. In the long run, stock price volatilities are the same whether or not prices are mean reverting. Short-run volatilities, however, are greater if prices are mean reverting than if they are not. As a result, the ratio of long-run volatility to short-run volatility is smaller if prices are mean reverting. The new statistical techniques use ratios of long-run volatilities to short-run volatilities to determine whether stock prices are mean reverting.

An example may help clarify this point. Suppose a stock's price will either rise 20 percent a year or fall 10 percent a year (solid lines in Figure 4). One measure of the volatility of this stock is the difference between the best and worst possible returns over the investment horizon. For a one-year investment, the best return is a 20 percent gain and the worst a 10 percent loss, so the volatility is 30 percent (20 percent less a negative 10 percent). For a two-year investment, the best return is 40 percent—20 percent in each of the two years—and the worst is a negative 20 percent, so the volatility is 60 percent. Thus, the volatility of the two-year investment is twice that of the one-year investment. More generally, the volatility of a k-year investment will be k times the volatility of a one-year investment if the market is efficient.[6]

The volatility of a k-year investment will be less than k times the volatility of a one-year investment, however, if prices are mean reverting. Because prices overshoot fundamental values in the short run but not the long run, prices are excessively volatile only in the short run. For example, prices might either rise 30 percent or fall 20 percent so that the volatility is 50 percent in the first year (dashed lines in Figure 4). If the price returns to its fundamental value by the second period, the best two-year return is 40 percent and the worst is a negative 20 percent, so that the volatility is 60 percent—just as in the efficient market. Thus, the volatility of the two-year investment is much less than twice the volatility of the one-year investment.[7]

Poterba and Summers have argued that the efficient market theory can be tested by looking at whether volatility rises proportionally to the investment horizon. They measured volatility by the variance of stock returns. If the market is efficient, the variance of k-year returns (r_k) should equal k times the variance of one-year returns (r_1).

$$Variance(r_k) = k \times Variance(r_1)$$

or

$$\frac{Variance(r_k)}{k \times Variance(r_1)} = 1$$

Figure 4
Investment Risk

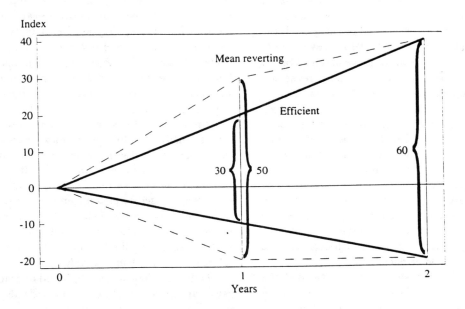

Thus, the ratio of the variances at all investment horizons should equal one if the market is efficient, but should be less than one if prices are mean reverting.

Poterba and Summers concluded that the stock market is inefficient because prices are mean reverting. They calculated variance ratios for investment horizons of two to eight years. The data were excess returns on the New York Stock Exchange (NYSE) from 1926 to 1985, measured as monthly NYSE returns less U.S. Treasury bill returns. The variance ratios were less than one for all investment horizons greater than two years. For example, eight-year returns should be eight times more variable than one-year returns if the stock market is efficient. Poterba and Summers found, however, that eight-year returns are only three-and-a-half times more variable than one-year returns. In addition, the eight-year variance ratio is significantly less than one in a statistical sense. Finally, Poterba and Summers showed that mean reversion is stronger for stocks of small firms than of large firms.[8]

Regression tests. Another way to test the efficient market theory is to regress stock returns on past stock returns. If stock prices rise at a constant rate as suggested by the efficient market theory, returns should be constant over time and, therefore, unrelated to past returns. That is, in a regression of stock returns on a constant term and past returns, the constant term should be positive, but the slope coefficient on past returns should be zero. On the other hand, if prices grow faster than trend initially but slower as they return to trend, returns should be above and then below normal. Thus, if prices are mean reverting, the slope coefficient should be negative.

Many researchers have regressed stock returns on past returns to test the efficient market theory. Most of the studies used returns over very short investment horizons, such as daily or weekly returns. Although the slope coefficients were generally found to be statistically significant, they were not economically significant because they were so close to zero. Thus, in a review of many of the early studies, Fama concluded that the stock market is efficient.

More recent studies have extended the early research by using multiyear returns in the regressions. Fama and French (1988a) tested for mean reversion by regressing multiyear returns on past multiyear returns for investment horizons of one to ten years. They used monthly data adjusted for inflation from the NYSE and various industry groups over the period from 1926 to 1985. For example, for a four-year horizon, the return from March 1935 to March 1939 was regressed on the return from March 1931 to March 1935.

Fama and French concluded that stock prices are mean reverting. They found that the coefficients on past returns became negative for two-year returns, reached a minimum for three-to-five-year returns, and then approached zero as the investment horizon increased to eight years. For example, the coefficient on past NYSE returns for the four-year horizon was -0.36 and statistically significant. Thus, for example, if returns were 10 percent above average over the past four years, they are likely to be 3.6 percent below average over the next four years. Finally, like Poterba and Summers, Fama and French found that mean reversion is stronger for stocks of small firms than of large firms.[9]

Another way to use regressions to test for efficient markets is to regress stock returns on the difference between stock prices and a measure of fundamental values.[10] If stock prices are mean reverting, returns should be negatively related to past differences between prices and fundamental values. For example, if a stock price is above its fundamental value, future returns should be small as the price returns to the fundamental value.

Fama and French (1988b) found that stock prices are mean reverting when dividends are used to measure fundamental values. Dividends are a measure of fundamental values because stock prices should be proportional to dividends in an efficient market (see equation 1). Thus, if prices are mean reverting, returns should be negatively related to the difference between prices and dividends. Using inflation-adjusted NYSE returns from 1926 to 1986, Fama and French found that two-year to four-year returns are negatively related to the difference between stock prices and dividends.[11]

Campbell and Shiller found that prices are mean reverting using dividends and earnings to measure fundamental values. Because dividends ultimately depend on earnings, earnings can also be used to measure fundamental values. Using excess returns and inflation-adjusted returns on the Standard and Poor's 500 stock index from 1871 to 1987, they found that prices are mean reverting over one-year, three-year, and ten-year horizons.

Why the stock market might still be efficient

Despite the evidence that stock prices are mean reverting, the stock market might still be efficient for two reasons. First, some critics argue the evidence for mean reversion is weak, either because the data samples are too small or because the evidence depends entirely on the behavior of stock prices before World War II. Second, some critics argue that mean reverting stock prices are, in fact, simply a characteristic of more sophisticated versions of the efficient market theory.

Small sample size. Some researchers argue there are not enough data to conclude that stock prices are mean reverting. In general, the tests used to determine whether a statistic is significant assume that the statistic is calculated from an infinite number of observations. Because a finite number of observations are actually used in any test, the tests are only an approximation. The larger the number of observations, however, the better the approximation. The problem with mean reversion tests is that the data sets are very small. For example, from 1925 to 1985, there are only 12 independent observations of five-year returns (60 years divided by five).

Using statistical tests that account for the relatively small number of observations, several studies have found that previous work overstated the statistical significance of the mean reversion evidence (Mankiw, Romer, and Shapiro; Nelson and Kim; Kim, Nelson, and Startz; and McQueen). In general, these studies have found that the evidence on mean reversion is only marginally, if at all, statistically significant. Thus, while the evidence is suggestive, it is not strong enough to conclude that stock prices are mean reverting.

Mean reversion is due to pre-World War II data. Some researchers argue that stock prices may have been mean reverting in the past, but not anymore. According to these critics, stock prices were mean reverting only before World War II—stock returns were high in the late 1920s, low after the 1929 Crash and during the Great Depression, and then high during and right after the war. Since the war, however, they argue that such regularities in stock returns have largely disappeared.

Some recent studies show that mean reversion does disappear when the early years are excluded. Using NYSE returns from 1947 to 1986, Kim, Nelson, and Startz found that stock prices are not mean reverting. Indeed, for large-firm stocks, prices move away from the mean at long horizons.[12] Fama and French (1988a) found that mean reversion disappears for all of their groups when returns from 1941 to 1985 are used.[13]

Critics of the studies of postwar data might argue that the studies omit the second half of the 1980s—a period in which stock prices appear to have been mean reverting. For example, the return on the Dow Jones Industrial Average over the three years prior to the October 1987 collapse was 112 percent, while the return over the three years after the

PART VI Monetary Theory

Chart 1
Variance Ratios

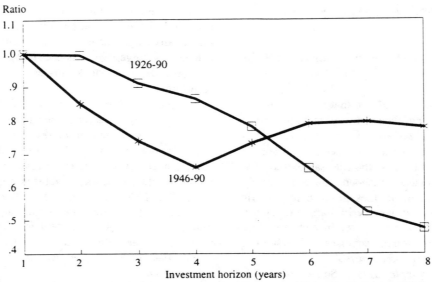

Note: Returns are monthly returns on the equal-weighted New York Stock Exchange portfolio less monthly returns on U.S. Treasury bills from 1926 to 1990 and 1946 to 1990. The variance ratio for a k-year investment horizon is calculated as the variance of the k-year return divided by k times the variance of the one-year return. The variance ratios are adjusted for small-sample bias as discussed in Poterba and Summers.

Source: Center for Research in Security Prices.

collapse was just 30 percent.[14]

Updating the postwar sample through 1990 does not significantly affect the results, however. The effect of updating the data is shown by calculating variance ratios over the 1946-90 period and comparing them with variance ratios calculated over the 1926-90 period (Chart 1). Mean reversion at long horizons has been weaker since 1946 than before 1946, although mean reversion at short horizons has been stronger over the postwar period. But because the sample is so small, these variance ratios are probably no more than marginally significant. Thus, overall, the postwar evidence casts doubt on the mean reversion evidence.

Sophisticated efficient market theories.
Even if stock prices are mean reverting, the stock market might still be efficient. Mean reversion implies that the simple efficient market theory described earlier—where the real interest rate is assumed to be constant over time—is incorrect. In the simple theory, expected real returns are constant over time

because the real interest rate is assumed to remain constant. But if real interest rates vary over time, returns should also vary over time in an efficient market. Indeed, if real interest rates are mean reverting, stock prices will also be mean reverting.

Real interest rates could vary for a variety of reasons. For a given riskless interest rate, changes in the riskiness of stocks or in investors' tolerance for risk would cause the risk adjustment factor, and therefore the interest rate, to change. Alternatively, for a given risk-adjustment factor, the riskless interest rate may change over time. Several researchers have developed sophisticated examples in which changes in risk tolerance and the riskiness of stocks cause interest rates, and therefore stock prices, to be mean reverting (Fama and French 1988b; Black; and Cecchetti, Lam, and Mark).

The basic idea underlying the sophisticated models is illustrated in Figure 5. Suppose that interest rates fall at the end of the first period. The decline could be due to a fall in the riskless interest rate, in the riskiness of stocks, or in the risk averseness of investors. According to equation 1, a decline in interest rates causes the current stock price to rise. At the same time, the lower interest rate implies that future prices will grow at a slower rate. As the figure shows, the stock price first jumps above the old trend and then slowly reverts to the old trend just as in the inefficient market theory. Indeed, Figure 5 looks very similar to Figure 2. Thus, if interest rates are mean reverting, perhaps because they fall during recessions and rise during recoveries, stock prices may appear mean reverting even if the stock market is efficient.

Poterba and Summers argue, however, that changes in the riskiness of stocks or the risk tolerance of investors cannot explain the mean reversion found in the data for two reasons. First, the degree of mean reversion in stock price data implies changes in the riskiness of stocks or in risk tolerance that are implausibly large. Second, although the behavior of stock prices in the feedback trader model and sophisticated efficient market theories are similar, they are not exact. Specifically, prices should move away from trend in the short run if they are mean reverting. In other words, as shown in Figure 2, if prices grow faster than normal, feedback traders should cause them to continue to grow faster than normal in the short run. In the sophisticated models (Figure 5), however, prices should immediately begin to grow slower than normal after a fall in interest rates. Lo and MacKinlay, and Poterba and Summers find that prices move away from trend for investment horizons of two years or less, which supports the feedback trader model.

CONCLUSIONS

Analysts have traditionally regarded the stock market as an efficient market. More recently, some analysts have argued that feedback traders cause the market to be inefficient. The major problem for the economy of an inefficient market is that investment funds are not directed to where they are most useful.

PART VI Monetary Theory

Figure 5
Stock Prices in an Efficient Market: Change in Interest Rates

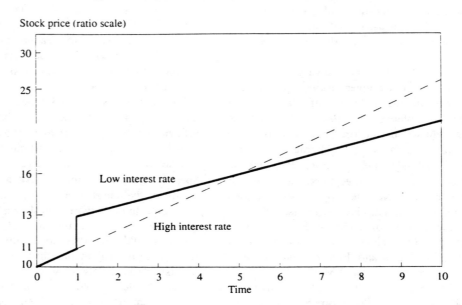

This article reviewed the mean reversion evidence on stock market efficiency. Some studies of stock prices suggest prices are mean reverting. However, it is too early to conclude that the stock market is inefficient for two reasons. First, other studies indicate that stock prices are not mean reverting. Some show that the statistical tests are relatively inaccurate due to a lack of long-horizon stock returns, while others show that the evidence in favor of mean reversion is much weaker if pre-World War II data are excluded. Second, even if stock prices are mean reverting, it may be that one of the more sophisticated efficient market theories is correct.

ENDNOTES

1. Investors cannot get higher than average returns by following simple investment strategies, however. In an efficient market, arbitragers work so quickly that investors cannot take advantage of any mispricing of securities.

READING 31 Challenges to Stock Market Efficiency

2. Because the real interest rate is used in equation 1, the price and dividend terms are also real values. Equation 1 would also hold if all values were expressed in nominal terms. Real terms are used to avoid changes in values induced by inflation. For expositional purposes, "real" will not be used as a modifier unless it is necessary for clarity.

3. More formally, the efficient market theory says that the price of a stock should equal the present value of all future dividends.

$$P_0 = \sum_{i=1}^{\infty} \frac{ED_i}{(1+r)^i} = \frac{ED_1}{1+r} + \sum_{i=2}^{\infty} \frac{ED_i}{(1+r)^i}$$

The expected price of a stock one period in the future is just the present value of all dividends from that time on.

$$EP_1 = \sum_{i=2}^{\infty} \frac{ED_i}{(1+r)^{i-1}}$$

Dividing EP_1 by $1 + r$ gives

$$\frac{EP_1}{1+r} = \sum_{i=2}^{\infty} \frac{ED_i}{(1+r)^i}$$

which is just the summation term in the second line of the P_0 equation. Thus, substituting $EP_1/1+r$ into the P_0 equation gives equation 1 in the text.

4. The dividend-inclusive price, q_t, is constructed so that the percentage change in price equals the total return from dividends and price appreciation. That is,

$$(q_t - q_{t-1})/q_{t-1} = (D_t + P_t - P_{t-1})/P_{t-1}.$$

One way to think of the dividend-inclusive price is that it is what the price of the stock would be if the stock did not pay dividends so that the total return comes from price appreciation.

5. The slope of the line is the percentage change in price instead of just the change in price because the vertical scale of the figure is a ratio scale. The slope equals the risk-adjusted interest rate because the dividend-inclusive price is constructed such that the percentage change in price equals the total return including dividends (see endnote 4). That is,

$$slope = (q_t - q_{t-1})/q_{t-1} = (D_t + P_t - P_{t-1})/P_{t-1} = r,$$

and r is assumed to be constant over time in the simple efficient market theory described in the text. More sophisticated efficient market theories allow r to vary over time. In those theories, expected returns will vary overtime with r. These theories will be discussed later in the article.

6. If risk is measured by the variance of returns, the variance of the return on a k-year investment is just k times the variance of the return on a one-year investment. For example, if p_t is the log of the dividend-inclusive price, the two-year return is

$$(p_t - p_{t-1}) + (p_{t-1} - p_{t-2}) = p_t - p_{t-2}.$$

The variance of the two-year return is

$$var(p_t - p_{t-2}) = var(p_t - p_{t-1}) + var(p_{t-1} - p_{t-2})$$
$$+ 2cov(p_t - p_{t-1}, p_{t-1} - p_{t-2}).$$

PART VI Monetary Theory

If the market is efficient, the covariance between the current one-year return and the lagged one-year return is zero. Assuming the variance of one-year returns is constant over time, the two-year variance becomes $2var(p_t - p_{t-1})$.

7. If risk is measured by the variance of returns, the variance of the return on a k-year investment is less than k times the variance of the return on a one-year investment. For example, if p_t is the log of the dividend-inclusive price, the two-year return is

$$(p_t - p_{t-1}) + (p_{t-1} - p_{t-2}) = p_t - p_{t-2}.$$

The variance of the two-year return is

$$var(p_t - p_{t-2}) = var(p_t - p_{t-1}) + var(p_{t-1} - p_{t-2}) + 2cov(p_t - p_{t-1}, p_{t-1} - p_{t-2}).$$

If prices are mean reverting, the covariance between the current one-year return and the lagged one-year return is negative. Thus, assuming the variance of one-year returns is constant over time, the two-year variance is less than $2var(p_t - p_{t-1})$.

8. Poterba and Summers report results for both value-weighted and equal-weighted NYSE returns. Value-weighted returns are calculated from a weighted-average price index for all stocks on the NYSE, where the weight on a stock's price is the market value of the firm's outstanding shares divided by the market value of all shares on the NYSE. Equal-weighted returns are calculated from a price index in which all stock prices have the same weight. The primary difference between the two measures of returns is that value-weighted returns are dominated by large-firm stocks.

The variance ratios for both types of returns are less than one for all horizons over two years. However, the equal-weighted statistics generally are smaller than the value-weighted statistics. For example, eight-year equal-weighted returns are three-and-a-half times more variable than one-year returns, while eight-year value-weighted returns are five-and-a-half times more variable than one-year returns. Because smaller firms carry a larger weight in equal-weighted returns than in value-weighted returns, these results suggest mean reversion is more prominent for stocks of small firms than of large firms.

Poterba and Summers report Monte Carlo estimates of the standard errors of the variance ratios for all horizons, but they report the statistical significance only for the eight-year horizon. The eight-year variance ratio is statistically different from one at the 8 percent level for the value-weighted returns and at the 0.5 percent level for the equal-weighted returns. It should be noted, however, that none of the variance ratios are more than two standard deviations from one.

The data used by Poterba and Summers end before the October 1987 stock market collapse. Extending the data through 1990, however, does not change the results.

9. Fama and French report results for value-weighted and equal-weighted NYSE returns, equal-weighted returns for groups of NYSE firms of similar size, and equal-weighted returns for various industries. In general, the coefficients for the three-to-five-year horizons are the most negative for all groups. Moreover, for most of the groups, the coefficients are more than two standard errors from zero only for the three-to-five-year horizons. The exceptions are the large-firm portfolios and the value-weighted returns, which are not more than two standard errors from zero at any horizon. Thus, like the Poterba and Summers results, mean reversion is more prominent for stocks of small firms than of large firms.

10. If the stock market is efficient, any difference between prices and a measure of fundamental value must be due to errors in measuring fundamental values. Because the measurement errors should cancel each other out over time, however, returns should not be systematically related to such measurement errors.

11. Fama and French actually regress returns on the log of dividends minus the log of prices and find that the slope coefficients are positive. This implies that the coefficient on prices minus dividends should be negative as discussed in the text. They report results for value-weighted and equal-weighted real returns. In general, the slope coefficients are larger in the equal-weighted regressions than in value-weighted regressions. Thus, they also find that mean reversion is more prominent for stocks of small firms than of large firms.

12. Kim Nelson, and Startz use the term "mean aversion" to describe the tendency of prices to move away from the mean. Like mean reversion, mean aversion is not consistent with the efficient market theory. However, no one has come up with a story that explains why prices should be mean averting over long horizons.

13. Poterba and Summers find that mean reversion does not disappear when returns from 1936 to 1985 are used. These results are apparently due to the fact that the sample still includes returns from the Great Depression.

14. The return over the three years prior to the 1987 collapse was calculated from monthly averages of the Dow Jones Industrial Average from September 1984 to September 1987. The return over the three years after the 1987 collapse was calculated from monthly averages of the Dow Jones Industrial Average from November 1987 to November 1990.

REFERENCES

Black, Fischer. 1990. "Mean Reversion and Consumption Smoothing," *Review of Financial Studies*, pp. 107-14.

Campbell, John Y., and Robert J. Shiller. 1988. "Stock Prices, Earnings, and Expected Dividends," *Journal of Finance*, pp. 661-76.

Cecchetti, Stephen G., Pok-Sang Lam, and Nelson C. Mark. 1990. "Mean Reversion in Equilibrium Asset Prices," *American Economic Review*, pp. 398-418.

Cutler, David M., James M. Poterba, and Lawrence H. Summers. 1990. "Speculative Dynamics and the Role of Feedback Traders," *American Economic Review*, pp. 63-68.

Fama, Eugene F. 1970. "Efficient Capital Markets: A Review of Theory and Empirical Work," *Journal of Finance*, pp. 383-417.

Fama, Eugene F., and Kenneth R. French. 1988a. "Permanent and Temporary Components of Stock Prices," *Journal of Political Economy*, pp. 246-73.

___. 1988b. "Dividend Yields and Expected Stock Returns," *Journal of Financial Economics*, pp. 3-25.

Kim, Myung Jig, Charles R. Nelson, and Richard Startz. 1991. "Mean Reversion in Stock Prices? A Reappraisal of the Empirical Evidence," *Review of Economic Studies*, pp. 515-28.

Lo, Andrew W., and A. Craig MacKinlay. 1988. "Stock Prices Do Not Follow Random Walks: Evidence from a Simple Specification Test," *Review of Financial Studies*, pp. 41-66.

Mankiw, N. Gregory, David Romer, and Matthew D. Shapiro. 1991. "Stock Market Forecastability and Volatility: A Statistical Appraisal," *Review of Economic Studies*, pp. 455-77.

McQueen, Grant. 1990. "Long Horizon Mean Reverting Stock Prices Revisited." Department of Finance, Marriott School of Management Brigham Young University.

Nelson, Charles R., and Myung J. Kim. 1990. "Predictable Stock Returns: Reality or Statistical Illusion?" Working Paper 3297. Cambridge, Mass.: National Bureau of Economic Studies.

Poterba, James M., and Lawrence H. Summers. 1988. "Mean Reversion in Stock Prices: Evidence and Implications," *Journal of Financial Economics*, pp. 27-59.

PART VI Monetary Theory

QUESTIONS

1. Why is stock market efficiency an important issue?

2. According to efficient market theory, what determines a stock's price and the behavior of its price over time?

3. What is meant by "mean reversion" of stock prices? Why might this occur?

4. Describe the tests for mean reversion and the results of those tests.

5. Why do Engels and Morris claim that it is too early to declare the stock market inefficient?

READING 32

Activist Monetary Policy for Good or Evil? The New Keynesians vs. the New Classicals

Tom Stark and Herb Taylor

Economic analysts and policy practitioners argue endlessly about how long it takes for monetary policy actions to affect output or employment, how long the effects will last, or how large they will be. But underneath it all, the truth is that economists cannot agree on how monetary policy affects the real economy in the first place. Theoreticians are offering two different explanations, each with its own implications for the way monetary policy ought to be conducted.

Perhaps the most popular explanation for money's impact was first proposed about 15 years ago by a group of economists now known as the New Classicals. These economists see episodes of money affecting economic activity as temporary aberrations that occur only when monetary policy actions happen to catch the public by surprise. Because they see these episodes as harmful, the New Classical economists think that central banks should avoid such surprises. They think that a central bank should just announce a simple money growth plan and stick to it. Such a policy, they say, would minimize economic disruptions and make inflation predictable.

In the last few years a group of economists labeled the New Keynesians has begun mounting a challenge to the New Classical view. The New Keynesians claim that under the right circumstances even widely publicized monetary policy actions can have a sustained impact on output and employment. And they claim that this impact can be used to help counteract what they see as the ecomomy's tendencies toward excessive volatility and unemployment. So the New Keynesians think that a good central bank conducts an activist monetary policy—it actively manages the supply of money and credit to keep the economy close to full employment.

Which side is right? Is an activist monetary policy good or evil? Neither side has all the answers, but both command serious attention in a very important policy debate.

THE NEW CLASSICALS' CASE AGAINST ACTIVIST POLICY

Like the great Classical economists of the last century, the New Classicals see the

Reprinted from Federal Reserve Bank of Philadelphia *Business Review*, March/April 1991, 17-25.

PART VI Monetary Theory

market system naturally bringing the economy to its peak level of efficiency. They see markets as a network of competitive auctions in which prices respond quickly and completely to changes in economic conditions. Basing their decisions on these market prices, households and firms automatically deploy the economy's real resources—its labor, raw materials, factories, and equipment—fully and efficiently. Activist monetary policy has no place in this world. Policy actions designed to alter the pattern of economic activity are ineffective and unnecessary.

Competition among many small households and firms makes the Classical economy efficient. In the Classical system, overall supply and demand conditions determine the prices people pay and the wages they earn. No business or individual is big enough to manipulate market conditions to its own advantage. Any firm that tried to charge above-market prices for its product would lose all of its customers to competing producers. Any worker that held out for above-market wages would lose his or her job to competing workers.

This environment may sound harsh, but it gives firms the incentive to perform at peak efficiency. Given the wage-price structure, each firm faces just one basic decision: how much to produce. And in its quest for profits, the firm will automatically choose a production level that balances consumer preferences with resource availability.

Consider the typical firm. For each unit it produces, it gets the market price. It also incurs costs equal to the price of the requisite labor and materials. The more it produces, the more it is prone to operating inefficiencies that push up per-unit production costs. At some point, the cost of producing another unit would exceed the product's market price. Expansion beyond that point would cut into profits, so the firm expands no further. Following this strategy not only maximizes the firm's own profits, it promotes overall economic efficiency as well. The product's market price measures its worth to the consumer. Wages and other input prices measure workers' and resource suppliers' valuation of their time and materials. So, in effect, the firm is producing only the units whose benefits to the consumer justify the burden their production imposes on workers and other resources.

Of course, economic conditions are constantly changing . Consumers' preferences shift away from one product and toward another; a new production technology comes along and displaces an old one. But in the Classical view, market prices and wages adjust quickly to changes in supply and demand, providing firms with the incentives to keep the economy's resources fully and efficiently employed. With the market system allocating resources so effectively, there is no reason to use monetary policy to alter the level of economic activity. But it's just as well. Because in the Classical world, any attempt at activist policy would fail.

The Classical economists developed the theory that money has no effect on economic activity. Clearly, prices are crucial to people's economic decisions in the Classical system. And usually we think of prices being quoted in terms of money. Yet the Classical economists maintained that changing the

READING 32   Activist Monetary Policy for Good or Evil?

money supply would have no impact on output or employment. How can this be?

The Classicals claimed that when the money supply changed, all prices and wages would change in equal proportion, leaving the relationships among them unchanged. Consequently, households and firms would stick by their original employment and production decisions, leaving the real economy unaffected.[1]

Suppose, for instance, that the central bank pumps up the money supply. This increases the overall demand for goods and services, pushing up market prices. But workers recognize that higher prices erode the purchasing power of their wages. So they are willing to work the same hours and expend the same effort only if they get wage increases commensurate with the increase in market prices. Firms, competing for workers, agree to pay for the raises out of their inflated sales revenues, and they maintain their original level of employment and output. All that remains of the money supply increase are higher prices and wages.

The Classical economists recognized that, as a practical matter, these adjustments to a change in the money supply would not always proceed as smoothly as their theoretical analysis might suggest. But their message comes through clearly enough: the money supply ultimately affects the level of prices, not the level of economic activity.

The New Classical economists reinvigorated the Classical argument that monetary policy is generally ineffective. The Classical perspective on money's role in the economy was among the casualties of the Great Depression. The Keynesian Revolution swept through the economics profession and gave birth to the activist monetary policies of the postwar period. But in the early 1970s, some economists resurrected the Classical viewpoint. In fact, by combining parts of the Classical tradition with the notion of "rational expectations," these New Classical economists emerged with an even stronger position: monetary policy cannot systematically affect the real economy. Instances in which monetary policy actions alter employment or output levels are occasional, random events.

The New Classical analysis of money's impact on the economy is a variation on the old adage "knowledge is power." In keeping with their Classical tradition, the New Classicals maintain that markets are competitive enough to drive the economy to full employment, and responsive enough to keep it there in the face of shifting economic conditions. To this they simply add that a key element in markets' responsiveness is market participants acting upon rational expectations about where the economy is headed. The New Classicals assume that market participants understand the underlying structure of the economy and use the available data on current economic conditions to formulate accurate forecasts about future economic performance. Presumably, participants' actions in the marketplace today reflect those rational expectations.

The New Classicals go on to argue that market participants pretty much know what to expect from the monetary authority. Competitive market prices and wages automatically reflect those expectations, thus neutralizing the impact of any anticipated policy actions on output and employment.

PART VI   Monetary Theory

Admittedly, policy actions that take people by surprise can affect economic activity. But, the New Classicals point out, such "surprises" must, by definition, be occasional and without pattern. So the monetary authority cannot systematically influence the level of output or employment.

The New Classicals emphasize that even when a monetary policy action does take people by surprise, its impact is temporary. It lasts only as long as it takes for the markets to find out what the central bank has done and respond. And in the interim, people—particularly workers—are not necessarily better off.[2]

Textbook versions of the New Classical view assume that product prices respond to sudden shifts in economic conditions more quickly than wages do. For one thing, wage agreements, whether formal or informal, may cover several months, a year, or even several years—all periods much longer than it takes for product prices to change. Even where wages are set more frequently, workers usually agree to a certain wage without the benefit of complete information on the prices of the products they intend to buy. Consequently, when an unexpected monetary expansion comes along and pushes up product prices, firms find they can retain, and perhaps even expand, their work force without raising wages very much. And they make the most of the opportunity. They pay a slightly higher wage, hire more workers, produce more output, and sell it at the new, higher prices. Hence the expansionary monetary policy boosts aggregate employment and output.[3]

Of course, the workers eventually catch on. They shop. They see the higher product prices. And the next time they negotiate a wage, they demand compensation for their loss in purchasing power. Once wages rise as much as prices have, firms revert to their original hiring and production patterns. So money is, in the last analysis, neutral.

Overall, the New Classical analysis of money's impact on the economy casts activist monetary policy in a very dim light. First of all, the New Classicals see the economy exhibiting a strong tendency toward full employment that makes it unnecessary for the monetary authority to focus on the level of economic activity. But even beyond that, attempts to conduct an activist policy do more harm than good. An expansionary policy anticipated by the public simply creates instant inflation. If, as occasionally happens, the policy is not anticipated by the public, it affects output and employment essentially by tricking people into producing at a pace they would not have chosen if they were fully informed.

Given this perspective, the New Classicals' advice to policymakers is straightforward: do not try any surprise moves. Choose a simple money growth plan consistent with your inflation goals. Announce the plan far enough in advance to allow markets to react. Then just follow the plan.[4]

THE NEW KEYNESIANS' CASE FOR AN ACTIVIST POLICY

The New Keynesians don't see things quite the way the New Classicals do. The

READING 32 Activist Monetary Policy for Good or Evil?

New Keynesians see an economy in which firms face only limited competition. These imperfectly competitive firms restrict their output to keep prices high and respond only partially to shifting demand conditions. As a result, the economy shows the tendencies toward underemployment and price "stickiness" that are very much a part of the traditional Keynesian perspective. The New Keynesians believe that in this world, regardless of how people form their expectations, monetary policy can and should be used to expand the level of economic activity.

Without strict market discipline, firms are less likely to achieve maximum economic efficiency. The difference between the Classical competitive firm and the imperfectly competitive firm is simple: the competitive firm must take the market price of its product as a given, whereas the imperfect competitor has the power to set price to its own advantage. And the right price structure for the imperfect competitor is not necessarily best for the overall economy.

In the competitive market, each firm is small and its output is nothing special. So its decision about how much to supply has no appreciable impact on the market price. If Farmer Jones decided to withhold some of his wheat from the market, how far could he drive up the price of wheat? If he tried to charge extra for Farmer Jones Wheat, who would pay the premium? No one.

Imperfect competitors have larger operations. Their product may have some special characteristic—real or imagined—that differentiates it in the mind of consumers. For these firms, size or special niche gives them some power over the price of their products. If General Mills were willing to cut its supply of breakfast cereal, cereal prices would rise. And if it decides to increase the price of Wheaties, some people would be willing to pay the premium.

In short, the imperfectly competitive firm has some advantage that frees its pricing structure from the strict discipline of the market. Of course, the firm is still subject to the Law of Demand: the higher the price it sets, the fewer units it will sell. So it must choose between setting a high price and selling to a limited number of customers, or setting a low price and grabbing the lion's share of the market. But one thing is for sure: it will not set as low a price as a Classical competitive market would establish. It will always find it profitable to set a higher price and maintain it by keeping output below competitive levels.

Exercising market power may make individual firms more profitable, but it imposes costs on society as a whole. From the social standpoint, imperfect competitors' prices are too high and their production is too low. Society would be better off if these firms would cut their prices to levels more consistent with resource costs. This would expand sales, production, and employment to more socially desirable levels.

Neither the notion of imperfect competition nor its impact on social welfare are original to the New Keynesians.[5] But the analysis offers them a rationale for their belief that the economy tends to underemployment. And it offers them something more—a jumping-off point for a new theory of how monetary policy can help alleviate the problem.

The New Keynesians believe monetary policy can work on imperfect competitors. Traditional theories of imperfect competition can explain underemployment, but they cannot explain why monetary policy should be effective in combating it. As long as prices and wages respond flexibly, the monetary authority is still powerless to affect firms' output and employment decisions. But the New Keynesians add a new wrinkle to the theory of imperfect competition: imperfectly competitive firms' prices are not as flexible as competitively established market prices. So real activity may respond to monetary policy actions.

In the Classical world, competitive markets adjust prices quickly and completely to every shift in economic conditions. In a world of imperfect competition, firms must set prices. When demand shifts are relatively small, these firms may not find changing prices worthwhile. It may be more profitable to maintain current prices and adjust production accordingly.

Economists have labeled the costs firms bear when they change their product prices "menu costs." That name captures the most obvious cost of repricing: printing new menus and catalogs and changing price tags and signs. But there are other costs as well. To find the new profit-maximizing price, the firm must estimate the likely nature, magnitude, and duration of the shift in customer demand. That kind of research and analysis uses up resources. In addition, frequent price changes may alienate customers and cost the firm some of its good will.

It's difficult to say how large menu costs are. It may seem that, as a practical matter, the cost of changing prices ought to be relatively small. But the New Keynesians emphasize that the benefits to changing prices can be small for imperfect competitors, too. So even small menu costs can thwart a price change.

When the demand for an imperfect competitor's product increases, the firm can respond in any number of ways. At one extreme, it can take the opportunity to raise its prices without losing sales. At the other extreme, it can hold the line on prices and take the opportunity to pick up sales volume. If the demand shift that the firm is experiencing is large, then choosing the right strategy can have a substantial impact on profits. But if the demand shift is relatively small, there is little advantage to choosing one over the other. A firm that simply maintains its original prices will not get as much as it could on each unit, but it will sell more units. So its profits will not be substantially compromised.[6] Once menu costs—even small ones—enter the equation, they can tip the scales in favor of maintaining current prices. Thus the profit-maximizing imperfect competitor may choose to accommodate a small demand shift without changing the price of its product.

This tendency for prices to be sticky in an imperfectly competitive environment affords the central bank some opportunity to influence overall output and employment. Suppose the central bank increases the money supply and thereby boosts overall demand for goods and services. Further suppose that individual firms decide that the demand increase is too small to make a price adjustment profitable. Instead, they decide to hold the line on prices and fully accommodate the increased demand for their products. In order to increase their output, they begin to hire more workers. So both output and employment pick up. Meanwhile, since product prices are not rising, workers are not demanding an inflation adjustment to their wages, so both wages and prices remain relatively constant.[7]

The New Keynesians recognize that the central bank's ability to raise output and employment in this way is circumscribed. If monetary policy actions create too large a demand shift, firms are more likely to raise prices than increase output. Furthermore, every firm faces different demand conditions and menu costs. Some will have lower thresholds for changing prices than others. So almost any policy action is likely to affect aggregate prices as well as aggregate output. In short, the New Keynesians acknowledge that a central bank cannot engineer dramatic or persistent increases in output and employment without driving up prices and wages. Nonetheless, New Keynesian analysis suggests that an activist policy can be successful, if used judiciously.

Overall, the New Keynesians see the potential for an activist monetary policy to improve the performance of an imperfectly competitive economy. Monetary policy may not be a cure-all, but it can help offset what New Keynesians see as the economy's chronic bias toward underproduction and underemployment in modern, imperfectly competitive economies.

Add to this underlying bias the fact that the economy is subject to sudden shifts in overall demand, and the New Keynesians' case for an activist monetary policy seems even stronger. For if price stickiness accentuates the impact of monetary policy on economic activity, it also accentuates the impact of other demand shifts as well. Thus a sudden decline in overall demand could drop the economy well below its potential level of performance. This suggests that monetary policymakers should be alert to these shifts and stand ready to offset them.[8]

WHO'S RIGHT?

Both the New Classicals and the New Keynesians offer explanations for monetary policy's impact on the economy. But the New Keynesian approach certainly casts activist monetary policy in a more positive light. Which explanation should we believe? One way to evaluate competing theories is to "let the data decide." But at this point, empirical tests do not provide a clear answer.

The New Classical theory has been around longer and been subjected to more empirical study. The results are not favorable to the hard-line New Classical view that only unexpected policy actions affect real activity. Statistical analyses seem to show output and employment responding to anticipated policy actions too. But, ironically enough, these kinds of results have prompted some New Classicals to support a theory that attributes even less potency to monetary policy actions: the *real business cycle* theory. According to this theory, monetary policy never causes fluctuations in economic activity. Rather, anticipated fluctuations in the economy cause the public to increase or decrease their demand for money. The central bank and financial system simply accommodate these demand fluctuations.[9]

The New Keynesian theory is relatively new, and empirical evidence is scantier. There is some supportive evidence, however. In countries where inflation is relatively low, which would suggest that expansionary monetary policies have not been pursued too aggressively, policy shifts seem to have more impact on real activity—as the New Keynesians would predict. But tests of the New Keynesian model are really in too early a stage to provide a convincing case one way or another.[10]

Empirical issues aside, there are unsettling aspects to both the New Classical and the New Keynesian models. Perhaps the most unsettling theoretical aspects have to do with the functioning of the labor market. Both groups admit they have trouble explaining why monetary policy actions that affect output have such a large effect on employment and such a small effect on wages. According to the New Classical theory, an unexpected increase in product demand induces firms to produce more because it pushes the product price up before wages have had a chance to rise in response. But firms need more workers in order to expand production. Won't that increased demand for labor itself push up wages?

The New Classicals' answer: some, but not much. True to their Classical perspective, they maintain that labor markets are competitive. They simply assume that labor supply is very sensitive to wage changes. Thus when labor demand increases, it evokes many more hours of work at only a slightly higher wage. The problem is that, as a practical matter, willingness to work does not seem to be all that sensitive to wage changes.

New Keynesians face a similar conundrum. According to them, when firms face a small increase in product demand, they hold the line on prices and expand output. Again, to expand output, firms need more workers. Granted, product prices are not increasing, so there is no inflation pressure on wages. But won't firms have to raise the wage they pay in order to induce more people to work? The New Keynesians' answer is no. True to the Keynesian tradition, they claim that there is a pool of involuntarily unemployed workers from which firms can always draw workers at the going wage. But to explain the involuntary unemployment, they must resort to some unconventional theories of the labor market.

Imperfectly competitive firms charge high prices, which restricts both output and employment. Nonetheless, the New Keynesians claim, these firms tend to pay the people they do employ relatively high wages. Different economists offer different reasons for this tendency. Proponents of the "efficiency wage" theory emphasize that by paying workers more than they would expect to earn if they had to go look elsewhere for a new job, the firm gives the worker the incentive to perform more effectively. Proponents of the "insider/outsider" theory emphasize that employees whose experience on the job is valuable to the firm can exact wage concessions from the firm. In either case, with wages high and employment opportunities limited, there is routinely a pool of willing workers unable to get jobs. Whenever firms want to expand output, they can tap this pool for workers without increasing the wage they pay.[11]

In short, both the New Classicals and the New Keynesians have a long way to go before either can proclaim their approach to be theoretically complete.

THE ACTIVIST POLICY DEBATE RENEWED

When the New Classical economics came on the scene in the early 1970s, it jolted academic economists and policymakers as well. The New Classicals were trying to explain precisely why monetary policy actions affect real activity. They concluded that money temporarily affects output and employment by tricking people into deviating from their preferred activity levels. This conclusion hardly cast activist monetary policy in the most favorable light, but there was little theoreticians could offer in rebuttal.

Now the New Keynesian school is offering an alternative explanation for money's impact on economic activity. That analysis, based on theories of imperfect competition, looks more favorably on activist monetary policy. The New Keynesians conclude that the economy tends toward underemployment and that an activist policy can help overcome the problem.

The New Keynesians can hardly claim to have overcome the New Classical paradigm. But they have reinvigorated the battle over the efficacy of an activist monetary policy.

ENDNOTES

1. To see this, suppose that initially bread costs $1 and workers earn $6 an hour, making a loaf of bread worth 10 minutes' work. If both prices and wages double, bread goes to $2 and wages go to $12, but a loaf of bread still trades for 10 minutes' work.
2. Thomas Sargent and Neil Wallace, in their article "'Rational' Expectations, the Optimal Monetary Instrument and the Optimal Money Supply Rule," *Journal of Political Economy* (April 1975) pp. 241-54, present a clear statement of the New Classical notion that expected monetary policy actions have no effect on economic activity.
3. Analyses stressing the role of wage contracts in limiting short-run wage flexibility can be found in Stanley Fischer's "Long-Term Contracts, Rational Expectations, and the Optimal Money Supply Rule," *Journal of Political Economy* (February 1977) pp. 191-205, and John Taylor's "Aggregate Dynamics and Staggered Contracts," *Journal of Political Economy* (1980) pp. 1-24. The idea that wages adjust imperfectly because workers are not completely aware of current product prices is more consistent with the original New Classical formulation by Robert Lucas in "Some International Evidence on Output-Inflation Tradeoffs," *American Economic Review* (June 1973) pp.326-34.
4. The New Classical argument for this approach to monetary policy has most recently been articulated by Bennett McCallum in *Monetary Economics: Theory and Policy* (Macmillan, 1989).
5. The term "imperfect competition" is used here as a convenient expression for "monopolistic competition" a market model that can be traced back to the work of E.H. Chamberlin in the 1930's. Texts such as Paul Samuelson's *Economics* (McGraw-Hill) provide readable discussions of this market type.

PART VI Monetary Theory

6. This idea is sometimes called the PAYM insight because it emerged from the work of economists Michael Parkin, George Akerlof, Janet Yellen, and N. Gregory Mankiw. Specific references are to Parkin's "The Output-Inflation Tradeoff When Prices Are Costly to Change," *Journal of Political Economy* (1986) pp.200-24; Akerlof and Yellen's "Can Small Deviations From Rationality Make Significant Differences to Economic Equilibria?" *American Economic Review* (September 1985) pp.708-21; and Mankiw's "Small Menu Costs and Large Business Cycles: A Macroeconomic Model of Monopoly," *Quarterly Journal of Economics* (May 1985) pp.529-37.

7. Olivier Blanchard and Nobuhiro Kiyotaki develop this argument formally in "Monopolistic Competition and the Effects of Aggregate Demand," *American Economic Review* (September 1987) pp.647-66.

8. Prospects for this kind of policy get some theoretical support in Lars Svensson's "Sticky Goods Prices, Flexible Asset Prices, Monopolistic Competition, and Monetary Policy," *Review of Economic Studies* (1986) pp.385-405.

9. Frederic Mishkin provides a more complete discussion of the evidence on the New Classical hypothesis in *A Rational Expectations Approach to Macroeconometrics* (University of Chicago Press, 1983). For a good discussion of the real business cycle view and its monetary policy implications, see "Monetary Policy with a New View of Potential GNP," by John Boschen and Leonard Mills, this *Business Review* (June/July 1990) pp.3-10.

10. This New Keynesian result is presented by Laurence Ball, N. Gregory Mankiw, and David Romer in "The New Keynesian Economics and the Output-Inflation Trade-Off," *Brookings Papers on Economic Activity* (1988:1) pp.1-65. For an up-to-date discussion of the empirical evidence on the New Keynesian economics, as well as a good evaluation of its theoretical underpinnings, see Robert Gordon, "What Is New Keynesian Economics?" *Journal of Economic Literature* (September 1990) pp.1115-71.

11. Lawrence Katz provides an excellent overview of these modern labor market theories in "Some Recent Developments in Labor Economics and Their Implications for Macroeconomics," *Journal of Money, Credit, and Banking* (August 1988, Part 2) pp.507-30.

QUESTIONS

1. Compare the positions of the New Classicals and New Keynesians regarding: (a) market competition; (b) flexibility of prices and wages; and (c) speed of price and wage adjustments.

2. According to the New Classical view, what can be accomplished with an activist monetary policy? Why? How would New Keynesians respond to the New Classical views?

3. If the New Classical view is correct, how should the Fed conduct monetary policy?

NOTES

NOTES

NOTES

NOTES